ESSAYS ON ANAPHORA

STUDIES IN NATURAL LANGUAGE
AND LINGUISTIC THEORY

HOWARD LASNIK

Dept. of Linguistics
University of Connecticut
Storrs, Connecticut U.S.A.

ESSAYS ON ANAPHORA

KLUWER ACADEMIC PUBLISHERS

DORDRECHT / BOSTON / LONDON

Library of Congress Cataloging-in-Publication Data

```
Essays on anaphora / [edited by] Howard Lasnik.
     p.   cm. -- (Studies in natural language and linguistic theory)
  Bibliography: p.
  Includes index.
  ISBN 1-556-08090-5 (U.S.).
  1. Anaphora (Linguistics) 2. Generative grammar.   I. Lasnik,
Howard.   II. Series.
P299.A5E87 1989
415--dc19                                             88-21813
                                                         CIP
```

Published by Kluwer Academic Publishers,
P.O. Box 17, 3300 AA Dordrecht, The Netherlands.

Kluwer Academic Publishers incorporates the publishing programmes of
D. Reidel, Martinus Nijhoff, Dr W. Junk and MTP Press.

Sold and distributed in the U.S.A. and Canada
by Kluwer Academic Publishers,
101 Philip Drive, Norwell, MA 02061, U.S.A.

In all other countries, sold and distributed
by Kluwer Academic Publishers Group,
P.O. Box 322, 3300 AH Dordrecht, The Netherlands.

Printed in The Netherlands

TABLE OF CONTENTS

PREFACE

The articles collected in this book are concerned with the treatment of anaphora within generative grammar, specifically, within Chomsky's 'Extended Standard Theory' (EST). Since the inception of this theory, and virtually since the inception of generative grammar, anaphora has been a central topic of investigation. In current research, it has, perhaps, become even more central, as a major focus of study in such areas as syntax, semantics, discourse analysis, and language acquisition.

Beginning in the early 1970's, and continuing to the present, Chomsky has developed a comprehensive syntactic theory of anaphora. The articles here are all related to stages in the development of that theory, and can best be understood in relation to that development. For that reason, Chapter 1 presents a historical survey of Chomsky's EST proposals on anaphora, along with brief indications of how the present articles fit into that history. Some of the articles here (e.g. Chapters 4, 8, and 9) proposed extensions of Chomsky's basic ideas to a wider range of phenomena. Others (e.g. Chapters 2, 3, and 7) suggested alternatives within the framework. Still others (e.g. Chapters 5 and 6) noted, and attempted to solve, conceptual problems with Chomsky's approach. Since a number of the proposals outlined in these articles were incorporated in one form or another into modern Binding Theory, this book can provide useful insight into the historical evolution of that theory. And since some of the empirical and conceptual difficulties still remain, the book can also be read as a commentary on the current status of Binding Theory.

The articles reprinted in this book appear in their original form, with the following exceptions: A few typographical and other minor errors have been corrected; bibliographic references have been updated; and Appendix A has been omitted from Chapter 3 since it is orthogonal to the concerns of the book.

I would like to acknowledge my vast intellectual debt to Noam Chomsky. None of this research would have been possible without his groundbreaking work, his advice, and his guidance. His specific comments over the years on these articles, as well as nearly two decades of discussion with me on issues in anaphora (and linguistic theory more generally), have been invaluable. Next, I offer my deep thanks to my co-authors represented here: Bob Fiengo, Bob Freidin, and Andy Barss. I have been fortunate, indeed, to have had the opportunity to collaborate with such outstanding linguists. I hereby thank them for their permission to reprint their co-authored articles. I also offer general thanks to the

holders of the copyrights for this reprinted material. Specific acknowledgements appear on a separate page. Finally, I would like to thank Frank
Heny, Martin Scrivener, and my wife, Roberta, for their encouragement in
this project, Sung-Ho Anh and Yasuo Ishii for invaluable editorial assist-
ance, and all of the members of the University of Connecticut Department
of Linguistics, and especially Department Head David Michaels, for
providing an intellectually stimulating atmosphere in which to work.

Storrs, Connecticut   HOWARD LASNIK
February 2, 1988

ORIGINAL PUBLICATION DETAILS

Chapter 1: written for this volume.
Chapter 2: reprinted from *Foundations of Language* **9** (1973), 447—468.
Chapter 3: reprinted from *Linguistic Inquiry* **5** (1974), 535—571, by permission of MIT Press.
Chapter 4: reprinted from *Linguistic Analysis* **2** (1976), 1—22, by permission of Elsevier Science Publishing Co.
Chapter 5: reprinted from *Linguistic Inquiry* **12** (1981), 39—53, by permission of MIT Press.
Chapter 6: reprinted from *Journal of Linguistic Research* **1**, **4** (1981), 48—58, by permission of Indiana University Linguistics Club.
Chapter 7: reprinted from *Linguistic Inquiry* **16** (1985), 481—490, by permission of MIT Press.
Chapter 8: reprinted from *Linguistic Inquiry* **17** (1985), 347—354, by permission of MIT Press.
Chapter 9: from R. Freidin (ed.), *Principles and Parameters in Comparative Grammar* (in press), by permission of MIT press.

HOWARD LASNIK

A SELECTIVE HISTORY OF MODERN BINDING THEORY

The articles in this book are concerned with the treatment of various anaphoric phenomena. The framework is that first introduced by Chomsky (1973) and successively revised and refined throughout the '70's and '80's. In this chapter, I will present a highly selective history of one line of investigation during that period in what has come to be known as Binding Theory (BT). I will be concerned with how Binding Theory as explicated by Chomsky has changed, but also with how it has remained the same (sometimes despite appearances to the contrary); with how changes in other modules of the theory have precipitated changes in BT; and with general theoretical concerns, for example, the rule of the desire to eliminate redundancy in the theory. Where appropriate, I will indicate how the articles comprising this book fit into the developments discussed. All references to Chapters will be to those in this book. In the interests of clarity, these articles will be referred to by their chapter numbers as well as by their original dates of publication, thus Chapter 4 [Lasnik (1976)]. It should be kept in mind that publication dates can be misleading as to history, since the large majority of the books and articles referred to in this chapter were in fairly general circulation in manuscript form long before they were actually published. It should also be kept in mind that because of the limited scope of the discussion, a number of important approaches to anaphora are ignored, including the influential Linking theory of Higginbotham (1983, 1985). Even within the approach discussed, questions of 'reconstruction' and of levels of representation relevant to BT will not be addressed. See Barss (1986) for discussion.

A number of now familiar themes were first introduced in Chomsky (1973). Perhaps most important is that there is one domain relevant to both disjoint reference effects and (indirectly) anaphoric dependence. The domain is characterized in terms of two constraints, the Tensed S Condition (TSC) and the Specified Subject Condition (SSC). These are presented, to a first approximation, in (1b) and (1a) respectively:

(1)   No rule can involve X, Y in the structure
        $\ldots$ X $\ldots$ [$_a$ $\ldots$ Z $\ldots$ WYV $\ldots$] $\ldots$
        where (a) Z is the specified subject to WYV
          or (b) a is a tensed S

(1b) straightforwardly excludes a passive such as (2a), while allowing (2b):

(2) a.   *John is believed [is happy]
    b.   John is believed [to be happy]

1

The embedded finite clause counts as α for (1b). Note in passing that it is the movement itself that is prevented by (1). While traces were introduced in Chomsky (1973), their treatment as anaphors was a later development, which I will discuss below. In fact, Chomsky (1973) had no 'interpretive' processes establishing relations between anaphors and antecedents. Reflexives were not discussed at all. Further, as just noted, the trace of NP movement was not treated as an anaphor. Reciprocal *each other* was also not treated in such terms. Here, too, the analysis was in terms of a syntactic transformation whose operation was constrained by (1). Following Dougherty (1970), Chomsky assumed a rule of *each*-Movement ultimately relating a more abstract structure like (3) to a more superficial one like (4).

(3)   The candidates each hated the others

(4)   The candidates hated each other

As in the case of passive, it is the movement that is constrained. In a footnote, Chomsky mentions the possibility, suggested by Jackendoff (1969), that the relevant process is a 'rule of interpretation' rather than one of movement. In Chapter 2 [Fiengo and Lasnik (1973)], that position is defended and discussed in detail.

While Chomsky (1973) had no direct coreference device, he did have an explicit non-coreference device, one whose effects are very similar to the ultimate effects of Condition B of Chomsky (1981). This was his RI (rule of interpretation) which

. . . applying to the structure NP-V-NP (among others) seeks to interpret the two NPs as nonintersecting in reference, and where this is impossible (as in the case of first and second person pronouns . . .), it assigns "strangeness," marking the sentence with *.

Among the examples Chomsky presented are the following:

(5)   *I saw me

(6)   *We watched me leaving (in the mirror)

(7)   He saw him

As noted, (5) and (6) are excluded by RI. (7), on the other hand, is allowed, but its interpretation is restricted in a particular way. Chomsky argued that RI, like passive and *each*-Movement, is constrained by (1) above. Thus, as long as the two NPs are separated by α, the rule seeking to interpret them as nonintersecting will be blocked. (8) does not display the "strangeness" of (5), nor does (9) display the strangeness of (6):

(8)   I think I will win

(9)   We think I will win

Note that the effect of (1) on RI is to allow additional sentences, or additional readings of sentences. This is the opposite of the effect of (1) on passive or *each*-Movement. This follows directly from the filter-like property of the former vis-à-vis the latter.

Thus far, the examples of the operation of (1) have all involved (1b), the Tensed S Condition. (1a), the Specified Subject Condition, is illustrated below. (10) shows how (1a) blocks *each*-Movement. In (10a), α is the complement infinitival clause, and in (10b), it is the object NP. In both examples, *Mary* is Z, the specified subject.

(10) a. *The men believe [Mary to like each other]
     b. *The men like [Mary's pictures of each other]

(11) displays the same paradigm, but with RI the relevant rule. *The men* and *them* may be coreferential.

(11) a. The men believe [Mary to like them]
     b. The men like [Mary's pictures of them]

I turn now to the notion 'specified subject' in (1a). In particular, under what circumstances might a subject not count as specified? Chomsky's answer is that the notion is determined relative to choice of X: Y is a specified subject with respect to X if it is not 'controlled' by X or a category containing X. Control here is both the relation between what is now called PRO and its antecedent (which is currently still called Control), and also the relation between a trace and the moved item that it is the trace of. A lexical Y is not controlled at all in this sense, hence is not controlled by X. Such a Y is thus always a specified subject, and this is taken as the core case. A non-lexical Y might or might not count as a specified subject, depending on what its controller is. In (12), PRO counts as a specified subject with respect to the matrix subject, but not the matrix object. This is because PRO is controlled by the latter and not by the former.

(12) a. *We persuaded Bill [PRO to kill each other]
     b. Bill persuaded us [PRO to kill each other]

Thus, SSC blocks *each*-Movement from the first person plural pronoun only in (12a). The pattern in (13) is precisely the reverse, in accord with the fact that *promise* takes subject control, rather than object control.

(13) a. We promised Bill [PRO to kill each other]
     b. *Bill promised us [PRO to kill each other]

The treatment of Wh-Movement, and of the interactions between this process and others, played a significant role in the theory. First, the contrast between (14a) and (14b) was treated in terms of (1), with (14b) excluded by the SSC.

(14) a. Who did you see [pictures of t]
  b. *Who did you see [John's pictures of t]

This, of course, immediately raises the question of why (15) and (16) are grammatical.

(15) Who do you believe [John to have seen t]

(16) Who do you believe [t saw Mary]

That is, why is Wh-Movement sometimes subject to (1) and sometimes not (while NP movement is apparently always subject to (1))? For (1a), the answer involves the nature of Wh-Movement and that of α. Wh-Movement was argued to be successive cyclic, involving movement into the most local COMP, then from there COMP to COMP. In addition, S', and not S, was taken to be the relevant sentential domain.[1] In both (15) and (16), then, the initial movement is into the lower COMP. This correctly renders SSC ineffectual for (15). The first movement is entirely inside α. For the second movement, from the lower to the higher COMP, movement is from a position outside the domain of the lower subject to a position that is still inside the only potential higher α.[2] (16) raised more difficult problems. The initial movement, that into the lower COMP, is once again in accord with the conditions. The movement into the matrix COMP is clearly in violation of (1b), however. The complement S', being tensed, is a relevant α. While the apparent SSC problem discussed just above received a natural solution in terms of independent properties, such is not the case with respect to the TSC violation now under consideration. In effect, Chomsky wound up stipulating that Wh-Movement from COMP is exempt from the TSC by restating that condition as in (17) (which replaces (1b) above).

(17) Y is not in COMP and α is a tensed S

Thus, when Y is in COMP, TSC is void. Note that this exemption is not available for (14b), since there is no intermediate COMP for Y, NP differing from S' in that regard. The necessity of including the complication in (17) suggests that (1) is irrelevant to Wh-Movement entirely. Chapter 5 [Freidin and Lasnik (1981)] argues at some length that this is, in fact, the case. This would leave (14b) unexplained, but, as Chomsky observes, entirely apart from the SSC, definiteness (or perhaps specificity) is relevant to Wh-extraction. He points out that while (18) is somewhat better than (14b), it is substantially worse than (14a).

(18) ?*Who did you see [the pictures of t]

(The question remains open whether or not (14b) should be entirely reduced to (18).)

  Of the three types of specified subjects, two have been examined so far:

lexical subjects, and PRO not controlled by (a category containing) X. I turn now to trace, the third type. Consider (19).

(19)   *We appeared to John [*t* to like us]

Chomsky considers a number of analyses of (19), ultimately concluding that in this case, the movement of *We* leaves behind a trace. But since the trace is (in Chomsky's terminology) controlled by *We*, it does not count as a specified subject with respect to *We*. Thus, RI applies, correctly starring the example. Consider now (20).

(20)   Which man did they expect [*t* to kill them]

This time, RI (between *they* and *them*) is blocked by the presence of the trace, since that trace is not controlled by *they*. As a result, those two pronouns are free to corefer. (21) is parallel, displaying a Wh-trace blocking *each*-Movement from *they*.

(21)   *Which man did they expect [*t* to kill each other]

One final case to consider in this regard involves a Wh-phrase as the 'antecedent' of *each other*, as in (22)

(22)   Which men did John expect [*t* to kill each other]

The analysis involves *each*-Movement on the first cycle prior to Wh-Movement. thus, neither SSC nor TSC is at issue, since *each*-Movement is entirely within α here. The interpretive analysis of reciprocals presented in Chapter 2 [Fiengo and Lasnik (1973)] is conceptually very similar to this approach. There too, the relevant rule is cyclic, thus preceding Wh-Movement. The difference is that the rule involves no movement, but rather the direct assignment of an antecedent for the reciprocal. In both analyses, the motivation for a cyclic process is that in late derived structure, the Wh-phrase is potentially too far from the reciprocal. While this is not the case in (22) (TSC is clearly not relevant, and the trace, being controlled by the Wh-phrase, does not count as specified), a simple modification of (22) immediately actualizes the potential problem. This can be seen in (23):

(23)   Which men did John expect [$_\alpha$ *t* would kill each other]

In (23), since α is a relevant tensed S, movement of *each* from the derived structure position of *which men* would be prohibited by TSC.

An alternative treatment of (22) and (23) could be constructed in which the relation between *each other* and its antecedent is established via an interpretive rule, as in Chapter 2, but where it is the trace, rather than the Wh-phrase itself, that counts as X. Interestingly, while Chomsky argues for the existence of traces, and while traces crucially count as specified subjects, Chomsky never uses them in the role of X. As we have seen, for the treatment of reciprocals, there was a viable alternative. However, one would expect, on the null hypothesis, that since traces are syntactically active, they could act as antecedents (i.e., as X). And, indeed, there are phenomena which seem to demand such treatment, even on the terms of Chomsky (1973). To see this, consider first a simple RI phenomenon in a Wh-question:

(24)   Who [t likes him]

The familiar phenomenon of disjointness obtains here. Purely syntactically, one might claim that it is the relation between *Who* and *him* that is constrained by RI.[3] Note that there is no α containing *him* and excluding *Who*, so SSC and TSC will not block the application of RI between these two NPs. However, such an analysis does not extend to (25):

(25)   Who do you think [t likes him]

Here, just as in (24), disjointness obtains. But if we assume, with Chomsky, that RI applies to a level of late derived structure, its application will be incorrectly blocked. True, SSC will not be relevant. t is controlled by *Who*, so it does not count as specified. Further, *Who* is contained in the matrix S', preventing that S' from counting as an α. On the other hand, TSC *will* be relevant. The embedded clause is clearly a finite clause containing *him* and not containing *Who*. Further, *him* is not in COMP. The operation of RI will thus be blocked, evidently an incorrect consequence. This problem is immediately overcome if we adopt the null hypothesis. Since the trace in (25) exists, RI should treat it as an X. Then, correctly, disjointness will obtain between the trace and *him*, since there is no α separating them.

Once it is established that a trace must be able to count as an X, a reconsideration of the notion 'specified' is in order. For example, in the treatment of Chomsky (1973), a Wh-trace never counts as a specified subject when the Wh-phrase itself is X, since 'control' obtains in this circumstance. But an alternative presents itself: in just that circumstance, the *trace* itself is X. And now note that the same reanalysis is available in the case of PRO as well. For example, Chomsky presents the following examples pertaining to RI.

(26) a. I (we) persuaded Bill [PRO to kill us]
     b. *I (we) promised Bill [PRO to kill us]

In (26a), PRO is not controlled by the subject of *persuade*. As a consequence, RI is prevented from applying with that subject as X and *us* as Y, and the example is acceptable. In (26b), on the other hand, the matrix subject does control PRO. PRO thus does not count as a specified subject with respect to the matrix subject; RI applies, forcing disjointness, and 'strangeness' results. Under the revision now being considered, instead of

PRO failing to block RI in (26b), PRO could itself be X. Then disjoint reference would obtain between PRO and *us*. This would, correctly, entail disjoint reference between the matrix subject and *us*, since PRO and the matrix subject must be coreferential.

A similar reanalysis is available in the case of reciprocals, particularly under an 'interpretive' treatment, such as that argued for in Chapter 2 [Fiengo and Lasnik (1973)]. One potential objection to such a reanalysis might be that in (27), for example, the interpretation would seem to indicate that the matrix subject, rather than PRO, is the antecedent of the reciprocal.

(27)   They want [PRO to visit each other]

As Higginbotham (1981) notes, (27) is paraphrasable as (28a), and not as (28b).

(28) a.   Each of them wants to visit the other
(28) b.   They want that each of them visit the other

This would follow under the syntactic analysis in Chomsky (1973), but not under the modification under consideration. However, there is reason to doubt the force of this objection. First, as discussed in Heim, Lasnik, and May (forthcoming), where an alternative account of (27) is offered, there is no general prohibition of PRO as the antecedent of a reciprocal. (29) seems easily paraphrasable as (30).

(29)   They agreed [PRO to work with each other]

(30)   They agreed that they each would work with the other

Further, it is not clear what principled basis there could be for entirely excluding the class of empty categories as antecedents. In addition, as Chomsky notes, even assuming a transformational account of *each other*, it is interpreted ". . . at least in part in terms of surface structure position". See Chapter 2 [Fiengo and Lasnik (1973)] for discussion of a number of relevant phenomena. Quite generally, then, it can be maintained that the full class of what came to be called 'empty categories' may serve as X for the operation of rules determining anaphoric possibilities. And if this can be maintained, the notion 'specified' will no longer be needed. (1a) can be stated simply as (31):

(31)   Z is the subject of WYV

That is, *all* subjects are specified subjects. The apparent cases of transparent subjects (those controlled by a category containing X) are now reinterpreted as cases of that subject itself functioning as X. While in retrospect this seems clearly the correct conclusion, removing, as it does, an unnecessary stipulation, the possibility of this sort of approach was overlooked at the time, and for some time subsequently. Thus, in Chomsky (1976), 'specified' is still assumed to play a crucial role in the statement of the conditions.

Beginning with the framework of Chomsky (1973), we have now seen evidence for two modifications. In particular, it has been suggested that Wh-movement does not fall under the constraints in (1). In addition, it has been argued that all subjects are specified subjects. Both of these modifications lead to simplifications in (1), and have empirical advantages as well, as seen above and in Chapter 5 [Freidin and Lasnik (1981)]. The first modification raises the question of whether it is plausible that certain rules should be exampt from the conditions. Chomsky himself claims, in passing, that there is a rule that does not fall under (1).

Notice that one rule that obviously does not satisfy the condition is Coreference Assignment (however it is formulated). Thus the pronoun can be anaphoric in *John said that he would leave*, for example. The same rule also applies within coordinate structures (for example, *John said that he and Bill would leave*) and others that block various types of rules.

On the other hand, in Chapter 4 [Lasnik (1976)], it is argued at some length that there is, in fact, no rule of coreference assignment responsible for the coreferential interpretation of pronouns in examples of the sort mentioned by Chomsky in the passage quoted just above. Based in part on the conclusion of this argument, Chomsky (1976) rejects his earlier claim. He seems to concede that if there were a rule associating *he* with *John* in the examples mentioned, this might undermine the approach developed in Chomsky (1973) and elaborated in Chomsky (1976). However, referring to Lasnik (1976), he indicates that

The rule of anaphora involved in the (normal but not obligatory) interpretation of [*John thought that he would win*] should in principle be exempt from the conditions on sentence-grammar, since it is no rule of sentence grammar at all.

This conclusion is not entirely unproblematic, however. While no sentence-grammar rule of *coreference* will be involved in the interpretation of pronouns, given the approach of Chapter 4 [Lasnik (1976)], there is, crucially, a sentence-grammar rule of *non-coreference* (or, more generally, disjoint reference) involved in the analysis presented. Consider (32):

(32)   He thought that John would win

The relevant property here is strongly reminiscent of that seen in such an RI example as (33):

(33)   John likes him

In particular, in both (32) and (33), we have two NPs that are assigned disjoint reference. In Chomsky (1973), as discussed earlier, the relevant rule for (33) was RI. In Chomsky (1976), essentially the same rule persists, but with a new name, 'Disjoint Reference (DR)'. This rule "assigns disjoint reference to a pair (NP, pronoun) ..." Crucially, of course, Chomsky's DR is constrained by TSC and SSC. Yet the rule implicated in (32), whose semantic effects are apparently identical to those of DR, clearly does *not* conform to the two constraints, as is immediately evident in (32) and (34):

(34)   He believes Mary to like John

In (32), the relevant interpretive rule, assigning disjoint reference, operates in apparent violation of TSC; and in (34), it operates in apparent violation of SSC. Thus, the problem noted by Chomsky (1973) still remains; only the rule has changed. In fact, this problem remained until the more radical reformulation of BT in Chomsky (1980), which will be discussed below.

In Chomsky (1976), we do find one rather significant departure from Chomsky (1973), namely, the conjecture that TSC and SSC are solely constraints on anaphoric relations of a particular type, rather than on the operation of transformations. Reciprocals are now treated in terms of a reciprocal rule which "assigns an appropriate sense to sentences of the form NP ... *each other*", as in Chapter 2 [Fiengo and Lasnik (1973)]. Further, it is proposed that the relation between an NP that has undergone NP-Movement and the position from which it moved is one of bound anaphora, as proposed by Fiengo (1974). As such, it would naturally fall under the same conditions as reciprocal interpretation. Chomsky thus tentatively concludes that

... we can regard SSC, in such cases, as a condition on surface structures applying quite generally to anaphora (hence to the NP-trace relation), rather than a condition on transformations.

Curiously, though, an equivocation remains concerning Wh-movement. It is suggested that this rule "seems superficially to violate ... SSC, and [TSC]". However, since the rule is (successive) cyclic and "movement is permitted from complementizer position in a tensed-S", there is no actual violation. As seen above, technically, the conditions can be made consistent with the properties of Wh-movement in this way. However, complications are required, with no obvious concomitant benefit. Further, if TSC and SSC are to be regarded strictly as constraints on anaphoric relations, as suggested above, there is no a priori reason to even expect them to be relevant to Wh-movement. This is so since, as Chomsky argues, the trace of Wh-movement does not have the properties of an anaphor, but rather, those of a name. Strong crossover is handled in just these terms, essentially following Wasow (1972). Thus, Chomsky compares (35a–c) with (36a–c) respectively.

(35) a. Who *t* said Mary kissed him
 b. Who did he say Mary kissed *t*
 c. Who *t* said he kissed Mary

(36) a. John said Mary kissed him
 b. He said Mary kissed John
 c. John said he kissed Mary

Strong crossover, the fact that *he* in (35b) cannot be understood as a variable bound by *Who*, thus reduces to just the disjoint reference phenomenon evidenced in (36b), but only if the trace of Wh-movement is treated as a name. However, as will be discussed shortly, this line of reasoning did not entirely settle the issue.

Weak crossover, as in (37), for example, was also investigated in Chomsky (1976).

(37) a. *Who$_1$ does his$_1$ mother love t_1
 b. *His$_1$ mother loves everyone$_1$

The core of Chomsky's analysis of (37a) is a constraint on the relationship between a pronoun and a variable antecedent: A variable cannot be the antecedent of a pronoun to its left. This analysis extends to (37b) on the assumption that the constraint is applicable to Logical Form, where the surface structure position of *everyone* will be occupied by a variable bound by *everyone*. A general, though brief, account of the circumstances under which pronouns can function as bound variables is presented in Chapter 4 [Lasnik (1976)]. There the structural requirement relevant to weak crossover, assumed to be precedence and kommand, is argued to be involved in the phenomenon of 'sloppy identity' as well, indicating that the latter also involves variable binding. See Reinhart (1983) for a detailed discussion of this correlation.

Chomsky (1980) presents the first major revision of modern binding theory. It is here that the notions 'bound' and 'free' are introduced, with their still standard definitions, as in (38a, b):

(38) a. An anaphor α is *bound* in β if there is a category c-commanding it and coindexed with it in β.
 b. Otherwise, α is free in β.

The SSC and TSC (actually called P(ropositional) I(sland) C(ondition) since Chomsky (1976)), are restated initially as (39):

(39)   If α is an anaphor in the domain of the tense or the subject of β, β minimal, then α cannot be free in β, β = NP or S'.

(39) is, of course, quite similar to Condition A of Chomsky (1981).

Chomsky calls (39) the "Opacity Condition", suggesting that Tense and Subject are "operators" making certain domains opaque to binding from without. He indicates that the Opacity Condition differs in important respects from earlier formulations. First, what was merely a conjecture previously is now fully implemented: here reciprocals, reflexives, and NP trace are all treated as anaphors; (39) does not directly constrain the operation of any transformation. Conceptually, this seems a desirable simplification, though, as discussed in some detail in Chapter 7 [Lasnik (1985)], rather surprisingly there are certain constraints on NP movement that cannot obviously be handled by conditions on the distribution of anaphors.

Second, the notion 'specified' is finally eliminated from the SSC, along the lines suggested above. As noted, this has both conceptual and empirical benefits. In particular, 'empty categories' are now full-fledged syntactic entities, serving as anaphors, as specified subjects, and, finally, as antecedents.

The basic Opacity Condition in (39) is modified in certain respects in Chomsky (1980). The first modification is motivated by a certain 'redundancy' present in (39), and, in fact, present in the earlier versions of the conditions as well. Consider (40):

(40)   *They told me [$_{S'}$ what I gave each other]

The reciprocal *each other* must find an antecedent; further, the antecedent must be plural, hence, not *I* in (40). (39) correctly prevents *They* from being the antecedent. However, as Chomsky notes, (39) prevents this in two different ways. *each other* is free in the domain of tense in the lower clause (the TSC/PIC); it is also free in the domain of the lower subject *I* (the SSC). More generally, PIC excludes free anaphors from both subject position and non-subject position of a finite clause, while SSC excludes free anaphors from non-subject position of both finite and non-finite clauses (and of NPs, as well). The conditions overlap with respect to non-subject of a finite clause. Chomsky proposes eliminating this redundancy by restricting the PIC to the subject of a finite clause. This is accomplished by limiting (39) to SSC effects, and adding an additional condition involving subjects of finite clauses. The revision of (39) is presented in (41), and the new condition is shown in (42):

(41)   If α is in the domain of the subject of β, β minimal, then α cannot be free in β.

(42)   A nominative anaphor cannot be free in S′.

Chomsky calls (42) the NOMINATIVE ISLAND CONDITION (NIC). Strictly speaking, this modification does not quite eliminate all redundancy between PIC and SSC, for there is still a small residue of redundancy between NIC and Opacity. In (43), the nominative anaphor *each other* is free in S', and is also free in the domain of a subject, *Mary*:

(43)   *The men think that Mary said [that each other would win]

But certainly the central instances of redundancy between the two conditions are now removed.

In addition to the advantage of eliminating a redundancy (or most of one, as it turns out), Chomsky argues that the reformulation in (41)—(42) is of empirical benefit also. Examples such as (44) constituted problems for TSC/PIC:

(44)   They expected [s' that pictures of each other (each other's pictures) would be on sale]

Compare (45):

(45)   *They expected [s' that each other would be there]

(44), unlike (45), is grammatical, but the PIC would incorrectly prohibit *They* from serving as the antecedent of *each other* in the former. In earlier work, Chomsky had suggested that PIC should be constrained by Subjacency. Since *each other* is not subjacent to *They* in (44), PIC would not take effect.[4] But now there is a simpler account available: *each other* is nominative in (45) but not in (44). Hence, only (45) is constrained by NIC (and, of course, neither example falls under SSC). And under this simpler account, Subjacency can be construed as strictly a property of movement rules.

Note that this discussion relies on something of an equivocation. Thus far, RI effects have not been considered; the disjoint reference in, say, (46) is not yet incorporated into the Chomsky (1980) framework.

(46) a. *I/We like me
     b. They like them

This omission is of potential significance in the treatment of (44), since not just an anaphor, but also a bound pronoun, is possible in the position under investigation. Consider (47):

(47)   They expected [s' that pictures of them (their pictures) would be on sale]

The pronoun in the 'picture NP' in these examples is free to corefer with the matrix subject. Thus, it will ultimately be crucial to keep RI from applying in certain contexts where bound anaphors are possible. Below, this point will be considered further, when the treatment of disjoint reference in Chomsky (1980) is presented. At present, it should be kept in mind that essentially all versions of Binding Theory from Chomsky (1973) through Chomsky (1981) are designed to capture the complementarity of anaphors and bound pronouns. This is a virtue of these versions of the theory, since such complementarity overwhelmingly obtains. But it is a defect as well, since, as just seen, the complementarity is not total.

There are two other points that should be noted, these concerning special properties of traces. First, since NP trace is an anaphor, it must conform to NIC and Opacity. And since it is created by movement, it must conform to Subjacency. Thus, Chomsky observes that (48) is not ruled out by either NIC or Opacity, since the trace is in a position permitting an anaphor, as seen in (44) above.

(48)   *The men were expected that pictures of t were on sale

But (48) (or its derivation) does violate Subjacency, and this violation provides an account for its ungrammaticality.[5] The second point to be mentioned concerns the trace of Wh-movement. Based on an argument of Rizzi (1980), Chomsky suggests that such a trace is not an anaphor for Opacity, not just in Italian, but in English, as well, the locality constraints on Wh-movement given by Subjacency instead for the relevant cases. This now partially unifies the treatment of Wh-trace, given the argument from strong crossover, discussed above, that Wh-trace has the behavior of a name. Interestingly, though, Chomsky explicitly limits the suggestion that Wh-trace is not an anaphor to Opacity effects, and not to NIC effects. Thus, he proposes that the difference between the mildly ungrammatical Subjacency violation (49) and the completely impossible (50) is to be attributed to the fact that NIC as well as Subjacency is violated in the latter.

(49)   ?What$_1$ [$_{S'}$ did you wonder [$_{S'}$ who$_2$ [$_S$ t_2 saw t_1]]]

(50)   *Who$_1$ [$_{S'}$ did you wonder [$_{S'}$ what$_2$ [$_S$ t_1 saw t_2]]]

Taraldsen (1978), Pesetsky (1981), and Kayne (1980) presented analyses along similar lines. Chapter 5 [Freidin and Lasnik (1981)] argues against any such treatment, based on strong crossover phenomena. It is true that the standard examples of crossover, such as those presented in Chomsky (1976), all involved object NPs (hence, were not inconsistent with the proposal that a *nominative* Wh-trace is an anaphor). However, alongside the strong crossover examples presented by Chomsky, such as (35b) above, there are also examples where the trace *is* nominative. And contrary to what might be expected, such examples are no better than (35b) on the relevant interpretation:

(51)   Who did he say t kissed Mary

Thus, to the extent that crossover provides a diagnostic, Wh-trace does not behave like an anaphor in NIC contexts any more than in Opacity contexts. Because of this, Chomsky (1981) rejects the NIC account of such an example as (50). To deal with this 'residue of the NIC' (RESNIC), Chomsky proposes a constraint specific to the distribution of traces, the E(mpty) C(ategory) P(rinciples), which will not be discussed here, but which is examined in detail in Lasnik and Saito (1984) [reprinted in Lasnik (1989)], Kayne (1984), and Chomsky (1986). See also Lasnik and Uriagereka (1988) and van Riensdijk and Williams (1986) and references cited in those books.

The technical details of Chomsky (1980) must now be considered, particularly with respect to the question thus far left open: How are disjoint reference effects to be handled? We begin with the theory of index assignment. First, movement involves obligatory coindexing of the moved category and its trace. Then, the remaining NPs in a sentence are indexed in 'top to bottom' fashion. ". . . an index is assigned to NP only when all NPs that c-command it or dominate it have been indexed." For anaphors, Chomsky assumes that indices are assigned by 'rules of construal', guaranteeing coindexation with an antecedent. As we will see, this introduces substantial redundancy into the system, since anaphors that are not bound in the appropriate local domain will be excluded regardless. To the extent that all relevant phenomena can be described in these terms, we will have a strong argument for free indexing.

The indices considered thus far, Chomsky calls 'referential indices'. A referential index is an integer. Nonanaphors are also assigned referential indices, though not, of course, by the same algorithm as in the case of anaphors. As before, the algorithm operates top down. But this time, contraindexing, rather than coindexing, is what is forced. Each nonanaphoric NP that has not already received an index (by movement) is assigned an unused integer as its referential index. (In this case, as well, the stipulation that the index be a new one is ultimately unnecessary.) In addition to its referential index (an integer), each nonanaphor is also assigned what Chomsky calls an 'anaphoric index'.[6] The anaphoric index of an NP is the set consisting of every integer that is the referential index of any NP c-commanding the NP in question. The (complete) index of a nonanaphor will be a pair (r, A) where r is the referential index and A the anaphoric index. Given all of this, we will have such representations as (52):

(52)   John$_{(2, \{\})}$ told Bill$_{(3, \{2\})}$ about him$_{(4, \{2, 3\})}$

It is the anaphoric index of an NP that is responsible for disjoint reference effects. This is instantiated in the following way.

We will interpret the anaphoric index $A = \{a_1, \ldots, a_n\}$ of α to mean that α is disjoint in reference from each NP with referential index a_i. Thus, *him* in [52] is disjoint in reference from *John* and *Bill*, and if *John* were to replace *him* (or *Bill*) in [52], the two occurrences of *John* would be disjoint in reference.

Notice that these indexing principles combined with this interpretive principle give the effects of both RI of Chomsky (1973) and the disjoint reference rule of Chapter 4 [Lasnik (1976)].[7] There is a conceptual difference, however. While the earlier analyses combined the syntactic and semantic aspects of disjoint reference into one rule, the proposal now under discussion separates the two aspects. There are syntactic rules and well-formedness conditions determining what syntactic representations are allowed. Then there is an interpretive principle assigning a meaning to a syntactically well-formed structure. In this clear separation of the syntax and semantics of anaphora, the analysis directly foreshadows that of Chomsky (1981), to be discussed below.

The present analysis in not yet complete. It does correctly rule out all cases of overlap in reference discussed in Chapter 4 [Lasnik (1976)]. Further, it rules out all cases covered by RI. But it does not yet capture the fact that RI showed TSC and SSC effects. Thus, it incorrectly excludes a coreferential interpretation for *John* and *he* or *him* in (53):

(53) a. John thinks he is clever
     b. John thinks Mary likes him

Chomsky proposes to capture this property and the corresponding property of anaphor binding simultaneously. Specifically, he first proposes that the binding conditions (now NIC and Opacity) can be construed "as deleting certain indices from the anaphoric index of a pronoun, thus in effect blocking certain cases of disjoint reference and permitting reference to be free." For an NP with no anaphoric index (i.e., an anaphor) the binding conditions operate on the referential index, altering it in a certain way rather similar to the way in which the anaphoric index is altered in the case of a pronoun. The binding conditions will thus affect the 'designated index' of an NP, where the designated index of a pronoun is its anaphoric index, and the designated index of an anaphor is its referential index (which is, of course, its only index). These notions are made precise as follows:

(54)   Suppose that α has the designated index j and i is an integer such that $i = j$ or $i \in j$. Then α is *free(i)* in β if there is no γ in β with index i that c-commands α.

(55)   Suppose that α has the designated index j and is free(i) in β ($\beta =$ NP or S′)
     where (a) α is nominative
        or (b) α in the domain of the subject of β, β minimal.
     Then $j \rightarrow 0$ if j is an integer, and $j \rightarrow (j - \{i\})$ if j is a set.

(55a) is the NIC and (55b) is Opacity. Consider the effects of (55) on the examples in (53). They will be initially indexed as in (56):

(56) a. John$_{(2, \{\})}$ thinks he$_{(3, \{2\})}$ is clever
     b. John$_{(2, \{\})}$ thinks Mary$_{(3, \{2\})}$ likes him$_{(4, \{2, 3\})}$

Then the NIC will cause the 2 to be eliminated from the anaphoric index of *he* in (56a), and Opacity will have the same effect on *him* in (56b):

(57) a. John$_{(2, \{\})}$ thinks he$_{(3, \{\})}$ is clever
     b. John$_{(2, \{\})}$ thinks Bill$_{(3, \{2\})}$ likes him$_{(4, \{3\})}$

The interpretive results will now be as follows: In (57a), neither *John* nor *he* is marked as necessarily disjoint from any other NP, hence these two NPs are free to corefer; in (57b), *him* is not necessarily disjoint from *John*, but *him* is disjoint from *Bill* and *Bill* is disjoint from *John*. Crucially, index substraction never applies in the case of full lexical NPs: SSC and NIC are irrelevant to disjoint reference in these instances, as noted in Chapter 4 [Lasnik (1976)].

Anaphors are treated in terms of roughly the same formalism as pronouns, as stated in (55). An example such as (58) will have as its initial indexing something like (59):

(58)   *John thinks Mary likes himself

(59)   John$_{(2, \{\})}$ thinks Mary$_{(3, \{2\})}$ likes himself$_2$

In (59), *himself* is free(2) in the domain of a subject (*Mary*) in the embedded S′. That is, in that domain, there is no NP with index 2 that c-commands *himself*. Thus, its index becomes $2 - 2 = 0$. To rule out the example, then, "It remains only to add that NP$_0$ is not permitted in LF, where 0 is the referential index."

Given this machinery, the mechanism specifically coindexing an anaphor with its antecedent becomes superfluous, as suggested above. Consider again (58), but now suppose that *himself* had been freely assigned an index, say 5:

(60)   John$_{(2, \{\})}$ thinks Mary$_{(3, \{2\})}$ likes himself$_5$

Now *himself* is free(5) in the domain of a subject in the embedded S′. Hence, just as before, the index will become 0 ($= 5 - 5$), again running afoul of the LF prohibition. Simple examples behave in the same way. In (61), if *himself* is assigned any index other than the index of *John*, Opacity will change the index to 0, thus ruling out the representation.

(61)   John likes himself

Further, even such an example as (62), where there is no potential antecedent, will be excluded in the same fashion.

(62)   *Himself left

No matter what index is assigned to *Himself*, NIC will change that index to 0. Thus, there is no need for an initial indexing algorithm for anaphors. Indices can be freely assigned to them, incorrect results all being filtered out by the interaction of NIC, Opacity, and the LF filter. All that is needed is to specify an interpretation for coindexation, in particular that two NPs with the same referential index are coreferential. See Chapter 5 [Freidin and Lasnik (1981)] for the first presentation of this argument; and see below, and Chapter 6 [Lasnik (1981)] for further discussion of this issue.

Note, incidentally, that it is now obvious why an anaphor does not have an anaphoric index. Suppose that this were not the case. Then an example such as (61) would have an initial indexing such as (63):

(63)   John$_{(2,\{\})}$ likes himself$_{(2,\;\;)}$

Since neither NIC nor Opacity is relevant here, (63) remains as the final representation. But the interpretive principle will now incorrectly demand that *John* and *himself* are disjoint in reference, a property that is not only not necessary here, but that is not even possible.

As with the formulation in (42) above, a certain class of long distance picture NP anaphors are permitted. Consider (44), repeated here as (64).

(64)   They$_{(2,\{\})}$ expected that [pictures of each other$_2$] would be on sale

In (64), *each other* is not nominative, nor is it free(2) in the domain of a subject. It is coindexed with the nearest c-commanding subject, *They*. Thus, neither NIC nor Opacity will apply, and *each other* will be allowed to keep its index. However, the potential problem noted earlier does in fact obtain. A coreferential pronoun in the position of *each other* in (64) is grammatical, yet it should not be. Consider (65).

(65)   They$_{(2,\{\})}$ expected that [pictures of them$_{(3,\{2\})}$] would be on sale

Once again, neither NIC nor Opacity operates, hence the designated index of the pronoun *them* is unaffected. But now the interpretive principle demands (apparently incorrectly) that *They* and *them* be disjoint in reference, hence, non-coreferential. Thus, the grammaticality of (64) provides but little support for this approach. After all, any approach based on complementarity between anaphors and pronouns will get at best, and at worst, half of these cases right.

Chomsky (1981), henceforth LGB, presents a second major revision of Binding Theory, motivated by what he terms a number of conceptual and empirical difficulties with the approach in Chomsky (1980), henceforth OB. One of the difficulties, I have already discussed — that NIC incorrectly included Wh-trace in its domain. Recall that this is problematic because, as indicated by crossover phenomena, Wh-trace has the behavior of a name rather than an anaphor. Among the further concerns that are addressed in Chomsky LGB, there are several more that are directly relevant to the present discussion. First, the properties of PRO were not all captured in the OB framework. In particular, the theory was too weak in not entailing that PRO occurs only in ungoverned positions (subject of infinitival or gerund), and too strong in excluding as SSC/Opacity violations certain cases of long distance control, as in (66).

(66)   They thought I said that [PRO to feed/feeding each other] would be difficult

In (66), *I* is a subject establishing an opaque domain in which an anaphor must be bound, but the antecedent of PRO, *They*, is outside of that domain. Chomsky argues that there are a number of other problems with OB that are more conceptual in nature. I turn now to some of those.

Chomsky points out a sort of 'redundancy' between the theories of Case and of binding. In effect, both theories distinguish subject of infinitives as special: this is the one basic NP position that is not (normally) marked for Case; and it is also the one position generally transparent with respect to anaphoric phenomena. Chomsky raises the question whether Opacity "cannot somehow be reduced to Case theory just as the [TSC] was reformulated in terms of considerations of Case within the OB-frame-work, as the NIC." A related question is what the two domains relevant for Binding Theory, subject of a tensed sentence and c-command domain of a subject, have in common. In terms of OB, these are in no way related.

Chomsky further suggests that the OB indexing conventions are another area where improvement is desirable. About these conventions, which were outlined in some detail above, Chomsky states,

While they work quite neatly, they are fairly complicated and it is worth asking whether it is not possible to eliminate the concept of "anaphoric index" entirely in terms of some more basic and simple notion . . .

It has already been noted that the convention for assigning *referential* indices is eliminable. Chomsky arrives at this conclusion in the course of his discussion. Momentarily, the issue of anaphoric indices will be considered. Chomsky further suggests that the phenomenon of disjoint reference itself is strange, the fact that pronouns enter into disjoint reference under the conditions where anaphors enter into coreference constituting "an odd state of affairs":

Why should languages have this peculiar design, which in fact gives rise to the complexity of the indexing conventions and of the notion 'free(i)' defined in OB? Why shouldn't pronouns have coreference, rather than disjoint reference, where, for example, reciprocals do?

To the extent that this state of affairs is problematic (and it is not entirely clear that it is), the problem is not really solved in the 'GB' framework of Chomsky (1981). Though the phenomenon is described in somewhat different terms, as we will see, it remains a basic unanalyzed property of pronouns that they show disjoint reference.

With these concerns as background, the central details of the GB approach to anaphora will now be presented. The indexing system assumed, contrary to the rather complicated one in OB, involves merely a single integer as the index of an NP. 'Bound' and 'free' are defined as in (67) and (68):

(67) α is bound by β if and only if α and β are coindexed and β c-commands α.

(68) α is free if and only if it is not bound.

The domain in which an anaphor must be bound and a pronominal free is the 'governing category' of the item in question. (69) is the first approximation of the characterization of this central notion:

(69) α is the governing category (GC) for β if and only if α is the minimal category containing β and a governor of β, where $\alpha = $ NP or S.

The concept of government relevant here is just the one relevant to Case theory, Chomsky indicates. Thus, there is a sort of unification in the theory as a whole, though no explanation is attempted for why the same structural relation should be relevant to both modules. As in OB, three basic types of nominals are assumed: anaphors, pronominals, and fully lexical NPs (here called 'R-expressions'). Recall that in OB, the differences among the three emerged in the mode of indexing, or reindexing. Anaphors received no anaphoric index, hence the designated index was the referential index. Pronominals and R-expressions had both anaphoric and referential indices, the former serving as designated index for a pronominal. Finally, R-expressions had no *designated* index, hence were not subject to reindexing at all. This three-way division now emerges in the form of the following three binding principles:

(70) A An anaphor is bound in its GC
     B A pronominal is free in its GC
     C An R-expression is free

All of these principles involve A-binding, that is, binding by an NP in a potential argument position. By A, anaphors are correctly excluded from nominative subject position, assuming that nominative Case, like other Cases, is assigned under government (by the agreement element AGR, presumably). Since no NP in an S c-commands the subject, a nominative anaphor will always be free in the minimal S containing it. This accounts for the ungrammaticality of the examples in (71), with *himself* and *each other* the anaphors in (a) and (b), and the trace of NP movement the anaphor in (c).

(71) a. *John$_1$ believes that himself$_1$ is clever
     b. *They$_1$ believe that each other$_1$ are clever
     c. *Mary$_1$ is believed t_1 is clever

Note that all of these are allowed with an infinitival complement:

(72) a. John$_1$ believes [himself$_1$ to be clever]
     b. They$_1$ believe [each other$_1$ to be clever]
     c. Mary$_1$ is believed [t_1 to be clever]

(72a, b) are straightforward. In both cases, the subject of the complement is not governed within that complement. Rather, each anaphor is governed by the exceptional Case marker *believe* in the higher clause. Thus, the matrix S is the GC in each case, and the anaphor is bound by the subject of the matrix. Similarly, in (72c), there is no governor of *t* in the complement, hence the complement is not the GC for *t*. At this point, there are actually two possibilities for *t* in this configuration: either *t* is governed by *believed* making the matrix the GC; or *t* is not governed at all, with the result that it has no GC. While both possibilities correctly allow (72c), shortly it will become clear that the first is the correct one.

Given (70b) and (70a), pronominals, as usual, are predicted to be free precisely where anaphors are bound. This is illustrated in (73) vs. (74):

(73)   *John$_1$ believes [him$_1$ to be clever]

(74)   John$_1$ believes that he$_1$ is clever

Thus, the effects of the NIC for both anaphors and pronouns follow directly from Principles A and B of the GB binding theory. The core SSC cases follow as well. Consider (75) and (76):

(75)   *John$_1$ believes [Mary to like himself$_1$]

(76)   John$_1$ believes [Mary to like him$_1$]

In these examples, the pronoun and anaphor are governed by the verb of the complement clause *like*. Hence, the GC for each is the complement clause. (75) is correctly excluded by Principle A, since *himself* is not bound in its GC. And (76) is correctly allowed by Principle B since *him* is free in its GC. Finally, Principle C gives the same distribution for R-expressions as was given by the OB assignment of anaphoric indices. The fact that locality is not relevant for R-expressions was captured by the lack of a reindexing algorithm for R-expressions, and is now captured by the irrelevance of governing category to Principle C. The examples in (77) are thus correctly excluded. While *John* is free in its GC, it does not satisfy the much stricter requirement of being entirely free:

(77) a. *He$_1$ believes that John$_1$ is clever
    b. *He$_1$ believes Mary to like John$_1$

With respect to the cases of anaphors and pronominals considered thus far, one of the problems Chomsky pointed out for OB has apparently been eliminated. It is now evident what nominative NP and NP in the domain of a subject have in common: both are governed internal to the minimal S dominating them, as seen in (73)—(76) above. Hence, both have that minimal S as a GC. Significantly, this result obtains with no stipulation. Seemingly, Chomsky has been successful in reducing two conditions to one. However, not all of the relevant phenomena have yet been considered in this new light. Recall that SSC effects show up not just in clauses but in NPs as well. For example, Chomsky (1981) presents the following contrast:

(78) a. *We$_1$ heard [their stories about each other$_1$]
    b. We$_1$ heard [some stories about each other$_1$]

In both (78a) and (78b), *each other* is governed by *about*. By (69), then, the bracketed NP is the GC for the anaphor. This correctly disallows (78a), but (78b) is incorrectly excluded as well. This is precisely the type of contrast captured in earlier work by the SSC, but it is not yet captured by the GB reformulation. Consequently, (69) is replaced by (79):

(79) β is a *governing category for* α if and only if β is the minimal category containing α, a governor of α, and a SUBJECT accessible to α.

Chomsky proposes that AGR is the SUBJECT in a finite clause; standard subject (NP of S) is the SUBJECT of an infinitival clause; and NP of NP (if present) is SUBJECT of an NP. Note first that this correctly distinguishes between (78a) and (78b). In the latter, the object NP has no SUBJECT, and the GC is thus the matrix clause, the desired result. In (78a), on the other hand, the NP does have a SUBJECT, hence constitutes a GC for the anaphor, with the result that the anaphor is, as desired, in violation of Principle A. Conversely, in these environments a bound pronoun will correctly be allowed. For clausal SSC cases such as (75) and (76), the change has no important consequence for the determination of GC, and the correct results are still obtained. Finally, the results are the same as before for NIC examples like (72)—(73): in these cases AGR now serves as both the governor for the nominative subject and as the relevant SUBJECT.

While (78) is now correctly handled, given the notion SUBJECT, it is somewhat less clear than before that the conceptual problem that concerned Chomsky has been entirely eliminated. The initial formulation of GC in (69) truly did reduce two domains (nominative NP, as in the NIC, and c-command domain of a subject, as in the SSC) to one. But for the

modification in (79), which was demanded by the facts in (78), much of
the reductive work is done by the definition of SUBJECT. And the two
parts of that definition are strikingly reminiscent of the original two
domains: AGR establishes a GC for a nominative subject, and subject
establishes a GC for any NP in its domain. Thus, the reduction is only
successful to the extent that INFL containing AGR, and subject constitute
a natural class. Chomsky suggests that they do:

The notion SUBJECT accords with the idea that the subject is the "most prominent
nominal element" in some sense, taking INFL to be the head of S.

This is not implausible, but it is not clear that this rationale provides the
correct division of cases. It is the head of S (rather than the subject of S)
that counts as the most prominent nominal in that domain, hence, the
SUBJECT. But it is crucially the subject of NP, rather than the head N of
NP, that counts as SUBJECT in that case. If this were not so, both (78a)
and (78b) would be excluded by Principle A, since, patently, both
bracketed NPs have nominal heads. Thus, in contradistinction to the
situation with Ss, presence or absence of subject is key here.

One final detail of (79), the mention of 'accessibility', remains to be
discussed. Recall that certain cases of long distance anaphors have been
problematic for most versions of BT. Example (64), repeated here as (80),
is representative:

(80)   They$_1$ expected [that [[pictures of each other$_1$] would be on
       sale]]

The embedded clause (and the subject of that clause) must not be a GC
for *each other* or Principle A will incorrectly be violated. The picture NP
has no SUBJECT, so it is immediately excluded from consideration. The
complement clause does, however, have a SUBJECT — AGR. Accessibility is defined precisely in such a way that AGR will not be an
accessible SUBJECT for *each other*:

(81) α is accessible to β if and only if β is in the c-command
       domain of α and assignment to β of the index of α would not
       violate (82).

(82)   *$[\gamma \ldots \delta \ldots]$, where γ and δ bear the same index.

(82) is often referred to as the '*i*-within-*i* condition'. Its incorporation into
(81) guarantees that a SUBJECT will not be accessible to a given anaphor
if that SUBJECT is (in fact) coindexed with a category properly containing the anaphor. Given that the subject of a finite clause is always
coindexed (via superscripts in LGB) with AGR, this being the instantiation of subject-verb agreement, that AGR will never be accessible to

anything within that subject. Consider (80) once again, but with AGR made explicit:

(83)   They$_1$ expected [that [[pictures of each other$_1$]^2 AGR^2 would be on sale]]

Here if we were to assign to *each other* the index of AGR, 2, an *i-within-i* configuration would be created, since the NP *pictures of each other* has an index 2. Thus, the embedded clause is not the GC for *each other*, and the latter is free to seek an antecedent in the matrix. Note incidentally, that AGR in the matrix clause will be accessible to *each other*, since that AGR is not coindexed with any category properly containing *each other*. The consequence of this observation is that the matrix is the GC in this case. In the present example, this is a matter of little import. But if a structure like (83) is further embedded, the GC will be correctly determined to be that embedded structure itself. As (84) shows, *each other* is not free to seek its antecedent in a larger domain:

(84)   *We$_1$ think [that they$_3$ AGR^3 expected [that [[pictures of each other$_1$]^2 AGR^2 would be on sale]]]

Simple NIC configurations will still be ruled out, as the *i-within-i* exemption will not be applicable. Consider (85):

(85)   *John$_1$ thinks that himself$_1$ AGR^1 will win

Assignment of the index of AGR to *himself* would not result in an *i-within-i* configuration. Hence, AGR is accessible to *himself*. Since AGR also governs *himself*, the GC for the latter is the embedded clause. Since it is not bound in that domain, Principle A is violated.

It might be noted that one minor problem noted above in connection with the OB approach is now eliminated. Recall that a small residue of the redundancy that Chomsky claimed to have eliminated still remained. While the change from TSC and SSC to NIC and Opacity removed the overlap in conditions in a simple example like (40), repeated as (87), (43), repeated as (88) was still ruled out by two binding conditions:

(87)   *They told me [$_{S'}$ what I gave each other]

(88)   *The men think that Mary said [that each other would win]

In (88), according to OB, *each other* is both free in the domain of a subject (*Mary*), and is a nominative anaphor free in S'. However, given the GB revision, (88) is excluded in precisely one way. Given the fact that an anaphor has (at most) one GC, there is no redundancy. The most deeply embedded clause in (88) is the GC for *each other*, and *each other* is free in that GC, in violation of Principle A.

Another somewhat more substantial problem still remains. Like OB, GB predicts essentially total complementarity between anaphors and pronouns. In the latter instance, this follows from the fact, stated in (70), that an anaphor must be bound and a pronoun free in precisely the same domain — the GC. But, as before, the device (in this case, accessibility) that allows long distance anaphor binding in limited circumstances, as in (83), will necessarily (and incorrectly) exclude a bound pronoun in the same circumstances:

(89)   They$_1$ expected [that [[pictures of them$_1$]^2 AGR^2 would be on sale]]

The GC for *them* in (89) is the matrix clause, and it is bound, hence not free, in that clause, in violation of Principle B. The problem of lack of complete complementarity is, thus, still not solved, or, indeed, even addressed. It is not until Chomsky (1986), to be discussed below, that Chomsky offers an account of this phenomenon.

A major innovation in the GB approach to anaphora involves the treatment of PRO, the base-generated null subject of non-finite clauses, as in (90)

(90)   John tried [PRO to leave]

As noted above, Chomsky argues that a defect of OB was that it failed to capture the central distributional fact that PRO must be ungoverned. Thus, the examples in (91) are all ungrammitical regardless of the index on PRO:

(91) a. *I like PRO
     b. *John believes PRO to be intelligent
     c. *Mary believes PRO is intelligent

The analysis of this fact offered in LGB is as follows. PRO is similar to overt pronouns in that it may have an antecedent, but not within its own clause or NP. On the other hand, PRO resembles anaphors in lacking intrinsic referential content. Rather, it is either assigned reference by an antecedent (the phenomenon of Control) or is indefinite in interpretation (so-called arbitrary PRO). Suppose, then, that PRO is a pronominal anaphor. By virtue of this, PRO is subject to both Principles A and B. If PRO has a GC, it must then be both bound and free in that GC, a contradiction, since free means not bound. Thus, PRO has no GC, hence, is ungoverned. The central property is therefore derived.[8]

This elegant deduction of the central distributional property of PRO clearly relies on the fact that the definition of GC makes reference to government. Is there independent justification for this aspect of the definition? Chomsky considers a simplification whereby GC (79) is changed to "binding category" as follows:

(92) β is a *binding category for* α if and only if β is the minimal
category containing α and a SUBJECT accessible to α

Principles A and B would then be stated in terms of (92):

(92) A   An anaphor is bound in its binding category
     B   A pronominal is free in its binding category

Chomsky observes that this modification has "no effects for elements that
are governed since for such elements the governor will always be contained in the binding category." For PRO, however, Chomsky shows that
the change leads to an incorrect consequence. Consider first (93), where
the modified theory still works correctly:

(93)   *John$_1$ expected [him$_1$ to win]

Here the GC for *him* is the entire sentence, since in the embedded clause
there is no SUBJECT accessible to *him*. (93) is thus correctly excluded as
a violation of (92B). The problem is that by exactly the same line of
reasoning, (94) will be incorrectly excluded.

(94)   John$_1$ tried [[PRO$_1$ to win]]

Just as in (93), the matrix is the binding category, since it contains a
SUBJECT, *John*, accessible to PRO (and no smaller domain contains
such a SUBJECT). Consequently, (94), like (93), violates (92B). Reference to government, as in (79) but not (92), is apparently necessary to
correctly distinguish (93) from (94): PRO in (94) is not governed, as an S'
boundary, a barrier to government, intervenes between it and *tried*. Thus,
there is at least a bit of independent evidence that the correct characterization of the domain relevant to binding theory involves government.

    As we have seen, if an item is ungoverned, then it has no GC. But there
is apparently an additional way for an item to have no GC, namely, for it
to have no accessible SUBJECT. This additional possibility has undesirable consequences. Consider (95):

(95)   *For each other to win would be unfortunate

In this example, though *each other* is governed (by *for*), it nonetheless has
no GC according to (79), as there is no SUBJECT accessible to it. (95)
then incorrectly fails to violate Principle A. One might imagine that (95)
simply lacks any possible interpretation, quite apart from any considerations of binding theory. However, Chomsky rejects such an account of
(95), observing that such an example as (96) could not be excluded on
such grounds.

(96)   *For each other$_1$ to win would be unfortunate for them$_1$

Chomsky argues that the simplest rule of interpretation for an anaphor would apply to any coindexed pair of NPs including the anaphor. But this simplest rule would, in fact, assign an interpretation to (96). Chomsky concludes that (96) must then fall under Principle A:

> The point is that the structural relation between the antecedent and the anaphor should be expressed in the binding theory, not by a (quite generally redundant) stipulation added to the rule of interpretation.

Consequently, (97) is added to the theory:

(97)   A root sentence is a governing category for a governed element

In both (95) and (96), *each other* is governed. Hence, the root sentence is a GC in each case, and the anaphor is not bound in that domain (in fact, is not bound at all). Both examples now violate Principle A, as desired. The identical account is available for (98), and even (99):

(98)   *Pictures of himself are on sale

(99)   *Pictures of PRO are on sale

In both examples, there is a governed anaphor, *himself* in (98) and PRO in (99). The root S is thus a GC, and the anaphor is free in that GC, violating Principle A, the desired result. Note, by the way, that the reference to government in (97) is crucial. To see this, consider an alternative such as (100):

(100)   A root sentence is a governing category for an element that otherwise has no governing category.

For the examples examined so far, it can be easily seen that (100) gives just the same results as (97). However, it has the completely unacceptable consequence that PRO will *never* be possible. This is so because given (100), PRO, like any other item, would invariably have a GC, even if it is not governed. But once it has a GC, the standard contradiction arises: it cannot be both bound and free in the same domain, hence either Principle A or Principle B would necessarily be violated. Thus, the required extension of the definition of GC must be (97), which grants the crucial exemption to an ungoverned item, rather than (100), which does not.

Chomsky points out a substantial conceptual change resulting from some of the essentially technical innovations discussed thus far with respect to LGB. Recall that in the OB approach, while disjoint reference was explicitly displayed in a representation (via the device of anaphoric indices), coreference between non-anaphors was not. That is, when a pair (R-expression, pronoun), say, were not marked as disjoint, then they were free to corefer or not. This was the formal instantiation of the free reference for pronouns of Chapter 4 [Lasnik (1976)]. Thus, as discussed in Chapter 6 [Lasnik (1981)], the OB theory made provision for three possible referential relations among NPs: disjoint reference (indicated by anaphoric index); bound anaphora (indicated by identical referential indices); and free reference. Since in LGB, every NP has exactly one index (the referential index of OB), only two possible relations between NPs are expressible. That is, two integers are either the same or different. Concerning these two possibilities, Chomsky proposes the following:[9]

> ... pronouns are "proximate" if they are coindexed with some other element and "obviative" if not coindexed with any other element ... This is ... a departure from the spirit of Lasnik's well-known proposal (Lasnik (1976)) that pronouns are free in reference, subject to other conditions.

As remarked earlier, the syntax of the LGB system is simpler than that of OB. But as also suggested, it appears to be *too* simple. That is, distinctions that evidently need to be made cannot. Chapter 6 [Lasnik (1981)] discusses this problem in detail, arguing that there are at least three linguistically significant referential relations among NPs: coreference, disjoint reference, and overlap in reference. Since the syntax provides but a two-way distinction, the theory is inadequate. It is for this reason that Chomsky (1981) concedes of the analysis that he develops that "The proposal does not appear to be feasible ..." Chomsky further suggests that this problem might be solved "by extending the theory of indexing to use of more complex indices ..." Chapter 9 [Lasnik (in press)] considers this possibility by exploring a theory in which a referential index is not a single integer but is, instead, a set of integers.

Chomsky (1982), henceforth C&C, adopts the LGB approach to binding, along with certain minor elaborations, modifications and extensions. First, an explicit feature representation of nominal types is introduced: NPs are combinations of [+/−a(naphoric), +/−p(ronominal)], with [+a] subject to Principle A and [+p] subject to Principle B. Pure anaphors, lexical ones and NP-trace, are [+a, −p]. Pure pronominals are the reverse, [−a, +p]. It is in C&C that the null analog of lexical pronouns, 'pro', is introduced. pro is argued to fill a gap in the paradigm of null NP types, and to provide a principled empty category to serve as subject in null subject languages. PRO is [+a, +p], hence subject to both Principles A and B. The PRO theorem thus holds precisely as in LGB. There is no lexical [+a, +p], since such a category would have to be both bound and free in the same domain if governed, but would be illicitly Caseless if ungoverned. Also as before, lexical R-expressions and Wh trace constitute a sort of default, having the negative value for both features — [−a, −p].

While Principles A and B are carried over unchanged from LGB, Chomsky argues that Principle C is eliminable. This argument relies on a particular approach to empty categories that Chomsky puts forward in C&C. According to this approach, there is but one empty category whose varied behavior is determined by the varied contexts in which it finds itself. The first version of the 'functional determination' algorithm deter-mining the treatment of an empty category is as follows: [10]

(101) (i)   An EC is a variable if it is in an A-position and is locally A'-bound.

(ii)   An EC in an A-position that is not a variable is an anaphor.

(iii)   An EC in an A-position that is not a variable is a pronominal if it is free or locally A'-bound by an antecedent with an independent theta role.

Following Koopman and Sportiche (1982), Chomsky argues that given (101), Principle C is rendered superfluous for strong crossover. Consider a standard example of crossover as in (102):

(102)   *Who$_1$ does he$_1$ think Mary likes e_1

Even though the empty category was created by Wh-movement, that does not suffice to make it a variable. Instead, (101) determines its status. But (101i) is inapplicable since e is not locally A'-bound; rather, it is locally A-bound, by *he*. Thus, by (101ii), it is an anaphor. Since it is free in its GC, (102) is excluded by Principle A. [(101iii) is applicable as well, but that is of no consequence for the example.] Consider now another case of crossover, (103):

(103)   *Who$_1$ does he$_1$ like e_1

Once again, (101i) is inapplicable while (101ii) and (101iii) both apply. In this instance, however, Principle A is satisfied, as e is bound in its GC (by *he*). But Principle B is violated. Examples (102) and (103) seem entirely representative. Thus, strong crossover is accounted for by Principles A and B. No appeal to Principle C is needed. According to Chomsky,

This suggests that Principle C can be entirely eliminated, since strong crossover was in fact the most important reason for maintaining it. Other cases that fall under Principle C would then have to be dealt with in other ways.

Chapter 9 [Lasnik (in press)] examines a range of these other ways and concludes that regardless of how crossover is treated, Principle C is *not* eliminable. Anaphoric epithets, first discussed in this context in Chapter 4 [Lasnik (1976)], are shown in Chapter 9 [Lasnik (in press)] to be particularly problematic for attempts to eliminate Principle C. In work subsequent to Chomsky (1982), Chomsky reinstates Principle C, even for strong crossover. This latter point is based on a number of arguments that functional determination is not the correct treatment of empty categories. Rather, as in work prior to C&C, empty categories, like lexical categories, are assumed to have intrinsic features. For the original arguments against functional determination, see Brody (1984) and Safir (1984), and for some discussion, see Lasnik and Uriagereka (1988).

Chomsky (1986), henceforth K of L, presents a number of rather substantial modifications in the theory of binding. The first to be discussed here, initially suggested in C&C, concerns Principle C. Chomsky (1977) had argued that so-called *tough*-Movement constructions, as in (104), involve Wh-movement of an operator.

(104)   John is tough [O [PRO to please *t*]]

Chomsky observes in C&C that the usual formulation of Principle C would have the incorrect effect of excluding such a representation, since *John* is presumably coindexed with *t*, resulting in the A-binding of the latter by the former. Noting that the O operator is also coindexed with the trace (via movement), Chomsky suggests that Principle C should be modified so as to preclude only *local* A-binding. In (104), though *t* is A-bound, it is not locally A-bound, because of the intervening A′-binder, *O*. The modification is instantiated as (105):

(105)   An R-expression must be A-free in the domain of the operator that A′-binds it.

In K of L, this is restated as (106), which is to be understood as in phonology as two disjunctively ordered principles:

(106)   An R-expression is A-free (in the domain of the head of its maximal chain).

In (104), the maximal chain of *t* is (*O, t*), and *t* is A-free in the domain of *O*, the head of the chain.

It is interesting to note that this is by no means the first time that problems involving *tough* constructions (and related ones) have necessitated certain complications in the theory. In fact, from the inception of modern Binding Theory in Chomsky (1973), these constructions have been problematic. Chomsky (1973) treated them by NP Movement, deriving (107) from (108).

(107)   John is tough [PRO to please *t*]

(108)   It is tough [PRO to please John]

Such an analysis captures the apparent relation between the two examples and, arguably correctly, makes the subject position a non-theta one. However, as Chomsky discussed, SSC would be violated by direct movement of the NP. Consequently, Chomsky proposed a two step derivation, with the first step involving 'PRO replacement':

(109)   It is tough [John to please *t*]

This movement is entirely within the embedded clause, and the second movement, producing (107), is from an accessible position, subject of an infinitive, just like standard raising. However, PRO replacement is quite a dubious operation, as it moves an NP into an argument position. Further, given the availability of such a derivation, it is difficult to see how to block a similar one whose first step is a legitimate instance of NP movement:

(110) a.   It is easy [e to be arrested John]
      b.   It is easy [John to be arrested t]
      c.   *John is easy [t to be arrested t]

Chapter 3 [Lasnik and Fiengo (1974)] is an early attempt to reanalyze these constructions in a way compatible with SSC but avoiding the problems just outlined. Certain aspects of the analysis were incorporated into that of Chomsky (1977), which, in its essentials, is still maintained in Chomsky (1986).

Chapter 7 [Lasnik (1985)] discusses a binding problem potentially involving the kind of redundancy considered on several occasions above. As will become evident, the proposals in K of L bear on this redundancy. The phenomenon at issue is of historical interest as well, since it is a rare case where SSC and TSC markedly diverge from Principle A: the NP movement in (111) would violate SSC and TSC, but, surprisingly, the trace *is* bound in its GC.

(111)   *John$_1$ is believed [(that) [he$_1$ likes t$_1$]]

An account of (111) in terms of Case, for example, via a prohibition of Case-marked NP trace, results in massive redundancy for (112), which would violate this Case constraint as well as the ECP and Principle A.[11]

(112)   *John is believed [(that) [t is intelligent]]

In part to eliminate a portion of this redundancy, Chomsky in effect excises the NIC from the binding principles, leaving only the SSC as the characterization of GC. As we will see, for Principle A, the revision amounts to the requirement that an anaphor must select the nearest potential binder.[12] Principle A has always had something of this flavor, except that AGR, which can never serve as an *actual* A-binder, nonetheless blocked access to a higher binder in standard NIC contexts. If, as proposed in K of L, AGR does not count as an accessible SUBJECT, conceptual simplification results.

Before we proceed to the precise details of the K of L proposal, one further phenomenon motivating the revision should be considered. As has been observed earlier, while the theory of binding has been based on complementarity between anaphors and bound pronouns, there are exceptions to this complementarity. (113) and (114) are two such configurations.

(113) a. The children like [each other's friends]
      b. The children like [their friends]

(114) a. The children thought that [[pictures of each other] were on sale]
      b. The children thought that [[pictures of them] were on sale]

As also noted earlier, and as discussed by Huang (1983), these paradigms suggest that the GCs for anaphor and for pronouns are different. The formulation about to be considered addresses both of the problems just mentioned: redundancy, and lack of total complementarity. In the following, 'CFC' stands for 'complete functional complex'. A CFC consists of a lexical head and all grammatical functions compatible with that head. According to Chomsky, what we want the theory to say is that

... the relevant governing category for an expression α is the least CFC containing a governor of α in which α could satisfy the binding theory with some indexing (perhaps not the actual indexing of the expression under investigation).

To the extent that the theory is able to state this, it will correctly allow both (113a) and (113b). In the former, though the object NP is a CFC, and though it has a governor for *each other* (since *each other* is assigned Case), there is no indexing on which the anaphor could be bound within that NP. Thus, the entire clause is the GC, and the anaphor is bound in that domain. In (113b), on the other hand, the object NP is the GC for the pronoun, since there is some indexing on which the pronoun is free within that NP. In fact, it is free in that domain on *any* indexing. The examples of (114) will also both be allowed. In (114a), there is no potential binder for *each other* nearer than the matrix subject. Hence, the matrix clause is the GC, and the anaphor is bound in that domain. In (114b), the NP *pictures of them* seems not to be a CFC, since a grammatical function compatible with the head *pictures* is not represented. If this is correct, then the fact that *them* is free in that NP does not suffice. However, the complement clause is clearly a CFC, and *them* is also free in that domain. Thus, there is some indexing on which BT could be satisfied in that domain. That clause is therefore a GC, and the pronoun is free in that GC. Note finally that, as desired, Principle A is no longer applicable to (112). There is no potential indexing on which *t* could be bound in the embedded clause, hence that clause is not a GC. A portion of the redundancy noted thus disappears: only ECP and Case requirements are relevant to (112).

This conception of BT does raise certain questions of its own. Before proceeding to these, I present in (115) and (116) Chomsky's formulation. I omit Principle C, since it is unaffected by the considerations under discussion. In (115) and (116), E is an expression with indexing I, α is an NP, and β is a domain. The indexing I and the pair (α, β) are 'BT-compatible' if α satisfies the binding theory in local domain β under indexing I. (116) is to be understood as a "licensing condition . . . for a category α governed by a lexical category γ in the expression E with indexing I . . ."

> (115)   I is BT-compatible with (α, β) if:
>   (A) α is an anaphor and is bound in β under I
>   (B) α is a pronominal and is free in β under I

> (116)   For some β such that (a) is true, I is BT-compatible with (α, β):
>   (a) α is an anaphor or pronominal and β is the least CFC containing γ for which there is an indexing J (not necessarily the actual indexing) BT-compatible with (α, β)

Since this theory is designed to allow environments in which either anaphors or bound pronouns can occur, the first question to ask is whether PRO is correctly excluded from such positions. That is, if a position is consistent with the requirements on anaphors, and independently consistent with the requirements on pronominals, why would it not be compatible with those of a pronominal anaphor, incorrectly allowing (117)?

(117) a.   *The children like [PRO friends]
      b.   *The children thought that [[pictures (of) PRO] were on sale]

The answer is, in some respects, a rather unsatisfyingly technical one. Consider, for example, (117a) in the light of (115)–(116). The object NP is the least CFC containing PRO and a governor for PRO. Further, there is a potential indexing, namely any indexing, under which PRO is free in that domain, in evident satisfaction of the licensing condition for pronominals. Now note that if PRO is coindexed with *The children*, the licensing condition for anaphors will be satisfied as well. The matrix is the smallest CFC containing a governor for PRO in which there is a potential BT-compatible indexing. But, by hypothesis, this potential indexing is once again the *actual* indexing, and the requirement seems to be satisfied. The solution to this apparent problem lies in the precise statement of (116): "For some β" takes scope over the entire constraint. Thus, there must be precisely one domain in which the licensing requirements are satisfied. The analysis of (117) presented immediately above is thus excluded, since it relied on two different β's, the object NP and the matrix S. This now raises the question of how PRO is *ever* possible, even in an ungoverned position. The answer is that the above licensing condition is strictly for *governed* α. Interestingly, it is still true that explicit reference to government cannot be avoided.

Exploring the details of K of L further, note that the stipulation (97) in

LGB, motivated by examples such as (98) and (99), repeated here as (118) and (119), is no longer needed.

(118) *Pictures of himself are on sale

(119) *Pictures of PRO are on sale

Recall that in the LGB theory, since *himself* and PRO in these examples had no accessible SUBJECT, they had no GC, an incorrect result. Consequently, it had to be stipulated that the root sentence is the GC in such cases. But now, the ungrammaticality of (118)—(119) follows directly. (116) is a licensing condition for a governed anaphor, but is not satisfied in either example, since in neither case is there a β with a possible indexing J BT-compatible with (α, β). That is, there is no NP that c-commands the anaphor. Thus, *himself* and PRO are not licensed. (120), on the other hand, will be allowed:

(120) Pictures of him are on sale

Here, the matrix is a CFC containing a governor for *him*, and there is a possible BT-compatible indexing J; in fact, any indexing is BT-compatible, since the requirement on a pronominal is that it be free.

Traditional SSC effects, as in (121), are easily accommodated:

(121) a. *John$_1$ believes [Mary$_j$ to like himself$_1$]
      b.   John$_1$ believes [Mary$_j$ to like him$_1$]

In (121a), licensing for *himself* fails. The embedded S is the least CFC containing a governor for *himself* in which *himself* could be bound, but it is not. In (121b), on the other hand, licensing succeeds. The embedded S is the least CFC containing a governor for *him* in which *him* could be free, and it is free in that domain.

Turning now to NIC effects, we have already seen that part of the motivation for the K of L theory is that it eliminates the redundancy evident in (112) between NIC and other conditions by, in effect, eliminating NIC. However, there were other traditional NIC effects involving no such redundancy, and these now are unexplained. Consider (122):

(122) *John$_1$ believes [(that) [himself$_1$ is intelligent]]

There is no potential binder for *himself* in the embedded clause. Consequently, the matrix is the domain in which (115A) must be satisfied, and it is so satisfied. Thus, there is no BT violation in (122). Further, since *John* and *himself* do not constitute an A chain, the Case requirement alluded to in connection with (112) is not relevant. Finally, the third constraint relevant to (112), the ECP, appears not to be relevant here, because there is no trace. However, based on a proposal of Lebeaux (1983), Chomsky argues that this is only an appearance. Chomsky suggests that at LF, lexical anaphors must undergo movement,

... rather in the manner of reflexivization in the Romance languages, with a reflexive clitic binding a trace ... English would have LF-movement of the anaphor corresponding to the S-structure representation in the Romance case ...

Then, if ECP is implicated in (112), it would also be relevant to (122). In both instances, there would be a trace in a position not susceptible to proper government. In a sense, in connecting conditions on traces and lexical anaphors in this way, the theory has come full circle. Recall that in OB, there was an attempt, abandoned in LGB in favor of the ECP, to derive a constraint on Wh-trace from the NIC. Now in K of L, we have the same connection, but in reverse: an analysis of NIC in terms of ECP.[13] The resulting theory handles a substantial range of cases in a reasonably straightforward way, and the rather problematic notion accessible SUBJECT is eliminated. With respect to the recurrent themes of this chapter, the near complementarity between anaphors and bound pronouns is accommodated in essentially the way that it always was, but now the residue of non-complementarity is handled as well. Further, virtually no redundancy remains internal to BT, and some of the redundancy between BT and other modules has also been eliminated.

Chomsky's successive modifications in BT have been summarized and illustrated in this chapter, but it is important not to overemphasize these changes. In important ways, the most recent theory discussed here, that of K of L, is still very closely related to the earliest, that of Chomsky (1973). Conceptually, the requirement that a pronominal must be free in a certain domain, which is now enforced by (115) and (116), is not drastically different from RI, illustrated in (5)–(7). Further, the central distinction between pronouns and anaphors, which was implicit in Chomsky (1973) and explicit in Chomsky (1976), is as important as ever. Even the notion of a domain defined (at least in part) by subject is in evidence early, the SSC (1a), and late, CFC. The extension of the insight behind RI, that the theory should incorporate a device disallowing coreference, from the local affects of RI to more distant ones in Lasnik (1976) remains in the form of Principle C. In fact, the developments explored here can best be seen not as a series of revolutionary upheavals in the study of anaphora, but rather as the successive refinement of one basic approach, and one that has proven remarkably resilient. Given that BT has become the subject of intensive investigation, with new phenomena in previously unexplored languages being constantly brought to bear, and all this while old problems from familiar languages remain, further refinements, or even revolutionary upheavals, are inevitable.

NOTES

[1] Chomsky appears to assert exactly the opposite of this, following his example (54). But this is only an appearance. His phrase structure rules reversed the convention of Bresnan (1970), on which they were based, and they were also the reverse of the now standard convention. Thus, instead of S′ → COMP S, he had S → COMP S′.

[2] It is interesting to note that successive cyclic movement is thus generally enforced by both (1) and Subjacency, the other major constraint first proposed in Chomsky (1973). This sort of 'redundancy' (though not this particular case) was already a concern in Chomsky (1973). It was to become a recurrent issue.

[3] Semantically, this would already be problematic, of course.

[4] Note, however, that SSC must not be constrained by Subjacency. (i) is generally not regarded as significantly better than (ii):

(i)   *They believe Mary likes each other

(ii)   *They believe Mary to like pictures of each other

[5] Later, this will be qualified, in light of the fact that the example is far worse than an ordinary 'island' violation.

[6] The terminology is somewhat unfortunate, since anaphors crucially do not have anaphoric indices. Only nonanaphors do.

[7] One obvious minor difference is that the rule in Chapter 4 is stated in terms of precedence and 'kommand', while subsequent work assumed the purely hierarchical c-command, introduced in Reinhart (1976). But see Chapter 8 [Barss and Lasnik (1986)] for some evidence that linear order might, in fact, be relevant to anaphora.

[8] Momentarily, we will see that the 'PRO theorem' does not follow in its entirety from these considerations. One further stipulation, albeit one with some independent justification, will be needed. It might also be noted that the PRO theorem rather strongly relies on Principles A and B involving the same domain. If, for example, the domain in which an anaphor had to be bound were larger than the domain in which a pronoun had to be free, then a governed pronominal anaphor would, in principle, be able to exist. Thus, apart from the near total complementarity of overt anaphors and pronominals, the fact that governed PRO is always ungrammatical provides further evidence that the relevant domains for Principles A and B are, at least, very similar.

[9] It is not entirely clear what the terms 'proximate' and 'obviative' in the following quotation mean. Earlier in LGB there is a characterization given, but it cannot be what is intended here, for it would be largely circular: "... we will call a pronoun or PRO "proximate" when it is coindexed with an antecedent and "obviative" when it is not."

[10] A category is locally A/A′-bound if its closest binder is in an A/A′-position. Note that (101) does not allow for a pure pronominal empty category. For this reason, (ii) is ultimately modified to allow optional assignment of [+a].

[11] The theory of Case developed in K of L extends to (i), since it is proposed that even adjectives and nouns assign Case (what Chomsky calls 'inherent Case'):

(i)   *John$_1$ is believed [(that) [he$_1$ is proud t_1]]

However, even this view of Case does not extend to (ii), since, crucially, inherent Case is only assigned under theta marking, and *belief* in (ii) does not theta mark the position of *t*.

(ii)   *John$_1$ seems [(that) [[his$_1$ belief [t_1 to be intelligent]] is absurd]]

        cf. It seems that John's belief that he is intelligent is absurd

See Lasnik and Uriagereka (1988) and Lasnik and Saito (in press) for further discussion.

[12] Earlier, Huang (1983) suggested an approach to the characterization of GC that was conceptually rather similar to this one, motivated by considerations to be considered immediately below.

[13] See Aoun (1985) for an approach to these phenomena conceptually similar to the one in OB, but foreshadowing certain aspects of the one in K of L.

THE LOGICAL STRUCTURE OF
RECIPROCAL SENTENCES IN ENGLISH
1973

1. INTRODUCTION

In the following investigation we will consider the syntactic behavior and semantic interpretation of reciprocal sentences. We will demonstrate that if the semantic interpretation of reciprocal sentences is effected by means of a cyclic interpretive rule, apparent irregularities can be explained. We will also provide both semantic and syntactic arguments that the analysis of reciprocals proposed by Dougherty (1970) is incorrect.

2. THE SYNTAX OF 'EACH OTHER'

We propose that *each other* never arises from a transformation, but rather is generated freely as a deep structure pronominal NP. We agree with Dougherty (1970) that there exists a rule of Quantifier Movement which moves distributive quantifiers from subject NPs into the auxiliary. Quantifier Movement operates on underlying structures such as (1) to yield (2) or (3). This rule is similar to Postal's rule of Q-Float:[1]

(1)   Each one of the men will hit Mary

(2)   The men each will hit Mary

(3)   The men will each hit Mary

The deep structure of the subject of (1) may be postulated to be roughly (4):

(4)

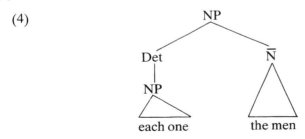

An optional transformation deletes *one* in structures such as (4); Q-Movement then optionally applies. If Q-Movement does not apply, the transformation which inserts *of* into structures such as (5) and (6) will operate on (4) to yield either the subject of (1), or (7), depending on whether the optional rule deleting *one* has applied:

(5)   the destruction of the city

(6)   the taming of the shrew

(7)   each of the men

We may postulate that Q-Movement applies if *one* has been deleted.

Only one quantifier will be generated per NP; thus ungrammatical sentences such as (8) will have no source.

(8)   *Each of the men will $\left\{ \begin{array}{l} \text{each} \\ \text{both} \\ \text{all} \end{array} \right\}$ hit Mary

The general factual proposal which we make is that there exists a transformational relationship between the placements of the quantifiers in subject and auxiliary positions, but no relationship between either of these positions and object position. In Sections 5 and 6 we will consider an analysis by Dougherty in which he argues for the existence of this second relationship. There we will provide arguments against such an analysis.

We will now propose a rule of semantic interpretation for reciprocal constructions. We will argue that this rule captures a number of semantic generalizations which Dougherty's analysis misses.

3. THE SEMANTICS OF RECIPROCITY

Consider first the meanings of (9) and (10):

(9)   each of the men is hitting the other

(10)   the men are hitting each other

(11)   each of the men is hitting the others

If there are only two men referred to in (9) and (10), the sentences are synonymous. In both sentences, each man both hit, and was hit by, the other man. Consider now sentences (10) and (11) when applied to the interaction of ten men. Sentence (11) states that every man is hitting every other man; every possible reciprocal hitting relationship is satisfied. We will refer to such a relationship as an *each-the-other* relationship. Sentence (10), on the other hand, does not necessitate that all possible pairwise hitting relationships be fulfilled. The truth conditions of (10) could be satisfied by a situation in which the men are standing in five distinct pairs. If there exists a reciprocal hitting relationship within the members of each pair, (10) can be used to describe the situation, but not (11). In other words, suppose that there are n men in a room and men 1 and 2 are hitting each other (i.e., 1 is hitting 2, and 2 is hitting 1); and men 3 and 4 are hitting each other (i.e., 3 is hitting 4, and 4 is hitting 3) . . . . This situation can be described by sentence (10) but not by sentence (11), since (11) requires that every member of the set under consideration be related to every other member of that set by the relationship asserted. That is to say, in (11) every possible pairwise relationship is fulfilled.

Suppose now that there are nine men in the room, divided into three groups of two and one trio as in diagram (12).

(12)

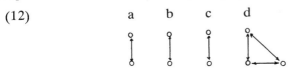

For (a), (b), and (c), each man is hitting the other; in trio (d), each man is hitting the others. It seems to us that (12) can also be described by sentence (10). In general, if it is possible to divide a set into subsets such that within each subset an *each-the-other* relationship holds, then the whole set of events can be described by an *each other* sentence such as (10). These intuitions may be described in the following manner (let S equal the set of men):

(13)   Every member of S hit every other member of S

(14) S can be divided into subsets S_i such that every member of S_i hit every other member of S_i

(13) defines an *each-the-other* relationship; (14) defines a reciprocal, or *each other*, relationship. Thus (13) is a special case of (14), namely, when the number of subsets = 1. Intuitively, then, an *each other* sentence can be appropriately used under either of two circumstances: when all of the members of the set are involved in one *each-the-other* relationship, or when the set can be divided into subsets such that an *each-the-other* relationship holds among the members of each subset.[2] In (13) and (14) *hit* is the particular relationship asserted by the sentence; we will use the symbol R to designate any semantic relationship in the more precise statements of these relationships below. When the conditions of (13) are fulfilled for some relationship R we will say that R is *each-the-other* in S; when the conditions of (14) are fulfilled we will say that R is reciprocal in S.

(15) R is *each-the-other* in S if $\forall_x \forall_y \in S, x \neq y \supset xRy$ where $\overline{\overline{S}} \geq 2$

(16) R is reciprocal in S if $\exists$ a partition of S into $s_1 \ldots s_n | \forall_i$, R is *each-the-other* in s_i

This formalism implies that when S has less than four members, n must equal 1, since we have required that the subsets be disjoint (by the definition of partition), that each subset have at least two members, and that x be distinct from y. When $n = 1$, (15) and (16) are synonymous.

(16) defines a relationship in a set. This set is the referent of the NP antecedent of the reciprocal pronoun *each other*. In Section 4, we will specify the input and form of a Reciprocal Rule (RR) that relates reciprocal structures to their semantic interpretations.

A further interesting semantic distinction between reciprocal and *each-the-other* sentences is the following. Reciprocal sentences often, but not always, require that the events referred to occur simultaneously, or in the same general time span. In *each-the-other* sentences there is never such a requirement. For example, consider (17) and (18):

(17)   Each of the cars bumped into the other; the Pontiac bumped into the Plymouth on Monday, and the Plymouth bumped into the Pontiac on Tuesday

(18)   The cars bumped into each other; *the Pontiac bumped into the Plymouth on Monday, and the Plymouth bumped into the Pontiac on Tuesday

The requirement that the events referred to in reciprocal sentences occur in the same general time span seems to be the result of the fact that the events characterized by reciprocal sentences are regarded as one general event. For example, consider (19) and (20), which are parallel to (17) and (18):

(19)   Each of the men stared at the other; John stared at Bill for 3 hours and then Bill stared at John for 3 hours

(20)   The men stared at each other; *John stared at Bill for 3 hours and then Bill stared at John for 3 hours

In (19), as in (17), distinct events at different times can be referred to. In (20), as in (18), one event at one time is referred to; in (20) a mutual staring, in (18) a collision.

These facts are not restricted to reciprocal sentences, but follow from general semantic properties of singulars and plurals. In the vast majority of cases, the joint reading of the plural is unmarked; that is to say, the reading in which one event is referred to is preferred. In (21), the preferred reading is that there was a single assault of the mountain by a group of climbers; in (22), the highly favored reading is that the musicians played together, not separately or at different times.

(21)   The men climbed Mt. Everest

(22)   The musicians played Beethoven's 5th

Since when the antecedent of a reciprocal sentence is the subject, the subject is plural, and since plural subjects favor a joint reading, it is not surprising that (18) and (20) require the joint reading. As we have seen in examples (21) and (22), the degree to which the joint reading is favored depends on the particular predicate. In (23) the non-joint reading is much less marked than in (21).

(23)   The women left

Similarly, in (24) there is the possibility that what is referred to is not a debate, but separate events.

(24)   The candidates criticized each other

Let us now consider the significance of this result with respect to the analysis given in Section 2. We have accepted that (25) and (26) are related by Quantifier Movement.

(25)   Each of the men will stare at the other

(26)   The men will each stare at the other

These sentences are synonymous in all respects, including the existence of the distinct-events reading. In (27), as we have noted, the distinct events reading is not available.

(27)   The men will stare at each other

We have proposed that the preference for a joint reading is based on plurality. The question arises as to where plurality is interpreted. In the analysis given in Section 2, (25) and (26) will have a singular subject in deep structure and (27) will have a plural subject in deep structure. Thus the semantic distinction which we have noted can be captured in deep structure.[3]

Because RR generates a semantic interpretation for reciprocal sentences which specifies that a relationship holds between non-identical items, RR produces semantic anomaly when the antecedent which it identifies is semantically singular. It is for this reason that (28) is anomalous:

(28)   *Balthazar hit each other

Thus *binoculars*, though syntactically plural, as (29) implies, cannot be the antecedent of *each other*.

(29)   The binoculars are on the table

(30)   *The binoculars are focused differently from each other (one pair)

There appears to be another difference between *each other* and *each-the-*

other sentences in addition to the semantic difference captured by (15) and (16). The fact that *each-the-other* sentences characterize each member of the set, while *each other* sentences can characterize the entire set, seems to be responsible for the fact that *each other* sentences allow vagueness in their interpretation. For example, if one walked into a room and a general brawl were going on, one could say (31), but not (32).

(31)   The men are hitting each other

(32)   Each of the men is hitting the others

We suspect that this vagueness represents the impossibility of discrete partitioning in an unclear situation. In terms of the formalism of (16), the subsets of *S* will be non-discrete. Therefore, in the vague interpretation, the condition is that every member of the set must be in a reciprocal relationship with another member sometime during the unclear situation.

Let us now consider some apparent counter-examples to the theory which we have proposed for the semantic interpretation of reciprocal sentences. Consider first symmetric predicates (that is, predicates for which aRb implies bRa) such as *equal, congruent mod 3, related by blood, similar, resemble*, etc., and in particular the following sentence:

(33)   The numbers in the list below are congruent mod 3 to each
        other
        2, 3, 4, 5, 6, 7, 8, 9, 10

(33) is clearly false even though there exists a partition of the list into three sets, namely $\{2, 5, 8\}$, $\{3, 6, 9\}$, and $\{4, 7, 10\}$, such that each set satisfies the *each-the-other* relationship. Thus (33) is an apparent counter-example to our analysis of *each other* sentences. Along the same lines consider (34):

(34)   The men in the room are the same height as each other

Sentence (34) cannot designate the situation illustrated in diagram (35):

(35)   5′7″○ ↔ ○5′7″
        6′2″○ ↔ ○6′2″
        7′1″○ ↔ ○7′1″

But this is not merely a fact about symmetric predicates; it is a general fact about stative predicates. Consider the following contrasts:

(36)   The men in the room are hitting each other

(37)   The men in the room know each other

(38)   The men in the room are looking at each other

(39)   The men in the room see each other

As we have argued above, (36) can be true if there exists a partition of *the men* such that within each subset the *each-the-other* relationship holds. For (37), however, the relationship *know* must hold for all possible pairs in the room. The distinction between (38) and (39) is parallel.

The generalization appears to be that stative predicates do not allow partitioning of S.[4] Above we gave examples of symmetric predicates which manifested this property; these symmetric predicates were stative. It can be seen, however, that the relevant distinction is between actives and statives, rather than between symmetrics and non-symmetrics, since active symmetrics *can* be interpreted with a partitioning of S. Consider the following active symmetric:

(40)   The men in the room are conversing with each other

The sentence 'A is conversing with B' implies that 'B is conversing with A'. Thus (41) is anomalous:

(41)   *A is conversing with B, but B isn't conversing with A

The verb *converse* is active, since it occurs in the progressive, can take imperatives, etc. (40) can, however, be given a partition reading; e.g. (40) can refer to three groups of men conversing in different corners of the room.

The behavior of reciprocals in stative environments seems parallel to the behavior of the progressive in stative environments. It is conceptually possible to iterate states; one can conceive of a situation in which John successively buys and sells the same car a number of times. But (42) cannot refer to this situation. Perhaps both of these facts can be explained by postulating that the linguistic entity 'state' is defined as non-partitionable, either by RR, or in the time continuum.[5]

(42)   *John was owning a car

With many symmetric predicates, the surface appearance of an object *each other* is optional. Thus each of the following sentences has the same meaning, whether or not *each other* is present.

(43) a.   The men met (each other)
     b.   The men were similar (to each other)
     c.   The men conversed (with each other)
     d.   The men are the same height (as each other)
     e.   The triangles are congruent (to each other)

Recall that the non-stative verbs, such as *converse* in (43)c, are partitionable. Thus sentences with verbs like *converse* behave like reciprocal sentences even when they do not manifest the reciprocal pronoun object. This suggests that (43)a—e undergo RR whether or not *each other* is present on the surface. One way to effect this is to specify that the set of

symmetric verbs obligatorily takes (prepositional) objects, and that there is
a rule which optionally deletes (*P*) *each other*, when it is semantically
redundant.[6]

We have seen that statives and actives behave differently with respect
to reciprocal constructions; in fact this distinction was captured rather
easily by our formal mechanism. We now wish to consider another
semantic class which behaves differently with respect to reciprocal constructions: the 'linear configurationals'. We would like to make it clear that
we know very little concerning this class, but we feel that the data has
considerable intrinsic interest. Some examples are as follows:

(44) a. a stack of trays
     b. a nest of pots

Linear configurationals define a set of objects which are in a common
linear configuration. That is to say, we wish to include cases such as (45)
and (46), but not (47) and (48).

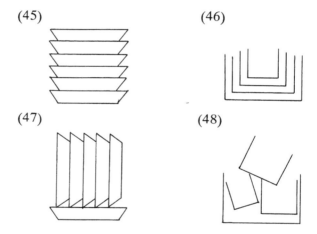

(45)   (46)

(47)   (48)

(45) can be described by the sentence 'The trays are stacked on top of
each other', but (47) cannot be so described. (46) can be described by the
sentence 'The boxes are nested in each other', but (48) cannot be so
described. Note, however, that if there is a line of men, with every man
hitting the man on his right, the situation cannot be described by the
sentence 'The men are hitting each other'. This situation seems analogous
to (45) and (46)' in the relevant respects. Thus, when a reciprocal
sentence is used to describe a linear configuration, there is not real
reciprocity, in the sense in which we have defined it. Apparently, all that is
necessary for the truth conditions of a sentence such as 'The boxes are
nested in each other' is that each box be inside of the preceding box. For
the sentence 'The trays are on top of each other' all that is required is that
each tray be on top of the preceding tray. Note that in the case of

sentences involving linear configurationals, the presence of the phrase containing the reciprocal is optional. That is, 'The trays are stacked on top of each other' is synonymous to 'The trays are stacked', and 'The boxes are nested in each other' is synonymous to 'The boxes are nested'. Thus, a linear configuration may be defined as in (49).

(49) $\forall_i, x_i R x_{i-1}$

where $i \geqslant 2$ and where R specifies a linear relation.

4. THE FORM AND ORDERING OF THE RECIPROCAL RULE (RR)

Consider the following sentences:

(50)   The men hit each other

(51)   *Each other hit the men

The ungrammaticality of sentence (51) indicates minimally that the rule of semantic interpretation RR selects an antecedent to the left of the reciprocal.

Now consider the following sentences:

(52)   *The men believed that each other had hit Mary

(53)   *The men insist that each other hit Mary

(54)   *The men want very much for each other to hit Mary

Sentences (52)–(54) indicate minimally that RR cannot relate *each other* to an NP across an intervening sentence initial complementizer. In contrast, consider example (54) with the complementizer absent.

(55)   *The men believed each other had hit Mary

(56)   *The men insist each other hit Mary

(57)   The men want each other to hit Mary[7]

A syntactic parallel to this semantic phenomenon has been discussed by Bresnan.[8] Bresnan argues that there exists a general constraint on transformations which states that the subject of a sentence cannot move across the complementizer of that sentence. Under this assumption, contrast (58) with (59), and (60) and (61) with (62):

(58)   *Who do you believe that hit Mary?

(59)   Who do you believe hit Mary?

(60)   *Who do you long for to die?

(61)   *Who do you long to die?

(62)   Who do you want to die?

The ungrammatically of (58) can be explained by Bresnan's Complementizer Constraint (CC). (59) is grammatical, since the complementizer has been deleted before Wh-Movement, which we will assume to be cyclic. This assumption implies that *for* and tensed *that* deletion are cyclic. (60) is explained by CC; (61) is ungrammatical since *for* cannot delete with the verb *long*, as (63) and (64) attest:

(63)   *John longed Bill to die

(64)   John longed for Bill to die

(62) is grammatical because the complementizer can delete with *want*.[9] Under this analysis, consider (65) and (66):

(65)   Who do you believe left?

(66)   *Who do you insist leave?

(65) and (66), assuming CC, argue minimally that *that*-deletion in tensed clauses and *that*-deletion in tenseless clauses are different phenomena. The ungrammatically of (66) may be explained by CC if we assume that *that*-deletion in tenseless sentences is a low-level post-cyclic rule. Thus, at the stage at which Wh-Movement applies, *that* is still present in (66). A fact which is consistent with this analysis is that for many speakers *that* cannot delete in tenseless clauses at all, whereas the possibility of deletion of *that* after verbs like *believe* is the general rule.

   Earlier, we proposed that *each other* is not the output of a syntactic rule, but that it is related to its antecedent by a semantic rule, which we have called RR. If CC can be generalized to constrain semantic rules, and in particular RR, the judgments in (52)—(57) above will be explained, with the exception of (55). (52)—(54) are ungrammatical, because in each case there is a complementizer between the reciprocal and its would-be coreferent. The ungrammatically of (56) will follow automatically from the assumption that RR is cyclic, since, as we have tried to argue, *that*-deletion in subjunctives is post-cyclic. (In this section we will give further arguments that RR is cyclic.) The last remaining problem in this section is the ungrammaticality of sentence (55). (55) may be ruled out if RR is made subject to the Tensed-*S* Constraint.[10]

   RR operates on structures roughly of the form

(67)   NP *X* each other

and links *each other* with NP. This formalism explains the fact that sentences (68) and (68′) are semantically well-formed, but makes the incorrect prediction that (69) and (69′) are well-formed.

(68)   The men gave slaves$_i$ to each other$_i$

(68')   The men$_i$ gave slaves to each other$_i$

(69)   *The men gave slaves$_i$ each other$_i$

(69')   *The men$_i$ gave slaves each other$_i$

However, the ungrammaticaly of (69) and (69') may be explained by the fact that *each other* is a pronoun, and thus cannot occur as the second NP in a double object construction. For example, (70) is also ungrammatical.

(70)   *John gave Mary it   (cf., John gave it to Mary)

John R. Ross has pointed out to us a further argument that *each other* is a pronoun. In verb particle constructions, pronoun objects can come only between the verb and the particle. ('John gave it up'. *'John gave up it'.) Full noun phrase objects can come after the particle as well. ('John gave the plan up'. 'John gave up the plan'.) As examples (71) and (71') demonstrate, *each other* behaves like a pronoun in this respect.

(71)   They gave each other up

(71')   *They gave up each other

For some speakers, there is a sharp contrast between sentences (72) and (73):

(72)   *The men asked John about each other

(73)   The men asked about each other

For these speakers, one might conclude that X in (67) above may contain no NP. But this is incorrect, since all speakers accept sentences like (74):

(74)   The men asked questions about each other

Thus, for those speakers who reject (72), it would appear that X can contain an NP, but only an NP which is semantically contained in R of definition (16). That is, *ask questions about* is a possible semantic relation linking two people, while the phrase *ask John about* is not. This is reflected by the fact that *ask questions about* has a roughly synonymous lexical item *investigate*, but there is no conceivable lexical item meaning *ask John about*. Along the same lines, there are speakers who accept (75), but reject (76):

(75)   The men told lies about each other (cf. slandered)

(76)   *The men told John about each other

A similar case is illustrated by sentences (77) and (78):

(77)   The men talked to each other about each other

(78)   *The men talked to John about each other

Some speakers reject (78), but everyone accepts (77). For those who accept (78) there is no problem explaining the grammaticality of (77). For those who don't accept (78), that is, for those speakers who require that an NP in *X* be in *R*, (78) is ungrammatical because *talk to John about* is not a possible *R*. But *talk to each other about* is a possible *R*; *discuss* can have this meaning.

We will now consider the ordering of RR. The following contrast demonstrates that RR cannot operate on deep structure, but must follow some transformations.

(79)   The men showed the women pictures of each other

(80)   The men showed pictures of each other to the women

In sentence (79), *each other* can refer to *the women*, and, for some speakers, sentence (79) is fully ambiguous. In sentence (80), however, *each other* can only refer to *the men* and cannot refer to *the women*. But sentences (79) and (80) are transformationally related (note that it makes no difference whether (79) is derived from (80) or vice versa). It follows that RR cannot operate on deep structure.

Consider now the following examples:

(81)   Which men does Mary believe to have hit each other?

(82)   The men who Mary believes to have hit each other

(83)   Which men do the women believe to have hit each other?

(84)   The men who the women believe to have hit each other

If we assume that Wh-Movement is cyclic, it follows that RR is cyclic. If RR were post-cyclic, in (83) and (84), *the women* could wrongly be selected as the antecedent of *each other*, since, as we have already shown, *each other* takes an NP to its left as its antecedent. Thus, under the post-cyclic hypothesis, (83) and (84) should be either ambiguous, or *each other* should refer uniquely to *the women*. The meaning of the strings, however, links *each other* uniquely to *the men*. Thus, the hypothesis that RR is post-cyclic cannot be correct. (83) and (84) should be contrasted with (85) and (86):

(85)   The men believed the women to have hit each other

(86)   *The men believed John to have hit each other

In (85), only *the women* can be the antecedent of *each other*, and (86) is ungrammatical. Thus if RR is post-cyclic, RR will have to be formulated to differentiate (85) from (83) and (84), and (86) from (81). This reformulation would be *ad hoc*, which provides direct evidence that RR is not post-cyclic. Note that there is no *a priori* reason why (83) could not have a reading in which *each other* refers to *the women*. If such a reading existed, (87) would be grammatical:

(87)   *Which man do the women believe to have hit each other?

(87) would mean: of what man is it true that woman A believes that man to have hit woman B, and woman B believes that man to have hit woman A. This meaning, though logically well-formed, is not available; its unavailability follows from ordering RR as a cyclic rule of semantic interpretation. Note too that (86) shows that RR must apply as soon as its structural description is met. There is not the option mentioned in note 7, in this case, of waiting until the next cycle.

One might argue that RR is last-cyclic and precedes the operation of Wh-Movement (which we again assume to be cyclic) on the last cycle. This is clearly impossible, since NPs like (82) above can be embedded indefinitely deeply. Hence, if RR were last-cyclic, its operation in sentence (88) below would necessarily follow the operation of Wh-Movement, causing the undesirable consequences discussed above.

(88)   I realized that John knows the men who Mary believes to have shot each other

An argument supporting the cyclic status of RR is as follows. Consider the following sentences:

(89)   I believe the men I met last night to have hated each other

(90)   I believe to have hated each other the men I met last night

We will accept the well-motivated position that Heavy-NP Shift applies only to objects, and that verbs like *believe* take Raising into object position. We will further assume that Heavy-NP Shift is cyclic and that Raising is cyclic. We have demonstrated above that RR only looks to the left to identify the antecedent of *each other*, yet (89) and (90) are synonymous and both are grammatical. These facts present no difficulty if RR applies at the end of each cycle. Thus, at the end of the embedded cycle, RR looks to the left and identifies *the men I met last night* as the antecedent of *each other*. It is not until the top cycle that Raising makes the Heavy-NP an object, allowing Heavy-NP Shift to apply. If RR were post-cyclic, it could never identify *the men I met last night* as the antecedent of *each other* in sentence (90) without an *ad hoc* extension of RR.

Though we have assumed that Heavy-NP Shift and Wh-Movement

were cyclic in the arguments above, we know of very little evidence that this is so.[11] In this light, consider the following sentence:

(91)   The men chained to each other the bicycles they had bought in the store

In sentence (91), *the bicycles they had bought in the store* is one possible antecedent of *each other.* Thus (91) demonstrates that RR precedes Heavy-NP Shift. If Heavy-NP Shift is cyclic, RR is interspersed among the transformations of each cycle. If Heavy-NP shift is post-cyclic, however, RR could be ordered after all of the transformations on each cycle.[12] We know of no data which would decide between these proposals.

5 THE MOTIVATION FOR DOUGHERTY'S SYNTACTIC ANALYSIS

In Dougherty (1970), an analysis of reciprocal constructions is proposed which would relate (92)a and (92)e transformatinally, with (92)b through (92)d as intermediate stages.

(92) a. Each of the men will speak to the others
     b. The men each will speak to the others
     c. The men will each speak to the others
     d. ?The men will speak each to the others
     e. The men will speak to each other

The deep structure which Dougherty proposes for (92)a must be (92)f, since *each* is a quantifier, not an NP, in his system.

(92) f. Each the men will speak to the others (DS)

If *each* remains on the subject NP, presumably a transformation inserts *of* and creates an NP with a PP complement, as in (92)a. Dougherty does not state this transformation. Under this analysis, Quantifier Postposition operates on (92)f to yield (92)b; *each* in (92)b is analyzed as the first element of the VP. Dougherty claims that Quantifier Movement then optionally applies to yield either (92)c or (92)d. Quantifier Movement is stated as follows:

(93)   (T6) SD: $[_s \, M_1 \quad \underset{[-\text{disjunctive}]}{Q} \quad \text{Aux} \, M_2]$

         SC: $[_s \, M_1 \, \text{Aux} \, \underset{[-\text{dis}]}{Q} \, M_2]$

         where $\underset{[-\text{dis}]}{Q}$ = each, all, both

         M = variable

Apparently, for Dougherty, (92)d is a necessary stage in the derivation, since the Each Other Transformation EOT (which Dougherty does not state) is claimed by Dougherty to operate on (92)d, producing (92)e. An examination of (93), however, shows that (92)d will never be produced, since in the SC the quantifier is immediately to the right of an element of the auxiliary, not of the verb. (93) might be reformulated to produce structures such as (92)d; the problem would then be to block sentences such as the following:

(94)   *The men will hit each children (from: Each of the men will hit the children)

(95)   *The men will hit each the other

Dougherty does not mention sentences such as (94); we assume that he has no way to block them. Dougherty's theory could best be revised as follows: a transformation, EOT′ could be postulated to relate (92)b (or perhaps (92)c) and (92)e directly. It is this theory which we shall argue against during the remainder of this section.

We will first propose counterarguments to existing syntactic arguments for the existence of a transformation such as EOT′. Consider the following sentences:

(96)   *Both of the men hit each other

(97)   *Each of the men hit each other

The ungrammaticality of sentences (96) and (97) has been used as evidence for the existence of EOT. The argument proceeds as follows. If reciprocals are not generated in the base, but only arise from movement, the ungrammaticality of (96) and (97) follows immediately from the fact that Dougherty's phrase structure rule schema inserts only one distributive quantifier[13] per determiner. In other words, there is only one slot for a distributive quantifier to fill, and the slot cannot be doubly filled. Therefore, under a movement analysis, sentences (96) and (97) have no source.

Note, however, that Dougherty's own analysis of the feature composition of predicates and distributive quantifiers can be used to provide an independent explanation, thus rendering the transformation superfluous. Dougherty argues that two of the relevant features of quantifiers are [±Totality] and [±Individual]. He shows that the feature composition of *each* and *both* is as follows:

(98)

	Totality	Individual
each	−	+
both	+	+

Furthermore he claims that "some predicates are subcategorized to require a [+tot, −ind] subject. The intransitive predicates *meet, collide, bump*, and *be alike* are this type".[14] Thus the ungrammaticality of sentence (99) follows from an incompatibility of features.

(99)   *The car and the truck both collided

But note that by a simple and natural generalization of the feature system, predicates such as *hit each other*, and in fact all reciprocal verb phrases, if generated in the base, could also be assigned the semantically appropriate feature complex [+tot, −ind]. Then the ungrammaticality of (96) and (97) would be completely parallel to the ungrammaticality of (99). Thus, under this analysis, sentences such as (96) and (97) offer no support to a movement analysis of reciprocals.

Dougherty offers a second argument to support *each* movement. He states: "Within the Conjunction Reduction Hypothesis, the fact that the reciprocal pronoun is *each other*, not *between other, yerba glark, rimmenow*, etc., is purely fortuitous, an *ad hoc* fact about English".[15] Dougherty assumes that a movement analysis explains this non-*ad hoc* fact. The truth of the matter is, however, that the similarity in shape between the quantifier and the reciprocal pronoun *is* an *ad hoc* fact about English synchronically. For example, in Latin the reciprocal pronoun is 'among themselves'; in Dutch, Karok, and Hausa the form is completely unrelated to quantifiers morphologically; in Russian the form is 'other other'; the reflexive is used in Serbo-Croatian, German, French, etc.[16]

Another argument which Dougherty offers in support of a movement analysis is that "In the PSR Hypothesis, the reciprocal pronoun *each other* fills a gap in a paradigm. Sentence (399) 'fits' into the set of sentences (396)—(399):

(396)   John and Bill each will speak to the other

(397)   John and Bill will each speak to the other

(398)   ?John and Bill will speak each to the other

(399)   John and Bill will speak to each other".

The circularity of this argument should be obvious; what the *each other* transformation claims is precisely that (396)—(399) form a paradigm. Thus, Dougherty is assuming what is to be proven. There is a considerable amount of semantic evidence that (396)—(399) do not form a paradigm; this evidence was discussed above. The syntactic evidence against the claim that (396)—(399) form a paradigm is compelling. (396), (397), and (398) seem to be related to each other just as (100)a, b, and c and (101)a, b, and c are, since these are positions generally accessible to these optional movement rules. But movement into determiner position, as in (399), is unique. Thus there is no *a priori* reason to accept (396)—(399) as a paradigm.

(100) a.   John often has spoken to the girl
      b.   John has often spoken to the girl
      c.   ?John has spoken often to the girl
      d.   *John has spoken to often girl

(101) a.   John himself has spoken to the girl
      b.   John has himself spoken to the girl
      c.   ?John has spoken himself to the girl
      d.   *John has spoken to himself girl

Not only do we know of no transformations which move elements into determiner position; we know of no transformations which move elements into noun phrases. It is possible that this is due to a universal prohibition against movement into NP's, parallel to Chomsky's (1965) constraint blocking movement into sentences. (Some apparent counterexamples are refuted in Lasnik (1972)).

There are, so far as we know, no further arguments which have been advanced in support of EOT; in the following section we will propose further arguments against EOT.

6. SOME ARGUMENTS AGAINST DOUGHERTY'S ANALYSIS

We will first reiterate that we agree with Dougherty that there exists a rule, which he calls Quantifier Movement, which optionally moves the quantifiers *each, both,* and *all* into auxiliary position, and which is responsible for sentences such as (92)c. Consider the following sentence:

(102)   Which men will hit each other?

Under Dougherty's analysis, (102) would be derived from something like (103).

(103)   *Each of which men will hit the others?

It might be claimed that (103) is ungrammatical only because Quantifier Postposition is obligatory in some cases, such as

(104) a.   *Each of John and Bill will hit Mary
      b.   John and Bill each will hit Mary

Note however that (105) is also ungrammatical:

(105)   *Which men each will hit the others

Quantifier Movement might be postulated to apply obligatorily in this environment as well, but (106) is also ungrammatical.

(106)   *Which men will each hit the others

In this case, EOT' must also be postulated to be obligatory. Thus, when the subject NP of a sentence is *each of which*, all of the transformations feeding EOT' are obligatory and EOT' must apply. Apparently, the structural description of EOT' must be met and the rule must apply, an absolute exception in the sense of Lakoff (1970). There is no non-*ad hoc* derivation for sentences such as (102) given Dougherty's assumptions.

A parallel argument can be constructed around the following sentence:

(107) $\begin{smallmatrix}\text{Some}\\\text{None}\end{smallmatrix}$ of my friends have met each other

(107) is perfectly grammatical, yet both (108) and (109) are ungrammatical.

(108)   *Each of $\begin{smallmatrix}\text{some}\\\text{none}\end{smallmatrix}$ of my friends have met the others

(109) $\begin{smallmatrix}\text{*None}\\\text{*Some}\end{smallmatrix}$ of my friends have each met the others

These sentences again suggest that the relationship between the Distributive Quantifier of the subject NP and the Q-moved Distributive Quantifier is transformational, but that the relationship between either of these and the reciprocal *each other* is not.[17]

A similar argument to this can be made on the basis of sentence (110):

(110)   All of the men will hit each other

Since Dougherty argued that there can be only one Distributive Quantifier per determiner, he proposed that (110) has as its source an embedded structure, as in (111):[18]

(111)   [$_{NP}$ each of [$_{NP}$ all of the men]] will hit the others

In the first place, (111) is ungrammatical; thus, the normally optional rule of Quantifier Movement must be postulated to apply obligatorily, yielding the ungrammatical

(112)   *All of the men each will hit the others

But then Q-Movement (normally optional) must obligatorily apply to yield the ungrammatical sentence (113):

(113)   *All of the men will each hit the others

EOT′ (normally optional) must obligatorily apply, producing the only grammatical output of (111), sentence (110). Again, EOT′ is an absolute exception in the sense of Lakoff (1970). Note further that if (111) is allowed as a possible deep structure, sentence (114) could be generated from deep structure (115).

(114)   *Both of the men hit each other

(115)   [$_{NP}$ each of [$_{NP}$ both of the men]] hit the others

In this case both the source and the output are ungrammatical.

7. CONCLUSION

This investigation has centered on the semantics of reciprocal constructions. A precise characterization of the meanings of reciprocal sentences has led us into the more general question of the form, operation, and ordering of interpretive rules. With respect to form, we have defined two relationships, the reciprocal and *each-the-other* relationships, and we have shown that the former is definitionally dependent upon the latter. Further, we have given evidence to support the claim of Chomsky (1973) that the operations of syntactic and semantic rules are subject to the same constraints. Finally, we have given arguments that RR is a cyclic rule of semantic interpretation. This supports the proposal of Jackendoff (1969) that interpretive rules can apply cyclically.

We found that the semantics of reciprocals could not be isolated from other semantic phenomena. As might have been expected, plurality was directly relevant. But stativity, which would seem unrelated to reciprocity, was found to be relevant as well. Both of these topics, as well as the formal properties of semantic rules mentioned above, deserve much further investigation.

ACKNOWLEDGEMENTS

We are indebted to Hu Matthews, Wayles Browne, and Thomas Wasow for helpful discussions of many of the issues raised in this paper, and to Hu Matthews, Paul Kiparsky, Noam Chomsky, Joan Bresnan, Wayles Browne, and Thomas Wasow, who commented on an earlier draft.

NOTES

[1] Paul Postal, MIT lectures (1971).

[2] Note that if three men are standing in a circle hitting one man and that one man is hitting the three men back, the sentence 'The men are hitting each other' seems inappropriate. This judgment is predicted by our formalism in that RR requires that it be possible to partition S, that is, divide S into non-overlapping subsets, such that the *each-the-other* relationship holds for each. For the circle case we have described above, the center man would be participating in three different sets. He would constitute the overlapping member, which our formalism disallows.

What is necessary is that every member belong to some subset which is non-overlapping. Thus (a) is disallowed, but (b) is allowed, because the extra *each-the-other* relationship creates the situation in which there is a division in which distinct *each-the-other* relationships exist.

        (a)   (b)

[3] Earlier we alluded to Dougherty's analysis, in which (25), (26), and (27) are derived from a common deep structure. In Dougherty's analysis, (26) is a stage in the derivation of (27). The interpretation of the joint — non-joint distinction cannnot take place before quantifiers have moved, since the sentences are identical at that level; all of the subjects are singular. The interpretation cannot take place after quantifiers have moved, since (26),

which is synonymous in all respects to (25), has a plural subject. There appears to be no non-*ad hoc* way for Dougherty to capture the semantic distinction which we have noted. It is interesting to note that the facts concerning plurality support Dougherty's basic claim that reciprocal sentences do not derive from conjoined structures, since 'John stared at Bill and Bill stared at John' is not synonymous to 'John and Bill stared at each other' in the relevant respect.

[4] There is one general class of exceptions. When the antecedent of the reciprocal defines natural pairwise relationships, the sentence will be true if the *each-the-other* relationship holds of each pair. For example:

    (a)   The husbands and wives in the room are similar to each other

[5] Thus, in terms of RR, *n* always equals 1 when R is a state, if it can be held that states are definitionally nonpartitionable.

[6] Paul Kiparsky has suggested to us that this rule may be an instance of a general principal that redundant lexical items can optionally delete. This rule would be universally stated, and would not exist in particular grammars.

[7] We impose the constraint that *each other* must ultimately find an antecedent. Thus, in the derivation of the sentence 'The men want each other to leave', *each other* won't be assigned an antecedent in the first cycle. However, in the second cycle, it will, and the sentence is allowed. '*Each other left*', on the other hand, is ruled out, since *each other* never receives an antecedent. Below, we argue at length for cyclic assignment of antecedent.

[8] Bresnan (1972).

[9] Bresnan (1972).

[10] For a detailed discussion of the Tensed-*S* constraint, see Chomsky (1973). An alternative to the Tensed-*S* constraint, in the case of the application of RR, would be to order RR after *for-deletion* but before *that-deletion*.

[11] The only argument that Wh-Movement is cyclic that we know of is given in Bresnan (1971, Appendix 2).

[12] Superficially, the same argument appears to hold for the relative ordering, on each cycle, of Wh-Movement and RR, since RR evidently applies prior to Wh-Movement in the following sentence:

            'Which women did John introduce to each other?'

But in this instance, both cyclic ordering of Wh-Movement and cycle-final ordering of RR can be maintained, if we adopt a proposal of Bresnan (1970). Bresnan has argued that the base rules produce structures like the following.

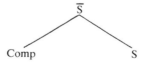

RR could then be ordered at the end of each *S* cycle, and Wh would apply in the $\bar{S}$ cycle.

[13] According to Dougherty (p. 872), the distributive Q's are *all, each, both, either, neither*.

[14] Dougherty (1970, 870).

[15] Dougherty (1970, 893).

[16] We don't mean to imply that *any* lexical item could serve as the reciprocal pronoun in a given language. We suspect that in English, and perhaps other languages as well, the reciprocal pronoun was transparent at an earlier stage. In earlier stages of English *each other* did not behave as a single lexical item. For example in 1615 (OED) sentences such as (a) were grammatical under reading (b).

    (a)   They were responsive each to others note

(b)   They were responsive, each of them to the others note

Thus a transformation moving *each* next to *other* may have come into existence and become obligatory, causing a reanalysis of *each other* as a deep structure NP.

[17] The following sentences provide counterexamples to Dougherty's analysis of the same form:

(a)   Only the stupid men shouted at each other

(b)   Many stupid men shouted at each other

(c)   Stupid people shout at each other

[18] Dougherty (1970).

COMPLEMENT OBJECT DELETION
1974

1. THE SYNTAX OF OBJECT DELETION

1.1. *Cases of Object Deletion*

There can be little doubt that there exists a process in English which deletes objects in sentences such as (1). We will call such processes Object Deletion (OD).[1]

(1)   Mary is pretty to look at ____.

This rule is obligatory, as example (1′) indicates.

(1′)   *Mary$_i$ is pretty to look at her$_i$.

It has been proposed that there exists an optional rule of *Tough* Movement, which would relate sentences (2) and (3).

(2)   It is easy to please John.

(3)   John is easy to please.

That such a transformation could not be operating in sentence (1) can be proven by the ungrammaticality of sentence (4).

(4)   *It is pretty to look at Mary.

Other examples, analogous to (1), are as follows:[2]

(5) a.   That flower is fragrant to smell.
    b.   That music is melodious to listen to.
    c.   That food is delicious to eat.

There is also a set of NPs the complements of which are subject to OD.

(6) a.   This room is a pigsty to behold ____.
    b.   Nureyev is a marvel to watch ____.
    c.   This problem is a hornets' nest to deal with ____.

Again, in these cases there is no motivation for deriving the sentences in (6) from underlying structures as in (7).

(7) a.   *It is a pigsty to behold this room.
    b.   *It is a marvel to watch Nureyev.
    c.   *It is a hornets' nest to deal with this problem.

In sentences (1), (5), and (6), the selectional restrictions on the object of the verb in the infinitival complement must be met by the subject NP. The following set of sentences demonstrates this.

(8) a.   Mary is graceful to dance with.
    b.   The flight of these birds is graceful.
    c.   *The flight of these birds is graceful to dance with.
    d.   *I danced with the flight of these birds.

These sentences argue that a rule of deletion under identity (in the sense of Chomsky 1965) is operating. There must be NPs in the underlying representations of (6); *behold* and *deal* (*with*) are subcategorized to require object NPs.

1.2. Too *and* Enough: *More Object Deletion Cases*

There also exist two adjective determiners which take complements exhibiting OD: *too* and *enough*. The ungrammaticality of (9b) and (10b) is evidence that the complements in (9c) and (10c) are complements to *too* and *enough*, as is diagrammed in (11), not to the adjectives *thin* and *soft*.

(9) a.   The mattress is thin.
    b.   *The mattress is thin to sleep on.
    c.   The mattress is too thin to sleep on.

(10) a. The football is soft.
     b. *The football is soft to kick.
     c. The football is soft enough to kick.

(11)

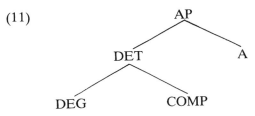

As in the previous examples, there is no plausible movement analysis to describe these data; but again the selectional restrictions on the object of the complement V are met by the subject of the sentence. There must have been objects in the underlying representations of (9c) and (10c), since (12) and (13) are ungrammatical.

(12)   *John slept on.

(13)   *John kicked.

The verbs *kick* and *sleep* (*on*) are subcategorized to require objects.

1.3. *Some Further Syntactic Properties*

There are also constructions with *too* and *enough* in which the missing subject of the complement is interpreted as identical to the subject of the matrix sentence.

(14) a. Mary$_i$ is shrewd enough ____$_i$ to win the election.
     b. John$_i$ is dumb enough ____$_i$ to blow up a bank.
     c. Max$_i$ is too dumb ____$_i$ to pass the exam.
     d. Einstein$_i$ is too well-known ____$_i$ to travel unnoticed.[3]

We will now consider some of the syntactic properties of the two types of sentences exemplified above — i.e. those with subjects deleted and those with objects deleted. We will demonstrate that these two constructions differ in certain respects and we will suggest that these differences reflect a structural difference.

First we will show that there is a complement *for-to* sentence in sentences such as (14). Consider the following sentence:

(15) Mary is too clever to be defeated in a debate by Bill.

Sentence (15) is in all respects parallel to (14), except for the fact that in (15) Passive has applied in the complement. Apparently, the complements in (14) and (15) are sentential and the normal rule of Equi has applied.

When the structural description of Equi is not met, sentences such as (16) arise.

(16) My campaign manager is $\begin{Bmatrix} \text{too stupid} \\ \text{smart enough} \end{Bmatrix}$ for me to win the election.

Thus the behavior of complements with *too* and *enough* is parallel to the behavior of complements of *want*:

(17) a. I want very much to win.
     b. I want very much to be accepted by the Knights of Columbus.
     c. I want very much for Bill to win.

Similarly, *There* Insertion may apply in the complements of *too* and *enough*.

(18) a. Mary is too clever for there to be any disagreement concerning her intelligence.
     b. Mary is dishonest enough for there to be an investigation of her activities.

We will now consider sentences such as (9c) and (10c), which we will call OD sentences. In some respects these sentences are similar to the sentences we have just considered, while in other respects they differ. Consider first the following examples which illustrate some of the differences.

(19) a. *Socrates$_i$ is dull enough (for me) to be bored by ____$_i$.
   b. *The policemen$_i$ are too stupid (for the demonstrators) to be captured by ____$_i$.
   c. *This music$_i$ is too cacophonous (for Bill) to be put to sleep by ____$_i$.
   d. *Mary$_i$ is too incompetent for this job to be offered to ____$_i$ by I.B.M.

It is apparent that Passive cannot apply in the complement of OD sentences. Apparently, *There* Insertion cannot apply in the complement of OD sentences.

(20) a. *George$_i$ is too obscure for there to be a book about ____$_i$.
   b. *This species$_i$ is common enough for there to be knowledge of ____$_i$.
   c. *This species$_i$ is too rare for there to be any knowledge of ____$_i$.

Bresnan (1971) demonstrated that the *tough* class of predicates manifests these same properties. She plausibly argued on the basis of these facts that the complement is a VP rather than an S. Later we consider this analysis in greater detail.
   Consider the following sentences

(21) a. This problem is too abstract for Bill to solve.
   b. This problem is too abstract for Bill to solve it.

One might be tempted to conclude that the only difference between them is the application of an optional transformation. The following two sentences demonstrate, however, that the parallelism of (21a) and (21b) is only apparent.

(22) a. For Bill, this problem is too abstract to solve.
   b. This problem is too abstract to solve, for Bill.
   c. *For Bill, this problem is too abstract to solve it.
   d. *This problem is too abstract to solve it, for Bill.

Evidently, (21a) is transformationally related to (22a and b) — the prepositional phrase can appear in only one of the three positions in any given sentence. On the other hand, in sentence (21b) *Bill* is the syntactic subject of a *for-to* complement sentence. As sentences (23a, b, and c) indicate, the subjects of *for-to* complements do not move.

(23) a. I want very much for Mt. Vesuvius to erupt.
   b. *For Mt. Vesuvius, I want very much to erupt.
   c. *I want very much to erupt, for Mt. Vesuvius.

We have shown that there exists a rule deleting objects in the complements of certain adjectives and of *too* and *enough*, and that *too* and *enough* take another kind of complement which seems syntactically identical to the complement of *want*. In those cases in which the object in the complement has been deleted, we have demonstrated that when a *for* phrase is present, it is not the syntactic subject of the complement.

2. TOUGH MOVEMENT REEXAMINED

2.1. *Previous Analyses*

We will now examine another set of phenomena, sometimes described with a movement rule — *Tough* Movement. After we have listed previous treatments, we will demonstrate that the arguments that have been given in support of *Tough* Movement are incorrect and we will provide arguments against the movement analysis. We will then examine the range of syntactic phenomena in the relevant sentences and show that these phenomena are identical to those we hve seen earlier.

The *tough* construction was first treated in Chomsky (1964, 61—65). Chomsky considered the following two sentences and noted that in the first, *John* is the understood object of *please*, whereas in the second, *John* is the understood subject of *please*.

(24)   John is easy to please.

(25)   John is eager to please.

Rosenbaum (1967, 107) proposed to explain these facts by postulating a rule which would relate sentences (26) and (27) transformationally, where (26) is the immediate source. Postal (1971, 27) later called a similar rule *Tough* Movement.

(26)   It is difficult for John to hit Bill.

(27)   Bill is difficult for John to hit.

Ross (1967, 231) suggested that sentence (28) is not derived by a rule of *Tough* Movement applying to (29), and proposed that (28) is derived by a rule of deletion operating on structure 6.122 (Ross's numbering).

(28)   John is easy to get along with.

(29)   It is easy to get along with John.

6.122

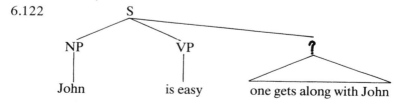

2.2. *Survey of Arguments Against* "Tough *Deletion*"

Since Ross (1967) there have been several arguments presented against the deletion analysis. We will now consider these arguments and show that they are incorrect.

2.2.1. *The Postal-Ross Argument*

Postal and Ross (1971) have presented an argument in support of *Tough* Movement based on the following sentence:

(30)   Getting herself arrested on purpose is hard for me to imagine Betsy being willing to consider.

Postal and Ross observe that *getting herself arrested* must in underlying structure have a subject coreferential with *Betsy*, since otherwise the presence of the reflexive *herself* is unexplained. they argue that if the underlying string is as in (31), the last occurence of *Betsy* may be deleted by the usual rule of Equi NP Deletion.

(31) $_S[_{NP}[_S[I$ imagine $_{NP}[_S[Betsy$ is willing for $_{NP}[Betsy$ consider $_{NP}[_S[Betsy_{Equi}$ getting herself arrested on purpose$]_S]_{NP}]_S]_{NP}]_S]_{NP}$ is hard for me$]_S$

Postal and Ross claim that under a *Tough* Deletion analysis a new rule of subject deletion would have to be proposed since *Betsy getting herself arrested on purpose* is not in a position where the normal rule of Equi would be expected to apply. Akmajian (1972) has observed, however, that just the sort of subject deletion which would be required under a *Tough* Deletion analysis is independently required in sentences in whcih any movement analysis is impossible. The relevant sentences are as follows (Akmajian's sentences 10).

(32)   Getting herself arrested on purpose is $\left\{ \begin{array}{l} \text{too crazy} \\ \text{just crazy enough} \end{array} \right\}$ for

me to imagine Betsy being willing to consider.

As Akmajian points out:

If it is correct to assume that (10) [our sentence (32)] derives by a deletion process and not by a movement process, then Postal and Ross's sentence (4) [our sentence (30)] cannot be used to motivate a [Tough] movement analysis . . .

We find Akmajian's argument convincing because there is no reasonable movement analysis for sentences such as (32). *Betsy getting herself arrested* must originate in subject position; therefore, there must exist a rule deleting identical subjects of complements in this position. It is not surprising that sentences with *too* and *enough* should be parallel to *tough* sentences in this respect, since, as we will show, the structures are parallel in other respects.

2.2.2. *Verb Phrase Idioms*

Another argument which has been given in support of a *Tough* Movement analysis is based on the following sentence:

(33) ?Headway is easy to make on problems like these.

We find sentence (33) questionable at best, though some speakers find it acceptable. The argument is based on the claim that *headway*, in general, only occurs as the object of *make*. Thus *Tough* Movement would explain the grammaticality of (33) for some speakers.

There exist several other VP idioms whose object NPs can be moved by transformations. Some examples are as follows:

(34) a. Someone kept tabs on Mary.
   Tabs were kept on Mary.
   b. Someone took advantage of Mary.
   Advantage was taken of Mary.
   c. Someone paid heed to our warning.
   Heed was paid to our warning.
   d. Someone paid attention to our problems.
   Attention was paid to our problems.
   e. Someone threw out the baby with the bathwater.
   The baby was thrown out with the bathwater.

Note, however, that the NPs in these cases cannot be the subjects of *tough* sentences.

(35) a. *Tabs were easy to keep on Mary.
   b. *Advantage was easy to take of Bill.
   c. *Heed is important to pay to such warnings.
   d. *Attention is difficult to pay to boring lectures.
   e. *The baby would be easy to throw out with the bathwater.

A *Tough* Movement analysis incorrectly predicts that all of the sentences in (35) are grammatical. Thus the behavior of *headway* does not seem to be representative. The fact that (33) is grammatical for some speakers is perhaps related to the fact that the occurrence of *headway* is much freer than that of the object NPs in (34). (36) seems marginally grammatical, while the sentences in (37) are ungrammatical.

(36) ?Our headway was insufficient.

(37) a. *Our tabs were close.
    b. *Our advantage was unfair.
    c. *Our heed was careful.
    d. *Our attention was close.

Similarly, *headway* relativizes, while the others do not.

(38)   The headway that we made was sufficient.

(39) a. *The tabs that we kept paid off.
    b. *The advantage that we took of Mary was frowned upon.
    c. *The heed that we paid to that warning was slight.
    d. *The attention that we paid to the lecture was careful.

Thus VP idioms cannot be used in support of the movement analysis, and in fact provide rather strong evidence against it.[4]

2.2.3. *Nominals*

We will now discuss what could be considered a strong argument in support of a movement analysis of *tough* sentences. Chomsky (1970) presents the following paradigm:

(40) a. John is eager to please.
    b. John is easy to please.

(41) a. John's eagerness to please
    b. *John's easiness to please

Chomsky assumes that (40a) is a possible deep structure frame and (40b) is not. Thus, if the lexicalist hypothesis is correct, it follows that (41a) is a possibe nominalization and (41b) is not.

We will present arguments that (40b) is a possible deep structure frame and suggest that there is an independent reason for the ungrammaticality of (41b).

Note first that this sense of *easy* and other predicates of this class have no corresponding infinitival nominals at all.

(42) a. *The $\left\{\begin{array}{l}\text{ease}\\\text{easiness}\end{array}\right\}$ (of) to please John

    b. *The difficulty (of) to understand algebra
    c. *The impossibility (of) to finish this paper
    d. *The amusement (of) to go to the circus

Thus, even assuming the lexicalist hypothesis, a movement analysis of (40b) is not sufficient to exclude all the missing nominalizations of *easy*.

Second, we have argued that (43) corresponds to a possible deep structure frame and that there is no possible movement source.

(43)   Mary is pretty to look at.

Note, however, that there is no nominalization of (43).

(44)   *Mary's prettiness to look at

This is true of all structures such as (43); the following are both un-grammatical:

(45) a. *Mary's beauty to see
     b. *That flower's fragrance to smell

Thus, in the cases which we have been discussing, the ungrammaticality of nominalizations apparently has nothing to do with movement.

2.3. *Arguments Against* Tough *Movement*

We will now present arguments that sentences such as *John is easy to please* cannot be derived by a rule of movement, except at great theoretical cost.

2.3.1. *The Progressive Aspect*

First, consider the following sentences:

(46) a. To please John is easy.
     b. It is easy to please John.
     c. John is easy to please.

Under a movement analysis, (46c) is derived from (46a), possibly via (46b). Now consider the following sentence, entirely parallel to (46c).

(47) a. John is being easy to please.

Note that the putative source and intermediate stage of (47a) under a movement analysis are ungrammatical.

(47) b. *To please John is being easy.
     c. *It is being easy to please John.

Under a *Tough* Movement analysis, the rule is optional; thus there appears to be no non-ad hoc way to account for the ungrammaticality of the examples in (47b, c). As one reviewer has remarked, in sentences containing adjective phrases or noun phrases in the progressive aspect, the property named by the adjective phrase must be under the control of the referent of the subject of the adjective phrase. For example, consider a situation in which height can be controlled by swallowing pills. Under these circumstances, the sentence *John is being tall* would be appropriate. However, if height varied from time to time but was not subject to control, the sentence *John is being tall* would not be appropriate, as it is not appropriate under present circumstances.

Apparently, this fact must be accounted for in terms of deep structure configurations, the principle being, in essence, that the progressive APs and NPs must select subjects which refer to higher animates. Whether or not the property is controllable appears to be a factual question, independent of the grammar. That this fact cannot be accounted for at the level of surface structure is indicated by the contrast between (47a and c) on the one hand and (47′a and b) on the other.

(47′) a.   *John is being certain to win.
      b.   *It is being certain that John will win.

In the latter case, as opposed to the former, neither version is grammatical. Notice also that various NP-moving transformations can move the subject indefinitely far from the progressive AP or NP.

(48) a.   What $\left\{ \begin{array}{c} \text{man} \\ \text{*book} \end{array} \right\}$ does everyone believe is being interesting today?

      b.   John, everyone thinks is being obnoxious.

2.3.2. *Try*

A similar problem arises with sentences such as (49).

(49)   John tries to be easy to please.

Again, there is no plausible source, as we see from the ungrammatical (50a and b):

(50) a. *John tries (for) to please $\left\{ \begin{array}{c} \text{John} \\ \text{him} \end{array} \right\}$ to be easy.

      b. *John tries (for) it to be easy to please $\left\{ \begin{array}{c} \text{John} \\ \text{him} \end{array} \right\}$.

Under a deletion analysis, (47a) and (49) undergo a straightforward derivation with the following as respective underlying structures:

(51) a.   John is being easy to please John.
      b.   John tries to be easy to please John.

OD will apply, obligatorily deleting the second occurrence of *John* in both cases.

One might be tempted to argue that *try* is a positive absolute exception (in the sense of Lakoff 1970) to the rule of Equi, and that therefore the examples which we give raise no difficulty for the *Tough* Movement analysis. This proposal cannot be considered a solution to the problem, but rather only a statement of it. There is another analysis of *try*, Perlmutter's (1968), which does not involve absolute exceptions and which is consistent with *Tough* Deletion and not consistent with *Tough* Movement. An analysis in which *try* takes a VP complement seems to us superior, however, as we suggest in section 3.2 below.

The last two arguments have been based on sentences which are in all respects parallel to sentences traditionally derived by *Tough* Movement, but which have no plausible source under an analysis using that rule. Now we will present a case in which *Tough* Movement converts a grammatical source into an ungrammatical output.

2.3.3. *Indefinite NPs*

Assuming the existence of a rule of *Tough* Movement, Postal (1971) noted that a constraint would have to be imposed on the rule, prohibiting movement of indefinites. The following examples illustrate this.

(52) a.   It would be easy to kill $\begin{Bmatrix} \text{a man} \\ \text{someone} \end{Bmatrix}$ with a gun like that.

    b.   *$\begin{Bmatrix} \text{A man} \\ \text{Someone} \end{Bmatrix}$ would be easy to kill with a gun like that.

(52′) a.   It was a delight to talk to someone interesting.
     b.   *Someone interesting was a delight to talk to.

The ungrammaticality of (52b) and (52′b) clearly involves indefiniteness, as the following examples indicate:

(53) a. It would be easy to kill John with a gun like that.
    b. John would be easy to kill with a gun like that.

(53′) a. It was a delight to talk to John.
     b. John was a delight to talk to.

The constraint that would be imposed is by no means general. First, note that indefinites can become the subject of a sentence by the oepration of some transformations. The following sentences demonstrate this:

(54) a. $\begin{Bmatrix} \text{A reporter} \\ \text{Someone} \end{Bmatrix}$ was arrested by the police.

    b. $\begin{Bmatrix} \text{A reporter} \\ \text{Someone} \end{Bmatrix}$ is certain to ask a stupid question.

In (54a), Passive has applied, in (54b), Raising into subject position. In both cases indefinites are made the subjects of the matrix sentences. (54b) not only demonstrates that an indefinite can become the subject of a sentence by the operation of a transformation; it also demonstrates that an indefinite can become the syntactic subject of an adjectival predicate. Under a movement analysis, however, this is precisely what is occurring in (52b).

Under a deletion analysis, (52b) would have something like (55) as its deep structure.

(55) $\left\{ \begin{array}{l} \text{A man}_j \\ \text{Someone}_i \end{array} \right\}$ would be easy to kill $\left\{ \begin{array}{l} \text{a man}_j \\ \text{someone}_i \end{array} \right\}$ with a gun like that.

In (55) *someone* and *a man* are the deep subjects under our analysis. But note that quite generally indefinites cannot be the deep subjects of predicates denoting characteristics.[5] Contrast (56) with the examples in (57).

(56) $\left\{ \begin{array}{l} \text{A bus} \\ \text{Someone} \end{array} \right\}$ left.

(57) a. *$\left\{ \begin{array}{l} \text{A building} \\ \text{Someone} \end{array} \right\}$ was tall.

   b. *$\left\{ \begin{array}{l} \text{A dog} \\ \text{Someone} \end{array} \right\}$ was strong.

   c. *$\left\{ \begin{array}{l} \text{A banker} \\ \text{Someone} \end{array} \right\}$ could be honest.

Under the assumption that (55) is the deep structure of (52b), nothing further need be said to explain the ungrammaticality of the latter. The deep structure constraint responsible for the ungrammaticality of the examples in (57) will also rule out (52b).

Postal further noted that his restriction only applies to nongeneric indefinites. The following sentences are grammatical:

(58) a. Beavers are hard to kill.
   b. A beaver is hard to kill.

(58a) and (58b) are only grammatical when the subject is interpreted as generic; the following examples are ill-formed.

(59) a. It was a pleasure to eat a bunch of bananas; there are their skins.
   b. *A bunch of bananas was a pleasure to eat; there are their skins.

For Postal, this phenomenon must be described by an additional condition on the rule of *Tough* Movement (actually a condition on a condition).

Under a deletion analysis, however, these facts follow from independently necessary restrictions. Although, as we have seen, a pure indefinite cannot be the subject of a characteristic-denoting predicate, generic indefinites can be. The following sentences demonstrate this:

(60) a. Beavers are fat (*they're over there).
     b. Birds are noisy (*they woke me up).
     c. A rose is pretty (*I have it on the table).

Thus both of the phenomena which Postal noticed and described by conditions on his *Tough* Movement transformation follow from general properties of indefinites and generics under the deletion hypothesis, but not under the movement hypothesis.

2.3.4. *Intentionality*

Consider now the following sentence:

(61)   John is intentionally easy to please.

Under a movement analysis, (61) would derive from (62a) or (62b).

(62) a. *It is intentionally easy to please John.
     b. *To please John is intentionally easy.

There appears to be no non-ad hoc way to block (62a) and (62b), since under a movement analysis, *Tough* Movement is optional. (62) provides evidence that the sources of sentences such as *John is easy to please* under a *Tough* Movement analysis can never be agentive. However, (61) demonstrates that sentences which would be the output of *Tough* Movement can quite generally be agentive. Thus, in any grammar in which such notions as "agent" are captured in the deepest level of representation, this fact constitutes the strongest type of counterargument. Since, under our analysis, *John* is the deep structure subject of *John is easy to please*, the fact that an agentive reading is possible follows as a natural consequence. (It should perhaps be emphasized that we are not claiming that all deep structure subjects can be interpreted as agents — the nature of the predicate is, of course, relevant.) Notice also that quite analogously to the patterning of progressives (section 2.3.1 above) it cannot be the surface structure subject that is relevant: *John is intentionally certain to win* is no better than *It is intentionally certain that John will win*. Further, in this case again, the understood agent of the *intentionally* clause can be indefinitely far removed from that clause in surface structure.

The clearest case of intentionality is the imperative construction. As we have already noted. *John is easy to please* can be intentional. Thus, as one would expect, the following sentence is grammatical.

(63)   Be easy to please.

We can think of no plausible syntactic source (not requiring absolute exceptions) under a movement analysis. Even if there is such a source, that source cannot be semantically intentional, as we have already argued. Hence (63) seems to raise insuperable semantic and syntactic problems for the movement analysis.

2.3.5. *Modals*

Consider now the following sentence:

(64)   John must be easy to please.

Sentence (64) is ambiguous: *must* can carry root or epistemic interpretation; it may be paraphrased by either (65) or (66).

(65)   John is required to be easy to please.

(66)   One can conclude that John is easy to please.

Now consider the semantic interpretation of (67).

(67)   It must be easy to please John.

(67) cannot be paraphrased by (65), while it can be paraphrased by (66). It is generally the case that verbs, in those cases where they take empty or sentential subjects, cannot take root modals. Thus root interpretation is impossible in the following sentences:

(68) a. It must be true that John is intelligent.
   b. It should be raining.
   c. That Bill left may seem strange to you.

As would be expected, the sentences in (69) can only carry epistemic interpretation, while those in (70) are ambiguous between root and epistemic interpretation.

(69) a. It may not be easy to please John.
   b. It should be hard to convince John.
   c. It could be hard to beat John.

(70) a. John may not be easy to please.
   b. John should be hard to convince.
   c. John could be hard to beat.

Under a *Tough* Movement analysis, one would expect that (64) and (70a—c) would uniquely carry epistemic interpretation. Thus the root interpretations of (64) and (70a—c) have no source under a *Tough* Movement analysis. Under a deletion analysis, the underlying structure of sentences such as *John is easy to please* is parallel to the underlying structure of *John is brave* in that *John* is the subject of adjectival predication. Thus the fact that the sentences in (71) can carry either root or epistemic interpretation is, in that analysis, parallel to the fact that the sentences in (70) can carry root or epistemic interpretation.

(71) a. John could be brave.
    b. John should be brave.
    c. John must be brave.

Here, once again, it is not obvious that any surface interpretation process could capture the generalization. As in the paradigms involving progressives and intentionality, the subject of a modal sentence can wind up indefinitely far from the modal in surface structure without affecting the possibility of root interpretation: *Who does everyone believe . . . must be brave?* Further, subject raising into subject position does not increase the possibility of root interpretation.

(71′) a. It may not be certain that John will win.
     b. John may not be certain to win.

3. OBJECT DELETION GENERALIZED

3.1. Tough *Deletion* = *Object Deletion*

The last sets of arguments have demonstrated that sentences such as *John is easy to please* are not derived by movement. Given the choices available within current linguistic theory, they must be derived by deletion. We will now show that the deletion rule required to derive *John is easy to please* has the same properties as the deletion rule we illustrated in the first sections.[6] As is obvious, in both cases it is the complement object which is deleted under identity with the subject of the sentence.

In both cases, it is demonstrable that whenever a *for* phrase is present, it is not the syntactic subject of the complement.

(72) a. John is easy for Bill to please.
    b. John is easy to please, for Bill.
    c. For Bill, John is easy to please.

Application of Passive is not allowed in the complement of either construction.

(73) a. *John is easy (for Bill) to be outsmarted by.
    b. *These arguments were impossible (for Max) to be convinced by.
    c. *Sam is tough (for us) to be misunderstood by.
    d. *The FBI is a breeze (for us) to be investigated by.

There Insertion behaves identically with respect to the two constructions.

(74) a. *North Vietnam is easy for there to be bombing raids over.
    b. *Max is impossible for there to be a book about.
    c. *The Pentagon would be amusing for there to be a raid on.

An additional similarity between the two constructions involves the interaction of Dative Movement with the deletion sites in the two constructions. Consider first the *tough* paradigms:

(75) a.   John was $\begin{cases} \text{fun} \\ \text{tough} \\ \text{impossible} \\ \text{a bitch} \end{cases}$ to give criticism to _____ .

    b. *John was $\begin{cases} \text{fun} \\ \text{tough} \\ \text{impossible} \\ \text{a bitch} \end{cases}$ to give _____ criticism.

(76) a.   Criticism was $\begin{cases} \text{fun} \\ \text{tough} \\ \text{impossible} \\ \text{a bitch} \end{cases}$ to give _____ to John.

    b. *?Criticism was $\begin{cases} \text{fun} \\ \text{tough} \\ \text{impossible} \\ \text{a bitch} \end{cases}$ to give John _____ .

Compare these sentences with the following:

(77) a.   My adviser is too meticulous to give this thesis to _____ .
    b.   *My adviser is too meticulous to give _____ this thesis.

(78) a.   This thesis is too sloppy to give _____ to my adviser.
    b.   *?This thesis is too sloppy to give my adviser _____ .

(79) a.   John is dumb enough to sell the Brooklyn Bridge to _____ .
    b.   *John is dumb enough to sell _____ the Brooklyn Bridge.

(80) a.   The Brooklyn Bridge is beautiful enough to sell _____ to John.
    b.   *?The Brooklyn Bridge is beautiful enough to sell John _____ .

While the judgments are delicate, we believe that the (b) sentences in (76), (78), and (80) are not fully grammatical; the (b) sentences in (75), (77), and (79) are totally ungrammatical. The significant fact is that the three paradigms above are parallel. Note, of course, that Wh-Movement distinguishes between direct and indirect object: *Who did you give a book?*; *What did you give John?*

3.2. *The Rule of Object Deletion and Its Syntactic Properties*

We have demonstrated a parallelism between sentences such as *John is easy to please* and sentences containing complements of *too* and *enough*. These sentences are all predicational, with the added complexity that the predicate phrase contains a complement whose sense specifies an action on the entity which is the understood subject of the predicate phrase. We have so far considered the commonest type of predicational sentences, copular sentences. Another type of relevant predicational sentence is the following:

(81) a. I call John $\left\{ \begin{array}{l} \text{a fool} \\ \text{stupid} \end{array} \right\}$.

    b. I call the voters $\left\{ \begin{array}{l} \text{easy to please} \\ \text{too smart to fool} \end{array} \right\}$.

We are now in a position to state an approximation of the rule of Complement Object Deletion.

(82)   *Complement Object Deletion*

$$X \, NP_i \, U_{NP \atop AP} [W \, NP_i \, Y] \, Z$$

$$\begin{array}{llllllll} 1 & 2 & 3 & 4 & 5 & 6 & 7 & \Rightarrow \\ 1 & 2 & 3 & 4 & \phi & 6 & 7 \end{array}$$

In many cases the rule would seem to produce ungrammatical sentences, but in these cases we will demonstrate that the sentences are ruled out on general grounds.[7]

Ross (1967, 228) was the first to notice some constraints on the process we have been discussing: "... a restriction must apparently be stated so that elements of clauses containing finite verbs will not be deleted: no grammatical sentences like (6.105) [our (83)] appear to exist."

(83)   *This rock is too heavy for us to try to claim that we picked up.

This condition does not have to be stated as part of the rule; this is merely an instance of Chomsky's (1973) Tensed S Condition.

As we have noted above, the following examples are ungrammatical:

(84) a. *George is too obscure for there to be a book about ____ .
     b. *This species is common enough for there to be knowledge of ____ .
     c. *The Pentagon would be fun for there to be a raid on ____ .

Here it is evident that the complements of *too, enough,* and *fun* are sentential and that *there* is the syntactic subject of the complement in these cases. Chomsky's Specified Subject Condition blocks the derivations.[8]

Berman and Szamosi (1972) have proposed an analysis of the *tough* sentences involving a movement rule which operates on structures such as (85) with the condition that "the rule of *Tough* Movement itself is prohibited when the embedded sentence contains a subject."

(85)

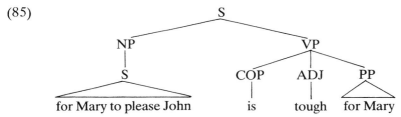

Since we have already given strong arguments that the *tough* sentences do not involve a movement rule and that they are parallel to the *too* and *enough* sentences, Berman and Szamosi's analysis cannot be considered well motivated. We will, therefore, consider an analysis which maintains the salient feaures of this proposal but which involves a deletion rule, and show that this revised analysis is also incorrect.

The revised analysis (as well as Berman and Szamosi's analysis) predicts correctly that the examples in (84) are ungrammatical, since *there* must be the subject of the complement. The analysis also works for sentences such as *John is easy for Bill to please.* The revised analysis would incorrectly predict, however, that the following sentences are grammatical.

(86) a. *Socrates is dull enough for me to be bored by.
     b. *The police are too stupid for the demonstrators to be captured by.
     c. *John is easy for Bill to be outsmarted by.

Again the Specified Subject Condition makes the correct prediction concerning these examples. Either *me, the demonstrators,* and *Bill* are the syntactic subjects of the complement, or *for me,* etc. are *for* datives, with *me,* etc. controlling subject position in the complement sentences. In either case, subject position in the complement counts as a specified subject. Note that the examples in (86) remain ungrammatical when the *for* and following NP must be analyzed as a *for* dative, as in (86′).

(86′) a. *Socrates is dull enough to be bored by, for me.
     b. *The police are too stupid to be captured by, for the demonstrators.
     c. *John is easy to be outsmarted by, for Bill.

This provides evidence for the strong form of Chomsky's Specified Subject Condition, that in which a deletion site controlled by a node other than one crucially involved in the rule functions like lexical material. However, if the complements in OD sentences are sentential, and the

Specified Subject Condition is therefore necessary to rule out the ungrammatical examples in (86) and (86′), then the following grammatical sentences cannot be generated.

(87) a. John is gullible enough for us to fool.
  b. The man is too tall for Max to outjump.
  c. John is easy for Bill to please.

Under the analysis in question, the subject of the matrix sentence does not control the subject of the complement; therefore, the deletion rule cannot apply, as it is blocked by the presence of a specified subject. It seems reasonable to conclude, then, that the complements in (87) are not sentences but VPs,[9] and that therefore even the revised Berman and Szamosi analysis is incorrect.

The notion of VP complement — that is, VP not immediately dominated by S — can plausibly be extended to other areas in English syntax. Likely candidates for such analysis are structures in which no subejct ever appears. One such instance is in the complement of *try*, briefly discussed in section 2.3.2 above. Briefly stated, if one assumes that this complement is sentential, it must be stated that the structural description for Equi must be met and the rule must apply. In addition to the general undesirability of such powerful mechanisms, this analysis incorrectly predicts grammaticality for all passives meeting the structural description of Equi. Under the VP analysis, neither an absolute exception nor an ad hoc condition prohibitng passive complements of *try* is required. Similar facts obtain for *endeavor, fail, manage*, etc. An exactly parallel line of argument can be made for the *force* class of verbs, including *persuade, convince, order*, etc.

It should be noted that *get* passives are far superior to *be* passives in the complements of the *try, force*, and OD classes of predicates.

(88) a. *John tried to be arrested by the police.
  a′. John tried to get (himself) arrested by the police.
  b. *Mary convinced John to be arrested by the police.
  b′. Mary convinced John to get (himself) arrested by the police.
  c. *The police are easy to be arrested by.
  c′. The police are easy to get (yourself) arrested by.

It has frequently been observed that predicates denoting states are not possible in the complements of *try* and *convince*. Thus examples such as *John tried to resemble Harry* and *Mary convinced John to resemble Harry* are anomalous. Note that *Harry is easy to resemble* seems bad in the same way. Observe further that quite generally those complements which under our assumptions would be analyzed as deep structure VPs not immediately dominated by S exhibit a uniform semantic behavior; they denote controllable actions. *Get* passives as opposed to *be* passives seem to be consistent with this hypothesis. The verb phrase of the former can be used to denote a controllable action, as in *Cowens got (himself) fouled by Kareem Fabbar on purpose*, where the specified intention is Cowen's. Such an interpretation is not generally available for *be* passives: *Cowens was fouled by Kareem Fabbar on purpose.*[10] Under most analyses of *be* passive, the operation of the rule involves the deep syntactic subject of the sentence. Consequently such passives would be excluded from VP complement structures. On the other hand, in the case of *get* passives, there is evidence that the deep and surface subjects of *get* are the same. NPs that are constrained to appear only as the objects of certain verbs can be the passive subject of *be* passives but not of *get* passives, as is shown by the ungrammaticality of **Heed got paid to our warning*. In addition, there is a selectional restriction on *get* requiring that its subject not denote an immutable entity, as evidenced by the impossibility of **The parallel postulate got (itself) chosen by mathematicians*. We conclude that *get* is a deep structure main verb, and consequently that *get* passives can occur as verb phrase complements.

At first glance, it might appear that the VP analysis would make it difficult to state rules such as those involving floating quantifiers, floating emphatic reflexives, and number agreement. This impression might arise from the widespread assumption that these rules must mention *subject* NPs. We will illustrate the rules mentioned and assumed to depend on subject NPs, with examples involving the verb *convince*.

(89) a. Melvin convinced the men to each solve the problem.

b. Joan convinced Susan to drive to N.Y. herself.

c. Harry convinced the men to become $\left\{ \begin{array}{l} \text{doctors} \\ \text{*a doctor} \end{array} \right\}$.

We see no reason, however, to make the radical assumption that transformations can make use of structural dependencies at all levels simultaneously. Since it is clear that the class of possible operations on trees involving only string conditions (as in Chomsky 1957) is a proper subset of the class of operations involving linear order and structural dependency, in the absence of any falsifying data the stronger theory — the former — must be maintained. Within current formalizations of transformational grammar, the operations mentioned would all involve X-NP-Y-A, where A is some item involved in the rules. Such a rule could not distinguish $_{VP}$[V NP VP] from $_S$[NP VP]. Hence there is no problem in accounting for the processes evidenced in (89) above within the VP framework; in fact it would be difficult to prevent the processes from applying. Further, we see no particular difficulty in extending this line of reasoning to include the interaction between the complement of *try* and the subject of *try*, and also that between object deletion complements and immediately preceding *for* prepositional phrases.

A related criticism might involve the claim that the VP analysis of certain complements leaves unexplained the "fact" that some specific NP in the matrix clause is always understood as the subject of the infinitive. There are two possible replies to this criticism. First, one could argue that whatever projection rules are responsible for the linkup between "real" subjects and following VPs would also be applicable to constructions in which a VP not dominated by S is preceded by some NP. That is, there would be no added cost to the grammar in extending the relevant interpretive principle. On the contrary, it would be costly to limit this process so as to exclude the NPs in question. Second, it is not implausible that the "understood subject" phenomenon is a consequence of entailments of readings produced. For example, in our framework, *try* could be analyzed as a two-place predicate taking an animate entity and an action as arguments. *Try* then establishes an [actor — attempted action] relationship between NP and VP, much as *give* establishes a [possessor — possessed] relationship between the two object NPs in *I gave Harry a book*. Clearly, this is only a beginning, but we feel that this framework holds enough promise of providing insights into the interaction between meaning and structure that it should not be rejected out of hand.

3.3. *Conditions on Applicability of Object Deletion*

In the discussion so far, we have not stated whether the rule of OD is optional or obligatory. It is clear that there are circumstances in which the rule is obligatory, as the following examples attest:

(90) a. *John is easy to please him.
     b. *Mary is pretty to look at her.

There are situations where a general condition blocks the application of the rule. In some such situations no grammatical output is produced, which is the usual case with a blocked obligatory rule:

(91) a. *Tensed S Condition and Specified Subject Condition*: *John is easy to demonstrate that Bill killed (him).
     b. *Coordinate Structure Constraint*: *John is easy to please Mary and (him).
     c. *Specified Subject Condition* (*NP case*): *Prime numbers are easy to prove Euclid's theorems about (them), (cf. Prime numbers are easy to prove theorems about (*them)).
     d. *Same as* (*a*), *and also Ross's Complex NP Constraint*: *John is easy to please a woman who likes (him).

Note that each sentence above has the further property that if any other NP is placed in the position of the pronoun, the sentence remains ungrammatical; that is to say, the structural description for the rule must be met. This fact should not be stated on the particular rule and apparently cannot be stated on particular lexical items; it is in fact a general property of obligatory deletion rules. Consider, for example, the following case, in which Gapping is the relevant rule.

(92) a. John kicked Harry, and Bill kicked Fred.
    b. John kicked Harry, and Bill ____ Fred.
    c. John kicked Harry, and Bill slapped Fred.

(93) a. *John kicked Harry, not Bill kicked Fred.
    b. John kicked Harry, not Bill ____ Fred.
    c. *John kicked Harry, not Bill slapped Fred.

In paradigm (93), the rule of Gapping is obligatory, as the ungrammaticality of example (a) shows. Example (93c) is also ungrammatical. Apparently, the conjunction *not* can only occur between sentences which contain the same verb. In paradigm (92), the rule of Gapping is optional, and the conjunction *and* can occur between sentences which do not contain the same verb. These two paradigms exemplify the usual properties of deletion rules. (See Fiengo 1974 for a more extensive discussion concerning other transformations.) We state the principle behind such phenomena as follows:

(94)   *Deletion Principle*
    A. If there is required identity between two strings, and if there is a rule deleting one string under identity with the other, then that rule is obligatory.
    B. If there is not required identity between two strings, and if there is a rule deleting one string under identity with the other, then that rule is optional.

Thus it is not necessary to state as part of the rule that it is obligatory in the OD sentences just discussed; Case A of the Deletion Principle guarantees that the rule will be obligatory in just these examples. The implicit claim of the Deletion Principle is that it is never necessary to mark identity deletion rules as optional or obligatory.[11]

Consider now the following sentences, in which the rule of OD has not applied:

(95) a. Senator Foghorn is too persuasive for us to like him.
    b. Nixon is conservative enough for us to vote for him.

These sentences raise an apparent difficulty, since the rule of OD has not applied, and yet the sentences are not ungrammatical (cf. 90a and b). Note, however, that the following sentences are also grammatical. By comparison with pardigms (22) and (23), the complements in (96a and b) can be seen to be sentential.

(96) a. Senator Foghorn is too persuasive for us to like his opponent.
     b. Nixon is conservative enough for us to vote for McGovern.

Thus exactly in those sentences where OD did not have to apply, a nonidentical noun phrase can also occur. This is what would be predicted by Case B of the Deletion Principle.[12]

There are, however, sentences with *too* and *enough* in which the deletion is obligatory.

(97) a. *Senator Foghorn$_i$ is too persuasive to like him$_i$.
     b. *Nixon$_i$ is conservative enough to vote for him$_i$.

(98) a. Senator Foghorn$_i$ is too persuasive to like ____$_i$.
     b. Nixon$_i$ is conservative enough to vote for ____$_i$.

Thus in some sentences containing complements to *too* and *enough* the deletion is optional, while in others the deletion is obligatory. It seems clear that the deletion is never obligatory when the complement is sentential and that the deletion is always obligatory when the complement is a VP. This would follow from the fact that in VP complements the presence of an identical NP is required while in S complements the presence of an identical NP is optional. In the following sentences, in which the complements are demonstrably sentential, good sentences are produced when an NP is present in the VP of the complement.

(99) a. John$_i$ is too obscure for there to be a book about him$_i$.
     b. John is too obscure for there to be a book about his wife.

(100) a. The police chief$_i$ is clever enough for us to be captured by him$_i$.
      b. The police chief is clever enough for us to be captured by his henchmen.

In accordance with Case B of the Deletion Principle, we wish to claim that the deletion is optional in the structures underlying (99) and (100); because of the presence of a specified subject in both cases, however, the rule cannot apply. Note that in both (99) and (100) the structural description of OD is met. It follows, therefore, that *too* and *enough* have dual subcategorization — they take both VP and S complements.

Earlier we pointed out that if the structural description of OD is met in the *tough* sentences, only ungrammatical sentences were produced when general constraints blocked the application of the rule. We pointed out the further fact that an identical NP was required in the complements of the *tough* class of predicates. On the basis of what we just concluded concerning the complements of *too* and *enough*, we may draw the following conclusion concerning the complements of the *tough* class of predicates: that the complements are always VPs.

A problem may now be raised concerning the structure underlying the following example.

(101) *This problem$_i$ is too abstract to solve it$_i$.

If the string *to solve it* is a VP complement to *too* in example (101), the ungrammaticality of example (101) is explained. Since the presence of an identical NP is required, the Deletion Principle necessitates that the rule of OD be obligatory. Thus, in one possible derivation, example (101) is ungrammatical since an obligatory rule failed to apply. One would expect, however, that example (101) would be grammatical on a derivation in which the complement is a subjectless sentence, since, in this case, the rule would be optional. We suggest that the ungrammaticality of example (101) has nothing to do with the Deletion Principle or the rule of OD, but rather follows from a principle proposed by Emonds (1970). Emonds's convention concerning obligatory nodes entails that subject position must be filled at some stage in the derivation of a sentence.

(102) a. This problem$_i$ is too abstract for us to solve it$_i$.
     b. This problem$_i$ is specific enough for there to be a solution to it$_i$.

In (102), the complements are sentential and the rule of OD does not have to apply.

Emonds's principle seems to entail that the complements of *try* and some other verbs are VPs, given our analysis. Consider the following contrast:

(103) a.   John is too stubborn to try to talk to.
     b.   *John is too stubborn to arrange to talk to.

The verb *arrange* is like *want*, taking a sentential complement. Emonds's principle predicts that example (103b) is ungrammatical; subject position in the complement of (103b) is never filled. If *try* took a sentential complement, the principle would incorrectly predict that (103a) is ungrammatical also. If our line of reasoning has been correct, we have additional confirmation for the VP proposal put forward in section 3.2.

Consider now the following examples:

(104) a.   *The policemen are too stupid to be captured by.
     b.   *The politicians are clever enough to be hoodwinked by.

In (104), the complement is sentential and the rule of OD, optional in this case, should be able to apply. Emonds's principle is not violated; subject position in the complement was filled prior to the application of Passive. We propose that a condition be added to Emonds's principle requiring that subject position (and perhaps all obligatory nodes) in a sentence be filled at *the end of the cycle on that sentence*.[13]

4. CONCLUSION

We have examined the process of complement object deletion and argued that the range of data which exemplify this process includes the *tough* class of sentences. In addition to showing that the arguments which have been given in support of *Tough* Movement are not correct, we have presented independent evidence against *Tough* Movement. We have also argued that *too* and *enough* have dual subcategorization, taking both VP and S complements, and that the *tough* class of predicates and the *pretty* class of predicates take only VP complements. The facts we have considered, stated in terms of our analysis, bear on several theoretical issues. In particular, specific details of our analysis have been seen to follow from more general conditions on the form of grammars. Chomsky's Specified Subject Condition and Tensed S Condition, Ross's Coordinate Structure Constraint, a strengthened form of Emonds's Obligatory Node Convention, and Fiengo's Deletion Principle have received additional confirmation from the analysis which we have presented.

APPENDIX: EXAMPLES OF SUBCATEGORIZATION TYPES

Type 1. Pure OD

Pure OD adjectives and nouns are those which can occur in the frame NP_i $be \left\{ \begin{matrix} ADJ \\ N \end{matrix} \right\}$ to $_{VP}[V(P)$ ___$_i$], as in *Mary$_i$ is pretty to look at* ___$_i$ but not in the frame *it be* $\left\{ \begin{matrix} ADJ \\ N \end{matrix} \right\}$ *to VP*. The following is a nonexhaustive list.

Adjectives	*Nouns*
pretty	hornets' nest
delicious	pigsty
fragrant	loony bin
graceful	bastard
melodious	tyrant
tasty	angel
cacophonous	prince
beautiful	
slippery	
pungent	
scratchy	

The adjectives and nouns in the list above denote a subjective evaluation; the subjective evaluation is almost always that of the speaker. The adjectives and nouns are subjective in that nonobjective criteria determine their sense. Thus adjectives such as *rectangular* and *black*, which are objective in this sense, cannot occur in this subcategorization frame:

(B.1)   *This room is rectangular to live in.

(B.2)   *Coal is black to look at.

Note that these adjectives and nouns in general do not allow *for* datives.

(B.3) a. ??Mary is pretty for Bill to look at.
      b. ??This music is melodious for Max to listen to.
      c. ??This room is a pigsty for Sam to work in.

The fact that the Pure OD adjectives and nouns are not subcategorized for *for* datives is probably due to the fact that the subjective evaluation denoted in general must be that of the speaker. Note the following contrast:

(B.4) a.   Apple pie is delicious to eat, but George doesn't like it.
      b.   *Apple pie is delicious to eat, but I don't like it.

The nouns in the Pure OD class are metaphorical; note that one cannot refer to a real pigsty with the following sentence:

(B.5)   This room is a pigsty to behold.

The preposition *like* serves to form a productive class of OD constructions with predicate nominals, as in the following constructions.

(B.6) a.   This paint is like concrete to work with.
      b.   *This paint is concrete to work with.

(B.7) a.   This coffee is like tar to drink.
      b.   *This coffee is tar to drink.

(B.8) a.   John is like Nixon to talk to.
      b.   *John is Nixon to talk to.

Type 2. Tough *Predicates*

The following adjectives and nouns are subcategorized both for the frames

NP_i *be* $\left\{\begin{array}{c} ADJ \\ N \end{array}\right\}$ *(for NP) to* $_{VP}[V\,X\underline{\hspace{1cm}}_i\ Y]$ and *it be* $\left\{\begin{array}{c} ADJ \\ N \end{array}\right\}$ *(for NP) to*

VP. A non-exhaustive list follows:

Adjectives	*Nouns*
easy	bitch
impossible	breeze
difficult	pleasure
hard	delight
simple	joy
tough	gas
unhealthy	pain in the $\left\{\begin{array}{c} \text{ass} \\ \text{neck} \end{array}\right\}$
stimulating	
boring	
interesting	
uninteresting	
entertaining	
amusing	
gratifying	

Our deletion analysis allows the relationship between *John is easy to please* and *John is an easy man to please* to be the same as that between *John is tall* and *John is a tall man. John is an easy man to please* will have the following structure:

(B.9)

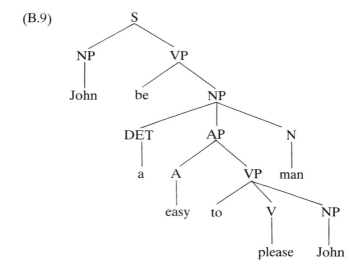

It may be possible to explain the ungrammaticality of *John is a certain man that God is dead* on the basis of a structural difference between *certain that God is dead* and *easy to please*. There is evidence that *certain that God is dead* is not an AP. The verb *call* requires an NP followed by a predicate NP or AP:

(B.10)   I call Mary $\left\{ \begin{array}{l} \text{easy to please} \\ \text{stupid} \\ \text{pretty to look at} \\ \text{too smart to fool} \end{array} \right\}$.

Notice that the phrases which can occur here can occur in attributive position as well:

(B.11)   Mary is $\left\{ \begin{array}{l} \text{an easy woman to please} \\ \text{a stupid woman} \\ \text{a pretty woman to look at} \\ \text{too smart a woman to fool} \end{array} \right\}$.

In contrast to paradigm (B.10) consider sentence (B.12).

(B.12) *I call Mary certain that God is dead.

This strongly suggests that *certain that God is dead* is not an AP. It probably has the following structure:

(B.13)

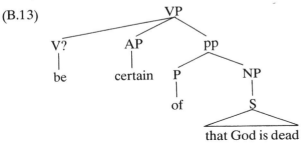

It is suggestive that whenever the complement of an adjective is intuitively felt to be the logical object of the adjective, the adjective and its complement do not seem to constitute an AP.

(B.14) *I call John $\left\{ \begin{array}{l} \text{certain that God is dead} \\ \text{proud of his children} \\ \text{eager for the world to end} \end{array} \right\}$.

None of these strings can occur in attributive position:

(B.15) *John is $\left\{ \begin{array}{l} \text{a certain man that God is dead} \\ \text{a proud man of his children} \\ \text{an eager man for the world to end} \end{array} \right\}$.

Type 3. Too *and* Enough

As we have argued, *too* and *enough* may take either VP or S complements. The following are two possible structures:

(B.16)

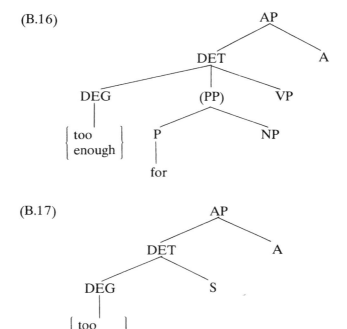

(B.17)

As we stated above, we have placed the complements in the determiners since the presence of the determiners is a necessary condition for the presence of the complements. The *for* phrase in (B.16) has been placed in the determiner because there seems to be a cooccurrence relationship between it and the VP. Although full sentences occur in the complements of *too* and *enough*, when they are present the *for* phrase is excluded:

(B.18) *The police are too slow for us for the firemen to work with them.

A rule (or rules) of Extraposition applies to structures (B.16) and (B.17) to produce the correct surface strings. This Extraposition is probably the same as that which operates in comparative structures (cf. Bresnan 1972).

ACKNOWLEDGEMENTS

We are grateful to Gary Milsark, C. L. Baker, several *Linguistic Inquiry* reviewers, Jay Keyser, and especially Noam Chomsky for many helpful suggestions. This work was supported in part by a grant from the National Institute of Mental Health (5 P01 MH 13390-07) and by the National Institutes of Health (grant 5 T01 HD 00111—09).

NOTES

[1] We do not wish to imply that the process which we will discuss must be formulated as a syntactic rule of deletion as opposed to a semantic rule of interpretation.

[2] Further examples of such predicates are given in Appendix, where we examine all of the subcategorization types discussed in this paper.

[3] Some sentences of this type are ambiguous; they may be interpreted as in (14), where the understood subject of the complement is interpreted as identical with the matrix subject; or as in (9c) and (10c) where the understood object of the complement is interpreted as identical with the matrix subject. All such sentences will be ones in which the embedded transitive verb does not require an object. The following are examples:

(i) a.   The chicken is too old to eat.
    b.   The chicken$_i$ is too old to eat ___$_i$.
    c.   The chicken$_i$ is too old ___$_i$ to eat.

[4] One *Linguistic Inquiry* reviewer, while accepting the data that we present in this section, presented several cases parallel to our (35) but for which grammaticality was claimed. In addition, the referee noted that in all such cases, "it is possible to construct relative clauses like [those in (39)] which seem perfectly acceptable." Far from nullifying our argument, as the reviewer supposed, these facts provide further support for it.

[5] Note that this concept cuts across syntactic categories.

(i)   Someone is interested in buying this house.
         *Someone is tall.

(ii)   Someone is swimming in the Charles.
         *Someone swims in the Charles.

The sentence *John swims in the Charles* indicates a general attribute. *John is swimming in the Charles* does not have this force. It is for the former type of predication that we reserve the term "characteristic".

[6] Berman (1974) discusses the *tough* predicates and, in passing, the Pure OD (*pretty*) type. She claims that the most important feature distinguishing these [Pure OD; HL & RF] sentences from Tough-moved sentences is that in these cases, selectional restrictions must hold between the subject and predicate adjective.

In support of this claim, Berman offers the following pairs:

(i)   This stew is delicious to eat.

(ii)   This stew is delicious.

We assume that Berman is maintaining that, for example, sentence (i) entails sentence (ii), because she goes on to state that when (i) is true, (ii) must be true. (Note that entailment is a much stronger relationship than shared selectional restriction, however.) There are relevant sentence pairs that Berman has not considered. The first sentence in each of the following trios must be produced by OD rather than by any movement rule, but in none of these instances is the second sentence entailed by the first.

(iii) a.   John is a bastard to work for.
     b.   John is a bastard.
     c.   John is a bastard to work for but a nice guy to live with.

(iv) a.   This floor is slippery to dance on.
     b.   This floor is slippery.
     c.   This floor is slippery to dance on but fine to walk on.

(v) a.   Harry$_i$ is too tall to cram ____$_i$ into a breadbox.
    b.   ?Harry is too tall.
    c.   Harry$_i$ is too tall to cram ____ into a breadbox (even though he's only 3 feet tall).

(vi) a.   Mary$_i$ is light enough to fit ____$_i$.
     b.   ?Mary is light enough.
     c.   Mary is light enough to fit ____$_i$ but not light enough to carry ____$_i$.

Returning to the original examples, we suggest that the apparent entailment arises because 'delicious to eat' is inherent in the meaning of the word *delicious*.

[7] For expository purposes, we have included one detail in the statement of the rule that is rendered unnecessary by a general condition. The referential indices need not be stated, since recoverability of deletion guarantees identity, as noted by Chomsky (1965, Ch. 3, fn. 13). We have not stated the fact that the first NP must command the second NP; this too follows from a general condition on deletion rules (see Fiengo (1974)). As the rule is stated, subjects of complements would be deleted. If Bresnan's Fixed Subject Constraint can be extended so that not only movement but also deletion of a subject is blocked when a complementizer is present, this problem will never arise. If Equi is stated so as to delete COMP NP, the Fixed Subject Constraint would not be applicable to it. The labelled bracketing in the rule is an artifact whose presence stems from our incomplete knowledge of the properties of deletion rules.

[8] Chomsky states the Specified Subject Condition as follows (Chomsky 1973, 28):

(123)   No rule can involve $X\ Y \ldots$ in the structure $\ldots X \ldots [\ldots Z \ldots -WYV \ldots]$
         $\ldots$ where Z is the subject of WYV and is not controlled by a category containing X.

One *Linguistic Inquiry* reviewer constructed a very ingenious counterargument to Chomsky's formulation. Correctly noting that Chomsky provides a "loophole allowing for action into or out of such clauses if the affected elements are in Comp and so is trigger or target," this reviewer constructed examples (i) and (ii), derived from (i′) and (ii′), by way of the escape clause.

(i)   *Which rock is too heavy for us to wonder is on the table.

(ii)   *That rock I think is too light for us to say we can't move.

(i′)   Which rock is too heavy for us to wonder which rock is on the table.

(ii′)   That rock I think is too light for us to say that rock we can't move.

A number of possible replies come to mind. First, if Object Deletion is an S cyclic (rather than $\overline{S}$ cyclic) rule, (i) and (ii) would not be produced since the loophole is not available until the trigger NP can also move into COMP, i.e. until the level of $\overline{S}$. Another possibility is that only movement rules are provided this escape route. Note, incidentally, that to the

exent that (i′) is grammatical at all, the two occurrences of *which rock* cannot be interpreted as coreferential. Consequently it is highly doubtful that OD would be applicable.

[9] Another possibility, that the complements are sentences with unfilled subjects, will be
examined below. For additional arguments supporting the existence of VP complements,
see Lees (1960), Emonds (1970), Newmeyer (1969), and Bresnan (1970).

[10] We have been informed that there are some speakers who accept *be* passives in the
environments discussed. Rosenbaum (1967) cites such examples as grammatical. Perhaps
for such speakers a suppletive relationship obtains between *get* and *be*.

[11] There are some apparent problems with (94b), but we believe that it will be possible to
handle these without sacrificing the Deletion Principle. For example, Equi appears to
violate B; (i) and (ii) are thus grammatical, but (iii) is not:

(i)   I want Bill to win.

(ii)   I want to win.

(iii)   *I want me to win.

However, there is some evidence that (iii) should not be excluded by making Equi
obligatory. Notice that when the structural description for Equi is met, but applying the
rule would be a violation of a general constraint, it is possible to leave the noun phrase
intact.

(iv)   I want (very much for) me and Harry to become friends.

(v)   I want (very much for) Harry and me to become friends.

This behavior contrasts sharply with that of Object Deletion. In (91), we showed that when
a general constraint prohibits the application of that rule, there is no possible good output.
The behaviour of Object Deletion, then, is quite representative of obligatory rules, while
that of Equi is not. We admit that we have no way, at present, to rule out (iii) above. It
seems, however, that some way must be found that does not also rule out (iv) or (v).

[12] Observe that in an S-complement, when the identical NP is inside of an island, the
sentence is grammatical:

(i) $John_i$ is too obnoxious for us to find a woman who likes him_i.

(ii) $John_i$ is too obscure for there to be a book about him_i and his wife.

This is as would be expected, since the rule of OD is optional in S-complements, as will be
discussed below.

Conceivably, various riders could be added to OD to prohibit its application in
sentences in which the complements to *too* and *enough* are sentential (see (99) and (100)
below, for further examples). However, this would be a cost to the grammar with no
concomitant benefit, since the riders would merely duplicate the effect of general conditions, including those exemplified in (91).

[13] It is worth noting that it follows as a consequence of this proposal that the object
preposing half of Passive will be obligatory, a fact that Emonds's principle could not
explain. It also follows that the part of the process of *There* Insertion that inserts *there* will
be obligatory, and that, if Extraposition is stated in the traditional way, the insertion (or
retention) of *it* will be obligatory.

HOWARD LASNIK

REMARKS ON COREFERENCE
1976

One of the more persistent topics in recent grammatical research has been that of pronominial coreference. Linguists have gained important insights into the syntax of pronouns and into the structural conditions permitting coreference. In this paper, I will examine two important approaches to these problems, the transformational and the interpretive, and show various formal and empirical difficulties encountered by each. In the course of this examination, I will sketch an alternative theory of personal pronouns that appears to be simpler and more descriptively adequate.

It is usually assumed that such a sentence as (1), from Postal (1966), is ambiguous.

(1)   Schwartz claims that he is sick.

On one reading, according to most linguists, *he* and *Schwartz* are co-referential and are related by some rule, either transformational or interpretive. On the second reading, *he* is not related to *Schwartz* by any rule, and is assumed therefore to refer to some individual other than the one designated by *Schwartz*. The former case, I will discuss at length below. For the latter case, there is a difference of opinion concerning the derivational history of the pronoun. For McCawley:

If a personal pronoun occurs in a sentence which does not contain an antecedent for that pronoun, then either the pronoun has an antecedent in some preceding sentence in the discourse (possibly a sentence uttered by someone other than the speaker) or that pronoun is used deictically (i.e., is a direct reference to someone or something physically present as the sentence is uttered and is stressed and accompanied by a gesture). [1970, 178]

Postal presents a contrary view:

The idea that a form like *she* in *she dances well* is a 'replacement' or 'substitute' for some other noun, say in 'discourse contexts' or the like, seems to me completely without basis. Such an assumption explains nothing for the quite simple reason that there is nothing really to explain. It is quite sufficient to indicate precisely that such forms refer to object-types whose particular referents are assumed by the speaker to be known to the person spoken to. [Postal 1966, fn. 3]

Surely Postal's claim, with its consequence that at least some pronouns are present in the base, is preferable to McCawley's. For example, there are trivial cases which are inconsistent with the latter. Consider a situation in which an unpopular man is present at a party. He is there for an hour during which period he is avoided by all, no one even mentioning his name. Finally, he storms out in a huff. It would be neither unacceptable, nor incomprehensible nor bizarre for someone at this point to remark, "Well, he's left." But McCawley's theory explicitly excludes such a use of a personal pronoun. Postal, on the other hand, could provide a natural way of explaining this fact, since the speaker could reasonably expect his audience to know who he was talking about. McCawley's theory could be weakened so as to encompass the relevant example. However, such a weakening would either remove from the theory all content in excess of Postal's theory; or it would drag the theory into a sort of mysticism in which the content of an idea or belief or memory or supposition, etc., can provide a noun phrase for the operation of a formal grammatical process.

Far preferable is Postal's explanation, in which the whole process is independent of the grammar. What we have is simply a principle of cooperation. By this I mean that a speaker must provide every reasonable means for his listener to know what he is talking about. Stated this way, the explanation can readily be seen not to be a claim about pronouns but rather about getting along with people, not about language, but about communication. And indeed, pronouns have no special status in this regard.

Thus far, I have argued, essentially following Postal (1966), that at least some instances of pronouns (third person pronouns included) are present in the base, and that a principle of cooperation limits the indiscriminate use of pronouns (as well as many other noun phrases). Hence, the reading of sentence (1) in which *he* and *Schwartz* are not assumed to refer to the same individual is not problematic.

It is to the apparent other reading, in which the two NPs are assumed to be coreferential, that I now turn. In many studies, linguists have argued for the existence of a set of rules resulting in the replacement of one full NP with a pronoun, under conditions of syntactic identity and coreference to another NP. It should be pointed out that the second of these conditions raises no problems for the transformational analysis even though it can be plausibly argued that "referent of a noun phrase" is not a syntactic property (or under certain assumptions even a semantic property) and hence is not information available to a syntactic rule. This is so because, contrary to the assumptions of nearly all linguists who have looked at problems of pronominalization,[1] the coreference condition (as well as the identity condition) need not be mentioned in the rule. A rule deleting one NP and leaving a pronoun in its place would necessarily be constrained by the principle of recoverability of deletion elaborated in Chomsky (1965). Since the hypothesized pronominalization transformation could not be formulated so as to delete a lexical item designated in the structural description of the rule, it could only delete an item that also appears elsewhere in the structure. Presumably (although this goes beyond Chomsky's claim) the nondeleted occurrence must be identical not only in syntactic shape but in sense and reference as well, or the deletion will not be recoverable. It is worth noting that these remarks apply with equal force to the transformational versions of such rules as Equi-NP-Deletion (whether or not the rule depends, as argued in Postal (1970), on prior pronominalization) and Object-Deletion, formulated and discussed in Lasnik and Fiengo (1974). Hence whatever the merits and shortcomings of transformational as opposed to "interpretive" deletion rules, the problem of identifying coreferent noun phrases is not an issue.

Syntactic processes of pronominalization have been discussed by Lees and Klima (1963), Postal (1966), Langacker (1969), and Ross (1967a), and many others. The differences between the analyses mentioned will not be relevant to the present discussion. Ross gives a pronominalization rule which actually contains two rules, one for forward pronominalization, and one for backward. I slightly restate the rule using Langacker's notion 'command'[2] in place of Ross' more cumbersome condition, and eliminate from the rule the requirement of identity, in line with the comments above.

$$(2) \quad \text{SD:} \quad X - \begin{bmatrix} NP \\ -PRO \end{bmatrix} - Y - \begin{bmatrix} NP \\ -PRO \end{bmatrix} - Z \quad \text{OBLIG}$$
$$\phantom{(2) \quad \text{SD:} \quad} 1 \qquad\quad 2 \qquad\quad 3 \qquad\quad 4 \qquad\quad 5$$

$$\text{SC: a.} \quad 1 \qquad 2 \qquad 3 \quad \begin{bmatrix} 4 \\ +PRO \end{bmatrix} \quad 5 \qquad \text{or}$$

$$\phantom{\text{SC:}} \text{b.} \quad 1 \quad \begin{bmatrix} 2 \\ +PRO \end{bmatrix} \quad 3 \qquad 4 \qquad 5$$

Condition: b is only possible when 2 does not command 4.

Ross notes that in some cases, pronominalization is optional, however. He gives an example noticed by Emonds.

$$(3) \quad \text{Willy washed his car and then he polished} \begin{Bmatrix} \text{his car} \\ \text{it} \end{Bmatrix}.$$

In example (3) it is clearly possible to understand the second occurrence of *his car* as designating the same entity as the first. It is important to note that the very sharpest instances of obligatory pronominalization are those in which one of the two identical noun phrases both precedes and commands the others.[3] Contrast examples (4), where this structural condition is met, with examples (5), where (as in (3) above) this condition is not met.

(4) a. Oscar finally realized that $\begin{Bmatrix} *\text{Oscar} \\ \text{he} \end{Bmatrix}$ is unpopular.

b. It surprises John that $\begin{Bmatrix} *\text{John} \\ \text{he} \end{Bmatrix}$ is so well liked.

c. Harry was really surprised that $\begin{Bmatrix} *\text{Harry} \\ \text{he} \end{Bmatrix}$ lost the race.

d. Nixon hates people who criticize $\begin{Bmatrix} *\text{Nixon} \\ \text{him} \end{Bmatrix}$.

(5) a. That Oscar is unpopular was finally realized by Oscar.
   b. That John is well liked proves that we ought to hire John as public relations director.
   c. That Harry won the race really surprised Harry.
   d. People who know Nixon hate Nixon.

These examples suggest that the relevant distinction is not that of forward as opposed to backward pronominalization, as indicated by Ross, but rather that of cases in which one NP both precedes and commands the other as opposed to all other structural configurations. Pronominalization could then be broken into two rules, one of them obligatory (involving NPs such that one precedes and commands the second), and the other optional. This will entail, correctly by and large, that whenever backward pronominalization is possible, forward pronominalization is also and there is the additional option of no pronominalization.

Even this improved proposal runs into significant difficulties, however. I have already argued, with Postal, that some pronouns are present in the base. Given this, as Postal and others have pointed out, a sentence such as (6) has two derivations, one from the more abstract structure (7) via pronominalization, and the other from a structure involving no relevant transformations.

(6) People who know him hate Nixon.

(7) People who know Nixon hate Nixon.

However, the usual claim that the two deep structures correlate with the two readings (coreferent versus noncoreferent) is mistaken. Certainly, a source resembling (7) can produce (6) under the assumptions being discussed. But there is no way to exclude a derivation in which *him* in (6) is present in underlying structure *with the same referential index* as *Nixon* has. This may appear to be a minor quibble — perhaps it is not important that (6) is structurally ambiguous, even on the reading where *he* and *Nixon* are assumed to be coreferent. But the significance of this fact is that it renders the pronominalization transformation superfluous. Since the virtue of pronominalization was that it accounted for an apparent ambiguity, and the supposed ambiguity is necessarily accounted for independently, little motivation exists for maintaining the transformation. Of the two hypothesized readings, one includes the other. It could be objected that the ungrammaticality of examples (4) can be accounted for, assuming the existence of a transformation, since an obligatory transformation has failed to apply. But this objection carries little weight, since examples (8) have a parallel ungrammaticality even though a pronominalization rule such as (2) would not be applicable.[4]

(8) a.   *He* finally realized that *Oscar* is unpopular.
   b.   *It surprises *him* that *John* is so well liked.
   c.   *He* was really surprised that *Harry* lost the race.
   d.   *He* hates people who criticize *Nixon*.

There is no obvious way to block the production of examples (8) beginning with a pronoun in the base carrying the same referential index (or equivalent device) as the full NP. These examples are particularly striking since the principle of cooperation alluded to above does not appear to be relevant. Even the existence of prior identifying information in the discourse is not sufficient to allow these examples a coreferent reading.

(9)   I spoke to *Oscar* yesterday. *He* finally realized that *Oscar* is unpopular.

The theory, then, is faced with the following difficulty: if pronouns can be generated freely in the base, how can we rule out a derivation of (8a), for example, in which the pronoun "by accident" has the same referent as the full NP? Note that (10) below is at worst rather uninformative, and (11) is impeccable even though parallel to (9).

(10)   He finally realized that Mary is unpopular.

(11)   I spoke to *Oscar* yesterday. *He* finally realized that Mary is unpopular.

I suggest that no system of optional and obligatory transformations could account for these facts, but rather, an additional filtering device is required. In particular, to prevent the ungrammatical "accidental" instances of coreference in question, a noncoreference rule must be postulated. Such a rule would mark pairs of NP's noncoreferent under certain circumstances. In (12) I give an approximation of the correct formulation:

(12)   If NP_1 precedes and commands NP_2, and NP_2 is not a pronoun, then NP_1 and NP_2 are noncoreferential.[5]

Rule (12) correctly excludes coreferent readings of (8) and (4) while
permitting coreference in (5) — and in modifications of examples (5) with
either NP replaced by a pronoun.

A set of transformational pronominalization rules augmented by rule
(12) results in a system quite similar to that of Lakoff (1968). But as
Wasow (1972) observes, Lakoff "offers no motivation whatever for the
postulation of the transformation". To summarize, any set of transformations postulated to account for the facts of pronominal anaphora must be
supplemented by a noncoreference rule to exclude the impossible coreference relations that could "accidentally" result from the presence of some
pronouns in the base. But now note that (12) is not only necessary to
account for the data I have presented, it is sufficient. Rule (12) correctly
accounts for the facts it was intended for, and also accounts for the facts
that motivated a transformation. It appears then that once pronouns are
permitted in the base, as they apparently must be, a noncoreference rule
such as (12) is needed. Then, by Occam's razor, rule (12) eliminates the
need for transformationally derived personal pronouns.

One interpretation of the resulting system, although certainly not the
only possible one, is that *he*, for example, means 'male human being', and
consequently, that pronoun can be used to refer to any member of that
class except under circumstances excluded by (12). Evidently, (12) applies
at some level of derived structure, since various transformations affect
coreference possibilities. Compare (8b), repeated below, with (8b′), its
nonextraposed counterpart:

(8) b.   *It surprises *him* that *John* is so well liked.
    b′.   That *John* is so well liked surprises *him*.

Under the interpretation of the theory suggested above, (8b′) could be
thought of as vague rather than ambiguous. That is, the possible referents
of *him* encompass all entities compatible with the meaning of that lexical
item. Then, one possible referent in (8b′) is excluded in (8b). In effect,
(12) is a semantic rule providing a sentence with an additional truth-
condition dependent on its syntactic representation. The theory under
consideration, which so far includes no syntactic or interpretive coreference device, accounts very neatly for whatever is correct in the 'anaporn
relation' discussed by Dougherty 1969. The substance of Dougherty's
position is that under any circumstances, a pronoun permits a nonanaphoric interpretation; and under some circumstances, a pronoun
requires such an interpretation.

Wasow (1972) insightfully discusses several putative counterexamples, offered by Postal (1972), to Dougherty's position. In all of the following examples from Wasow [1972, Chap. 1 (38)] coreference is required between the italicized NPs:

(13) a. *Mary* washed *her*self.
   b. *The chairman* gnashed *his* teeth.
   c. *The losers* had to buy beer, didn't *they*.
   d. *The man who shot Liberty Valance, he* was the bravest of them all.
   e. *He* is a very wise man, *the Maharishi*.

Wasow points out that in all of these examples, the pronouns can be plausibly analyzed as arising from copying transformations. Examples (a) and (b) are produced by the reflexivization transformation, which is convincingly argued by Helke (1971) and Wasow (1972) to insert a pronominal copy of some NP into the determiner of certain nouns. Examples (c), (d), and (e) are derived via Tag-Formation, Left Dislocation, and Right Dislocation, respectively. After presenting the foregoing data, Wasow continues:

These facts are highly suggestive. If all counter-examples to the anaporn relation are pronouns resulting from the application of copying transformations, then it might be possible to salvage the anaporn relation in spirit by stipulating that copying transformations which involve an NP always produce a pronoun whose antecedent is that NP.

In support of this claim Wasow presents several arguments to which the reader is hereby referred.[6]

   The hypothesis that understood coreference within a sentence is not (or need not be) the result of a coreference rule of some sort permits one to claim that the following two examples illustrate basically the same process:

(14)   A: I hit *John*.   B: What did *he* do then?

(15)   After I hit *John, he* screamed.

If the possibility of coreference in (15) is accounted for by a rule, one would be forced to discriminate sharply between (14) and (15). This is so since, as I argued above in support of Postal, grammatical processes are sentence internal. I have gone further than Postal, however, and argued that even sentence internal cases of coreference are not produced by any rule. Notice that an interpretive rule of coreference, such as those proposed by Jackendoff (1969; 1972), encounters the same difficulties as a transformational rule. Here again (14) and (15) would receive radically different treatments since an interpretive rule, being a rule of grammar, must also be constrained so as to apply essentially sentence internally. Further, the problems emphasized earlier emerge in this framework as well. For example, a coreference rule, like a pronominalization transformation, provides no obvious way to rule out (16), and in addition, fails to rule out (17).

(16)   *_He_ finally realized that _Oscar_ is unpopular.

(17)   *_Oscar_ finally realized that _Oscar_ is unpopular.

I will not go into all of the details of Jackendoff's coreference rule here, but its domain of operation includes the environment of the standard pronominalization transformations discussed above. The relevant part of the rule is given in (18).

(18)   Jackendoff's pronominalization rule:
Enter in the table [of coreference HL]: NP^1 + coref

$$\begin{bmatrix} NP^2 \\ +PRO \end{bmatrix}$$ unless NP^2 both precedes and commands NP^1.

OPTIONAL

Jackendoff recognizes the difficulty presented by such examples as (16) and (17). That is, such examples could "by accident" have a coreferent reading. Consequently, he augments his grammar with an additional inter-pretive device, a noncoreference rule.

(19)   Jackendoff's noncoreference rule:
If for any NP^1 and NP^2 in a sentence, there is no entry in the table NP^1 + coref NP^2, enter in the table NP^1 − coref NP^2.
OBLIGATORY

Jackendoff explicates (19) as follows:

This rule says that any noun phrases that have not yet been related by a rule of coreference are noncoreferential.

There are two problems with this treatment, however. First, the non-coreference rule is too general. Notice that the coreference rule is only operative when at least one of the two NPs is a pronoun. Consequently, (19) will rule out coreference between any two full NPs in a sentence. However, Jackendoff is incorrect in assuming that, "any two nonpronominal noun phrases in the same sentence, morphologically identical or not, are always noncoreferential." As I indicated above, this restriction should probably be limited to situations in which one of the NPs both precedes and commands the other (cf. (3) and (5)). Presumably, rules (18) and (19) could be modified in some manner to overcome this defect, but the resulting noncoreference rule would then be completely equivalent to my rule (12). That is, a correct formulation of Jackendoff's noncoreference rule would render his coreference rule superfluous.

I would now like to explore some further ramifications of the system I have tentatively proposed. One advantage of the analysis is that it generalizes in a straightforward way to so-called anaphoric epithets. Jackendoff (1972) has shown that to some extent phrases such as *the bastard* behave like pronouns. Further, he has persuasively argued that these phrases could not arise via the operation of a pronominalization transformation since there is no one-to-one semantic relationship between a definite description and a coreferent epithet. Jackendoff concludes,

> In an interpretive framework, we can mark epithets as special lexical items which may function as pronouns in certain contexts of the pronominalization rule, adding their lexical meaning to the intended attributes of the person they refer to.

To the extent that anaphoric epithets behave like pronouns, however, the difficulties that arise in Jackendoff's treatment of pronouns are also present in the case of epithets. Further, Jackendoff is presumably committed to calling epithets pronouns in order to capture the parallelism between (15) and (20):

(20)   After I hit *John, the sissy* screamed.

Jackendoff equivocates about the identification of the two types of expressions, but it is not at all clear how the equivocation can be captured in the coreference rule. Notice that just in case some NP both precedes and commands an epithet, the two cannot be understood as coreferential.

(21) a. *_John_ realizes that *the sissy* is going to lose.
      b. *_He_ realizes that *the sissy* is going to lose.

(22)   *The sissy realizes that *the sissy* is going to lose.

But this is exactly what would be predicted by my rule (12), assuming that epithets are *not* pronouns.

Another traditional problem in pronominalization (cf. Stockwell et al. 1973) involves sentences like the following:

(23)   After John talked to Mary, they left the room.

Clearly (23) can be used when the intended referent of *they* is John and Mary. However, there is no single NP in the structure designating John and Mary. Consequently no formulation of a pronominalization transformation can account for the occurrence of *they*. Further, as Stockwell et al. point out, an interpretive rule of coreference runs into exactly the same difficulty. Within the system I have proposed, however, (23) is not problematic, for the same reason that the discourse situations alluded to by Postal are not problematic. That is, no coreference rule is needed to explain (23), because there is nothing to explain. *They* in (23) can be used to refer to any group of entities; under many discourse situations, however, John and Mary are the only likely candidates. It is informative to compare (23) with an example involving the determiner of a reflexive NP, i.e., an instance of required anaphora.

(23′)   *John asked Mary about themselves.

I turn now to a complex phenomenon hinted at in Jackendoff (1969) and Postal (1972) and discussed at length in Wasow (1972). Wasow points out that there is no reading of (24) on which the three italicized NP's can all be understood as coreferential.

(24)   *The woman *he* loved told *him* that *John* was a jerk.

However, it appears that independently, *he* can be coreferential to *him* and *he* can be coreferential to *John*:

(25) a.   The woman *he* loved told us that *John* was a jerk.
     b.   The woman *he* loved told *him* that we were all jerks.

Wasow notes that the impossibility of (24) can only be accounted for in a system like Jackendoff's if there is a noncoreference rule as well as a coreference rule. Otherwise, (24) would be allowed because of the transitivity of coreference. If there is a noncoreference rule such as (19), (24) can be directly accounted for by the transitivity of the relationship *coreferent to*, since *him* and *John* will not meet the structural description for Jackendoff's coreference rule and will therefore by obligatorily susceptible to the noncoreference rule. Wasow concludes that the principle responsible for the ungrammaticality of (24), which he calls the Transitivity Condition, could be regarded as primitive instead.[7]

(26)   Wasow's Transitivity Condition (TC):
       If A, B, and C are three elements in a sentence such that an anaphoric relation holds between A and B and an anaphic relation holds between B and C, then the sentence is marked ungrammatical unless an anaphoric relation holds between A and C.

Notice that this condition can account for (24), since, as I noted above, *him* and *John* will not be anaphorically related (i.e., will not be susceptible to the coreference rule).

(27)   *I told *him* that *John* was a jerk.

The flaw in Wasow's argument is that he assumes Jackendoff introduces his noncoreference rule solely for the purpose of dispensing with (26) as a primitive condition. But this view overlooks an important fact: given that coreference in (27) is not possible, either Wasow's TC or Jackendoff's noncoreference rule will label (24) as ungrammatical. However, the TC says nothing about (27) and curiously, Wasow provides no way to exclude

(27) on the coreference reading. True, his anaphora rule will not apply in
(27). But Wasow explicitly stipulates that "the failure of two NPs to be
related anaphorically does not entail that they have distinct referents."
Here again, no provision is made for disallowing "accidental" coreference.
I argued earlier that regardless of whether there is a pronominalization
transformation or an interpretive coreference rule, a noncoreference rule
is required to account for the ungrammaticality of such examples as (27).
In fact, I concluded that both types of coreference devices can be dispensed with, since the following three systems are descriptively equivalent,
for the data range under consideration, and that the noncoreference rule
cannot be dispensed with.

(28)   Three descriptively equivalent theories of coreference phe-
        nomena:
        a. Noncoreference rule (12)
        b. Noncoreference rule (12) plus a coreference rule
        c. Noncoreference rule (12) plus a pronominalization transforma-
           tion

But notice now that if noncoreference rule (12) must be included in the
grammar, the Transitivity Condition becomes superfluous, at least for
NPs. For if some sentence contains three NPs, A, B, and C, and the
noncoreference rule marks A and C as noncoreferential, then it is clear
that A, B, and C cannot all be understood as coreferential.

Thus far, I have presented a noncoreference rule and shown that it can
be used to explain a range of facts handled in a variety of ways in existing
theories.[8] I have also suggested that this rule can account for certain facts
usually left unexplained. At this point, I will offer a few refinements of the
theory, and then proceed to deal with some apparent anomalies. Wasow
(1972) presents the following data. The judgments are Wasow's. I concur
with them except that I find examples (29) fully grammatical.

(29) a. (?)*His* mother loves *John*.
     b. (?)*Their* maid speaks well of the *Smiths*.
     c. (?)*Her* friends gave *Mary* a going away present.

(30) a. **He* loves *John's* mother.
     b. **They* speak well of the *Smith's* maid.
     c. **She* gave *Mary's* friends a going away present.

All of examples (29) and (30) would be ruled out by (12) as I formulated
it. It should be noted here that, as we might expect, replacement of the
pronouns by full NPs in (29) does not make the sentence worse.

(31) a. *John's* mother loves *John*.
     b. *The Smith's* maid speaks well of *the Smiths*.
     c. *Mary's* friends gave *Mary* a going away present.

Thus, the examples in (29) display normal "backward pronominalization" behavior. I have already indicated that whenever a pronoun can appear to the left of its antecedent, a full coreference NP can appear in the same position. Now notice that the examples in (30) are not improved by the substitution of a full NP:

(32) a. *John* loves *John's* mother.
  b. *The Smiths* speak well of *the Smith's* maid.
  c. *Mary* gave *Mary's* friends a going away present.

Thus, (30) represents the customary "forward and downward" paradigm. The difficulty here is that (12) does not discriminate between (29) and (30). A modification of (12), along the approximate lines suggested by Wasow, might be the following:

(33)   If NP_1 precedes and kommands NP_2, and NP_2 is not a pronoun, then NP_1 and NP_2 are noncoreferential.[9]
       definition: A *kommands* B if the minimal cyclic node dominating A also dominates B.

To motivate one final modification, I turn now to some examples similar to (23). I suggest that any sort of coreference rule will run into difficulty in trying to capture the readings of *After John talked to Mary, they left.* In fact, other such examples create problems for the noncoreference rule as well. Consider the following example:

(34)   They assume that Bob will talk to Tom.

Notice that *they* in (34) cannot be understood as having *Tom* and *Bob* as intended referents. However, noncoreference rule (33) is not sufficient to block such an interpretation. Rule (33) will label *they* and *Bob* noncoreferential, and also *they* and *Tom*. But that misses the point, and provides no way of eliminating the reading. In fact, even without (33), it is clear that the NPs cannot be coreferential, since they disagree in number. What (33) cannot do is tell us that *they* on the one hand, and *Bob and Tom* on the other hand designate distinct entities, since the latter does not appear in the structure. Another example of the same type is (35).

(35)   They hate the man who forced Tom to hit Harry.

In (36), unlike (35), *they* can be understood as designating Tom and Harry.

(36) a.   The man who forced Tom to hit Harry hates them.
  b.   The man who hates them forced Tom to hit Harry.

Thus, the crucial structural configuration again appears to be one NP both preceding and commanding another. Further, as (37) indicates, 'kommand' rather than 'command' is relevant.

(37)   Their parents told Mary to play with Susan.

I tentatively propose that (33) should be replaced with (38) in light of examples (34—37).

(38)   If NP_1 precedes and kommands NP_2 and NP_2 is not a pronoun, then NP_1 and NP_2 are disjoint in reference.[10]

Rule (38) will suffice to exclude the undesired reading in (34) since if *they* and *Bob* are disjoint in reference, for example, the sentence cannot have a reading in which *they* designates Bob and Tom. The correct generalization appears to be that in any structural configuration in which coreference between two NPs is precluded, overlap in reference is also precluded. Notice that the implications of (38) extend beyond situations involving pronouns or identical NPs. The following sentence, for example, has the relevant structural configuration and, although the judgment is delicate, no reading in which *soldiers* is understood as including *officers* seems to be available.

(39)   The soldiers think that the officers are competent.

Contrast (39) with (40), in which *soldiers* can be understood in the wider sense.

(40)   The man who spoke to the soldiers praised the officers.

In conclusion, I have argued that every theory of coreference requires a noncoreference rule in some form, to account for sentences in which a pair of NPs is prohibited from designating the same entity. When existing analyses are augmented with such a rule, the coreference devices in those accounts are found to be superfluous. Hence, it appears that a rule with the general properties of (12) is not only necessary but sufficient to account for reference interactions among NPs.

APPENDIX

PRONOUNS AS BOUND VARIABLES

It has been noted in the literature that there is a class of noun phrases including *no one, someone*, etc., that diverge from definite descriptions in their relationship to pronouns. Postal (1970), for example, claims that when a definite pronoun is to the left of an NP, the NP must be definite in order to serve as antecedent. Wasow offers such examples as the following. Note that the asterisk indicates ungrammaticality only on the relevant reading, in the examples of the appendix.

(A1)   *The fact that he lost disturbed each candidate.

(A2)   Each candidate was disturbed by the fact that he lost.

(A3)   *The woman who loved him impoverished every businessman.

(A4)   Every businessman was impoverished by the woman who loved him.

Wasow (1972) suggests that the relevant distinction is between referring expressions, which he calls "determinate," and other NPs. The former class includes specific NPs (which he used to designate an entity), and generic NPs (which are used to refer to a class). Nonspecific nongenerics are, in Wasow's terms, indeterminate.

The following examples hint at the extent of the phenomenon. Note particularly that kommand relationships, as well as other structural relationships, play a role. It will also be important to keep in mind that each starred example can be made grammatical by the substitution of a suitable determinate NP in place of the indeterminate one.

(A5) $\begin{Bmatrix} \text{Everyone} \\ \text{No one} \end{Bmatrix}$ seriously believes that he is unattractive.

(A6)   *He seriously believes that $\begin{Bmatrix} \text{everyone} \\ \text{no one} \end{Bmatrix}$ is unattractive.

(A7)   *$\begin{Bmatrix} \text{Everyone's} \\ \text{No one's} \end{Bmatrix}$ mother thinks he is unfriendly.

(A8) $\begin{Bmatrix} \text{Everyone} \\ \text{No one} \end{Bmatrix}$ thinks his wife is unfriendly.

(A9)   *$\begin{Bmatrix} \text{Everyone's} \\ \text{No one's} \end{Bmatrix}$ mother doubts that he will succeed.

(A10) *Because $\begin{Bmatrix} \text{everyone} \\ \text{no one} \end{Bmatrix}$ walked, he sat down.

(A11) *After he walked in, $\begin{Bmatrix} \text{everyone} \\ \text{no one} \end{Bmatrix}$ sat down.

(A12) $\begin{Bmatrix} \text{Everyone} \\ \text{No one} \end{Bmatrix}$ sat down after he walked in.

In general, it appears that the NPs in question can only be related to the pronouns when the NP both precedes and kommands the pronoun. A more complete specification of the nature of this relatedness is in order. While the relationship is often characterized as coreference, this seems quite inappropriate. Presumably, two NPs can be coreferential only if they are both referring expressions. More simply, how can two NPs designate the same entity unless each of them can designate some entity? By this criterion, *no one* and *he*, for example, can never be coreferential. Rather, the relationship should be characterized as that holding between a quantifier and the variable that it binds. Evidence for this suggestion is provided by the fact that the structural requirements in the present case are exactly those of established instances of quantifier scope such as the scope of negation, discussed in Lasnik (1972; 1975).

Another situation in which "coreference" seems a similarly inappropriate description is exemplified by the following:

(A13)   Who thinks he can handle this job?

Patently, *who* fails to refer. Its function in a sentence appears to be that of an operator, rather than that of a definite description. Here too, the relationship between the NP in a question and its related pronoun should perhaps be analyzed as variable-binding, rather than coreference. Notice that kommand appears to be relevant in this instance as well.

(A14)   *Whose mother thinks he can handle the job?

If it is accepted that the relationship between Wh-words and pronouns is distinct from coreference, the way is cleared for a solution to a number of "cross-over" problems presented in Postal (1971). Compare (A15) to (A16):

(A15)   Who thinks he can solve the problem?

(A16)   *Who does he think can solve the problem?

When the relationship between *who* and *he* in (A15) is incorrectly taken to be that of coreference, as it is in most of the literature on the subject, very serious difficulties, first noted by Postal, arise. One might be tempted to argue that pronominalization precedes Wh-Fronting, and cannot apply backward and upward. That is, such a process (whether transformational or interpretive) could not apply to (A17), since the pronoun precedes and commands the full NP.

(A17)   He thinks who can solve the problem.

The problem arises in the consideration of (A18).

(A18)   Who that *John* knows does *he* think can solve the problem?

Example (A18) is grammatical, yet its structure at the point in its derivational history hypothesized as the input to pronominalization does not meet the structural requirements of that rule.

(A19)   He thinks who that John knows can solve the problem.

Postal (1971) proposes the Cross-over Principle as an explanation; Wasow (1972) provides an alternative based on the special properties of movement rules. Obviously, ordering does not suffice, since pronominalization in these examples cannot both precede and follow Wh-Fronting. However, *John* and *he* can properly be said to be coreference in the relevant reading of (A18). On the other hand, in (A15) *who* should be said to bind *he*. Since the phenomena at hand must be described by two different processes, no ordering paradox need arise. For example, if the scope of a Wh operator is assigned cyclically[11] (that is, following the application of all syntactic rules on a cycle) and the noncoreference rule is applied last cyclically (following the syntactic rules on the final cycle), only the unstarred sentences above will be produced. In (A18), *John* and *he* will not be marked as noncoreferential, since *he* does not both precede and kommand John. Example (A16) *will* be blocked, since in (A17), *who* will be assigned a scope on the first possible cycle, and consequently, *he*, which is not included in the first cyclic domain, will not be bound by *who*.[12]

Pursuing this line of inquiry further, it may be instructive to examine other relationships between NPs with regard to the structural requirements involved. One relationship of interest is that of "sloppy identity" first discussed in Ross (1967a; 1969). Sentence (A20) illustrates deletion under sloppy identity, on the reading where it is synonymous to (A21).

(A20)   Harry believes he is intelligent, and Bill does too.

(A21)   Harry believes himself to be intelligent and Bill believes himself to be intelligent.

By and large, it appears that deletion under sloppy identity[13] is only possible when the antecedent of the deleted pronoun both precedes and kommands the pronoun. Compare (A20) with (A22), which has no sloppy reading.

(A22)   The woman who emulated Harry believes he is intelligent and the woman who emulated Bill does too.

The following example, as well, seems to lack a sloppy reading.

(A23)   Harry's mother believes he is intelligent, and Bill's mother does too.

Notice that it is not always correct to inquire as to what pairs of NPs are coreferential in instances of sloppy identity, since the phenomenon exists even in the absence of a referring antecedent:

(A24)   Every linguist thinks he's terrific and every philosopher does too.

Here, variable-binding rather than coreference is exhibited. An informal logical representation for (A24) is given in (A25).

(A25) $\forall x((x \text{ is a linguist}) \rightarrow (x \text{ thinks } x \text{ is terrific}))$ and
$\forall y((y \text{ is a philosopher}) \rightarrow (y \text{ thinks } y \text{ is terrific}))$

Intuitively, the deleted VP in (A24) corresponds to the second consequent in (A25). But since x and y are *bound* variables, the two consequents are identical (rather than sloppily identical) open sentences, and the mystery of deletion under nonidentity disappears. It is not inconceivable, given the structural requirements illustrated in (A20—A23), that the missing pronoun in (A20) is also an instance of a bound variable (bound in this situation by a definite description operator, perhaps). I don't claim to have solved the problem with these brief remarks, but the parallelism between sloppy identity and variable-binding is sufficiently striking to be worthy of investigation.

One final aspect to pronominal behavior that may bear on the question of variable-binding is illustrated by so-called Bach—Peters sentences, presented in Bach (1970). Example (A26), on the relevant reading, is an instance of the Bach—Peters Paradox.

(A26)   The pilot that shot at it hit the mig that chased him.

Karttunen (1971) and Wasow (1972) have discussed the semantic possibilities of (A26) at some length, and I have little to add. It is interesting to note, however, that here again, we may not be dealing with coreference, per se. The next example seems to parallel (A26) even though the "antecedent" of one of the pronouns is a quantifier, rather than a referring expression.

(A27)   Every pilot that shot at it hit the mig that chased him.

If, in line with my suggestions about sloppy identity, *him* in (A26) can similarly be said to be bound by an operator, no infinite regress develops, since it would not be appropriate to substitute some full NP in place of *him*. One would predict, given these assumptions, that Bach—Peters phenomena would be limited to the structural configurations allowing variable-binding. My intuitions on this matter are not crystal clear, but when the full NP does not both precede and kommand the pronoun, as in (A28) and (A29), a crossing interpretation seems much less available.

(A28)   After the pilot that shot at it landed, the mig that chased him crashed.

(A29)   The story about the mig that chased him amused the pilot that
        shot at it.

ACKNOWLEDGEMENTS

I would like to express my gratitude to Janet Fodor, Avery Andrews, Noam Chomsky, and especially Bob Fiengo for many helpful suggestions. I have also profited greatly from the important discussions of coreference in Jackendoff (1969; 1972) and Wasow (1972).

NOTES

[1] For example, Ross (1967b) includes in his pronominalization rule the condition that $NP_1 = NP_2$. Lees and Klima (1963) had the same condition. Jackendoff (1972, 108) argues that

If a transformation produces pronouns, it must be able to make use of coreference relations. However, transformations cannot mention coreference relations: there is no rule, for example, that preposes a noun phrase if it is coreferential with some other noun phrase. Thus in stating pronominalization ... transformations that refer to intended coreference, we are implicitly granting transformations power which they do not in general possess.

[2] Node A is said to command node B if the minimal S node dominating A also dominates B. It should be pointed out that command is not statable as a Boolean condition on analyzability. Indeed, this fact forms the basis for a genuine argument against a pronominalization transformation. The theory of transformations would have to be considerably enriched for command to play a role in the statement of a transformation. Further arguments are considered by Wasow (1972).

[3] This generalization owes much to the important insights of Lakoff (1968), particularly section 1.1.5.3.

[4] Coreference between NP's has been indicated by italicizing them in these examples.

[5] This rule blocks all coreferent readings that seem to be universally unavailable. Speakers vary in their acceptance of such examples as (6) and (7) above. Perhaps rule (12) is augmented or expanded in certain dialects. It should be noted that the unacceptability of (6) and (7) for some speakers does not bear on the basic thesis of the present study, namely that a noncoreference rule in some form is necessary in an adequate account of English. I note in passing that it is possible that the notion of coreference in this rule, and elsewhere in this discussion, should be replaced with that of intended coreference.

[6] It seems likely that the general condition proposed by Wasow can be extended so that it becomes, in effect, the mirror image of Chomsky's principle of recoverability of deletion. That is, an insertion process could only insert a specific lexical item named in the rule (Do-Support is a candidate), or a copy of a constituent appearing elsewhere in the structure. Noam Chomsky has pointed out to me that the anapom phenomena can also be described without assuming the existence of syntactic copying rules. The constructions exemplified in (13) could be base-generated, if the pronouns are marked as necessarily anaphoric.

[7] Wasow's argument is actually considerably more complex. He does not simply claim that the Transitivity Condition is a possible replacement for the noncoreference rule. Rather, he attempts to show that in principle, no noncoreference rule could be compatible with the facts of human languages. Wasow alludes to an argument given by Postal (1972).

as Postal argues, the failure of two NPs to be related anaphorically does not entail that they have distinct referents. This can be seen from

a.   Leon Trotsky and Leon Bronstein were the same person.

b.   If you have seen the morning star, you have seen the evening star.

While *Leon Trotsky* and *Leon Bronstein* may be used to refer to the same thing, as may *the evening star* and *the morning star*, no anaphoric relation holds between these pairs in [(a) and (b)]. Wasow (1972, 20—21).

(Recall that Jackendoff's noncoreference rule applies whenever two NPs have not been marked coreferential. My noncoreference rule (12) above is slightly different since my system includes no coreference rule, but Wasow's argument would presumably be as relevant to my rule as to Jackendoff's.) It is not at all clear to me that this argument goes through. First, the logical structure of example (a) is open to question. Notice that (ii) below is no better than (i).

(i)   *Leon Trotsky* and *Leon Trotsky* were the same person.
(ii)   *Leon Trotsky* and *he* were the same person.

It may be that the NP's in (a) are not referring expressions at all, in which case non-coreference would not be relevant. Geach 1962 in discussing a similar sentence, states,

I shall not here discuss the difficult question . . . whether "Tully is Cicero" exemplifies the classical uses of "Tully" and "Cicero" as names, or whether we should rather regard it as a proposition about these names in this use. [In the latter case, a paraphrase would be] something like "In history books the names 'Tully' and 'Cicero' are commonly used for the same man."

In line with this possibility, (iii) might be a suitable paraphrase for (a).

(iii)   'Leon Trotsky' and 'Leon Bronstein' designate the same person.

Example (b) above does not appear to be problematic since it does not meet the structural description of the noncoreference rule. Example (b) is of some interest in its own right, however. Many philosophers assume that *the morning star* and *the evening star* are simply alternative names for the planet Venus. This position seems to me to be quite mistaken. Notice that in even the most transparent of contexts, the names are not interchangeable. Example (iv) is surely not a true statement when uttered at 6:0^ AM, but (v) could well be true.

(iv)   I see the evening star.
(v)   I see the morning star.

Hence, it would seem that *the morning star* and *the evening star* differ not only in meaning but in reference. A similar circumstance is evidenced in such a location as *the six o'clock train*, which seems to designate a complex of entities and events, including, but not exhausted by, the locomotive and cars involved.

[8] For a survey of some recalcitrant cases see Lakoff (1968), Postal (1972), and especially Wasow (1972, Chap. 4).

[9] Both (33) and (12) appear, at first sight, to rule out a wide range c˙ grammatical sentences. For example, several linguists have indicated to me that I have left myself no way to generate (i).

(i)   Nixon believes that the president should have absolute authority.

Notice that I carefully avoided indicating that *Nixon* and *the president* are core˙erential. In fact, I don't believe that they are coreferential, because, minimally, if two NPs are coreferential they must both be referential. By this, I do not mean that they necessarily have a referent, but rather, that each be used as a referring expression. But clearly *the president* in (i) is used in an attributive rather than a referential way. (See Donnellan (1966) for a discussion of this distinction.) A rough paraphrase for (i) might be (ii).

(ii)   Nixon believes that anyone who is the president should have absolute authority.

Notice that examples quite parallel to (i) are ungrammatical when an attributive use is precluded.

(iii)   *Nixon believes that the president ate dinner at 6:00 PM yesterday.

[10] This formulation is a modification of the rule mentioned in Chomsky (1973), which "seeks to interpret . . . two NPs [in certain configurations] as nonintersecting in reference."

[11] See Lasnik (1972) for arguments that the scope of negation is assigned cyclically.

[12] An alternative analysis along roughly the lines of Wasow (1972) is also available assuming the trace theory of movement rules, if it is stipulated both that variables bound by the same operator must be coreferential, and that a trace is not a pronoun.

[13] I ignore the question of whether such a process as VP-Deletion is syntactic or interpretive in nature. See Wasow (1972) for discussion. My remarks here appear to be equally applicable to either formulation.

ROBERT FREIDIN AND HOWARD LASNIK

DISJOINT REFERENCE AND WH-TRACE
1981

This article explores the ramifications of an analysis of disjoint reference for the theory of core grammar.[1] The analysis we will adopt accounts for coreference possibilities between pronouns and Wh-traces and, following May (1981), also provides an explanation for the COMP-to-COMP condition on Wh-Movement of Chomsky (1973). The central assumption of the analysis — that Wh-trace binding is exempt from the Propositional Island Condition (PIC) and the Specified Subject Condition (SSC) — allows for a simplification of the theories of binding and indexing, and also provides an argument that the Subjacency Condition is properly interpreted as a condition on representations rather than a condition on derivations.[2]

The organization of this article is as follows. Section I deals with the theoretical framework presupposed in the discussion. Section 2 contains an explication of indexing and binding as applied to the various NP-types (e.g. lexical NP vs. NP-trace). This section gives the analysis of disjoint reference under which Wh-traces must be exempt from the PIC and SSC. Discussions of the resulting simplification in the analysis of binding and indexing follow in section 3. Section 4 deals with the consequences of our analysis for the *[that—e] filter and Subjacency.

1. THEORETICAL FRAMEWORK

The following discussion presupposes the general framework of the Extended Standard Theory as developed in Chomsky (1975), Chomsky and Lasnik (1977), and Lasnik and Kupin (1977) — including in particular trace theory (see Chomsky (1980) and the references cited there). In addition, it will be assumed that the PIC and SSC constitute principles of binding (Chomsky (1980) and Freidin (1978)) rather than conditions on rules of grammar (Chomsky (1973; 1976)).

Following Chomsky and Lasnik (1977), the organization of core grammar is taken to be roughly as shown in (1).

(1)
              I. a. Base
                 b. Transformations (movement and insertion)

II. a. Deletion	III. a. Quantifier interpretation
b. Filters	b. Control
c. Phonological rules	c. Binding principles

(See Lasnik and Freidin (1981) for a discussion of how Case theory (as

110

discussed in Chomsky (1980)) relates to this organization.) The components of (I) constitute "the Syntax"; those of (II), "the Phonology"; and those of (III), "Logical Form". (I) maps base structures onto S-structures, the output of the transformational component.[3] (II) maps S-structures onto phonetic representations; and (III) maps S-structure onto representations in logical form (LF), one aspect of semantic representation. According to (1), the rules of the phonology in no way determine semantic representations and the rules of LF in no way determine phonetic representations. (1) constitutes an empirical hypothesis and therefore comes with the usual caveats. We return to (1) in section 3.

With respect to indexing, we adopt part of the formalism given in Chomsky (1980). Every NP is assigned a *referential index*, consisting of a single integer i ($i \geq 1$). In addition, every nonanaphoric NP is assigned an *anaphoric index*, given as a set of integers which consists of the referential indices of all *c*-commanding NPs. An index $(i, \{j\})$ indicates that an NP whose referential index is i may not have the same intended referent as an NP whose referential index is j. The relation between the referential and anaphoric indices of an NP is that of disjoint reference (DR). Anaphors are not assigned anaphoric indices; only nonanaphoric NPs enter directly into the relation of DR. Under this analysis, the (i)-examples of (2) would be assigned the indexed representations of the corresponding (ii)-examples.

(2) a. *Pronouns*:
     i. John saw him.
     ii. John$_{(1)}$ saw him$_{(2, \{1\})}$

  b. *Names*:[4]
     i. John saw the boy.
     ii. John$_{(1)}$ saw the boy$_{(2, \{1\})}$

The algorithms for assigning indices and their location in the grammar will be discussed in section 4.

2. INTRODUCTION TO BINDING

In this section it will be assumed that the SSC and PIC are properly construed as principles of binding which hold for the relations of bound anaphora and disjoint reference. We will show that while anaphors and pronouns (in contrast to names) fall under these principles, Wh-traces (like names) do not.

Considering for the moment just bound anaphora, one formulation of the PIC and SSC as binding principles could be (3).

(3)   *NP_i, NP_i an anaphor, unless NP_i is bound in the domain of
        (a) a subject (the SSC)
    or (b) tense (the PIC).

We take (3) to be a filter at the level of LF (cf. Freidin (1978)). The *domain* of a category α is taken to be all the categories c-commanded by α. An anaphor is *bound* in a domain when there is a c-commanding NP with the same referential index in that domain. This formulation has advantages over previous formulations of the SSC and PIC — for example, the one in Chomsky (1980) — as will be discussed in section 3.

(3) accounts for the standard paradigm of bound anaphora, where the class of anaphors includes reflexive pronouns, reciprocals, and also Wh-traces. Some of the relevant data are given in (4).

(4) a. *Lexical Anaphors:*
    i.   *Harry$_1$ suspected [$_{\bar{S}}$ Celia to be insulting himself$_1$]
    ii. *Harry$_1$ suspected [$_{\bar{S}}$ that himself$_1$ was insulting Celia]
    iii. Harry$_1$ suspected [$_{\bar{S}}$ himself$_1$ to be insulting Celia]

  b. *NP-trace:*
    i.   *Harry$_1$ was suspected [$_{\bar{S}}$ Celia to be insulting e$_1$]
    ii. *Harry$_1$ was suspected [$_{\bar{S}}$ (that) e$_1$ was insulting Celia]
    iii. Harry$_1$ was suspected [$_{\bar{S}}$ e$_1$ to be insulting Celia]

The anaphors in the (i)-examples are free in the domain of the complement subject and are therefore prohibited by the SSC (3a). The anaphors in the (ii)-examples are free in the domain of the complement tense and are therefore prohibited by the PIC (3b). In contrast, the anaphors in the (iii)-examples are in the domain of a subject and tense with respect to the matrix S, but not the complement S. In the matrix domain the anaphors are bound and thus not prohibited by (3). This formulation of the binding principles generalizes automatically to anaphors in simple sentences, as shown in (5).

(5) a. *Lexical Anaphors:*
    i.   *Himself$_1$ left
    ii. *John$_1$ insulted herself$_2$

  b. *NP-trace:*
    i.   *e$_1$ left
    ii. *John$_1$ insulted e$_2$

The (i)-examples fall under the PIC (3b); the (ii)-examples, under the PIC and the SSC (3a). Previous formulations of the SSC and PIC, with the exception of Chomsky (1980), applied only to complex sentences. As a result, an account of (5) required additional stipulations (cf. Freidin (1978, (8))). Given (3), these are unnecessary.

Ordinary pronouns also should fall within the domain of the SSC and PIC, as discussed in Chomsky (1973; 1976). In the case of pronouns, however, the relevant property is obligatory disjoint reference (Lasnik

(1976), Chomsky (1976)) rather than obligatory coreference as in the case of anaphors. Because of this, the filtering formulation of the SSC and PIC in (3) cannot be extended to account for the facts of disjoint reference. Therefore, the SSC and PIC as stated in (3) must be reformulated. A reformulation is given below.

In the formalism for indexing of section I, obligatory disjoint reference is expressed in terms of an anaphoric index. Under the procedure for constructing anaphoric indices stated above, the pronoun cases analogous to (4) will be assigned the indexed representations (6a–c).

(6) a. Harry$_{(1)}$ suspected [$_{\bar{S}}$ Celia$_{(2, \{1\})}$ to be insulting him$_{(3, \{1, 2\})}$]

  b. Harry$_{(1)}$ suspected [$_{\bar{S}}$ that he$_{(2, \{1\})}$ was insulting Celia$_{(3, \{1, 2\})}$]

  c. Harry$_{(1)}$ suspected [$_{\bar{S}}$ him$_{(2, \{1\})}$ to be insulting Celia$_{(3, \{1, 2\})}$]

The representations (6a) and (6b), in contrast to (6c), are incorrect because the pronouns *him* and *he* are not interpreted as obligatorily disjoint in reference from *Harry* in the corresponding sentences (7a) and (7b).

(7) a. Harry suspected Celia to be insulting him.

  b. Harry suspected that he was insulting Celia.

The pronouns in (7a, b) are free in reference with respect to *Harry* — that is, coreference is possible though not necessary.

In terms of indexing, a pronoun is free in reference with respect to an NP with referential index i when the anaphoric index of the pronoun does not contain the integer i. Given this, the correct representations for (7a, b) are (7′a, b), respectively.

(7′) a. Harry$_{(1)}$ suspected [$_{\bar{S}}$ Celia$_{(2, \{1\})}$ to be insulting him$_{(3, \{2\})}$]

  b. Harry$_{(1)}$ suspected [$_{\bar{S}}$ that he$_{(2)}$ was insulting Celia$_{(3, \{1, 2\})}$]

In the framework of Chomsky (1980), (7′a, b) would be derived from (6a, b) by deleting the member 1 from the anaphoric index of each pronoun. In (6a), the member 1 is not *bound* (as defined for (3)) in the domain of a subject. In (6b), the member 1 is not bound in the domain of tense.[5] Thus, the deletions occur when the member 1 fits the structural circumstance inherent in (3) — i.e. free (= not bound) in the domain of a subject or tense. (7′a, b) are derived from (6a, b) by reformulating the SSC and PIC as reindexing rules which carry out the required deletion under the stated structural circumstances. These rules can be formalized as follows:

(8)   When a pronoun with anaphoric index j ($j = \{a_1, \ldots, a_n\}$) is free(i) in the domain of subject or tense, $j \rightarrow j - \{i\}$. (Cf. Chomsky (1980, appendix).)

A pronoun is *free(i)* in a domain when there is no *c*-commanding NP with referential index *i* in that domain.

This type of analysis can be extended to the anaphor cases, as Chomsky shows. For anaphors, the SSC and PIC affect *referential* indices. For example, the SSC and PIC as reindexing rules should map (4ai) onto (9a) and (4aii) onto (9b).

(9) a. $Harry_{(1)}$ suspected $[_{\bar{S}}$ Celia to be insulting $himself_{(0)}]$
    b. $Harry_{(1)}$ suspected $[_{\bar{S}}$ that $himself_{(0)}$ was insulting Celia]

It must be assumed that an NP with a zero referential index is ill-formed — i.e. $*NP_{(0)}$. The appropriate reindexing rule can be formalized as follows:

(10)   When an anaphor with referential index i is *free(i)* in the domain of subject or tense, $i \rightarrow 0$ (i.e. $i - i$). (Cf. Chomsky (1980, appendix).)

The definition of *free(i)* with respect to pronouns extends without modification to anaphors. An anaphor is *free(i)* in a domain when there is no *c*-commanding NP with referential index i in that domain.

Given this system, we will now show that a Wh-trace has an anaphoric index which is not subject to the reindexing rules, SSC and PIC. Thus, a Wh-trace is distinct from an anaphor and also from a pronoun. The relevant evidence involves coreference possibilities between a Wh-trace and a *c*-commanding pronoun. (11) gives the paradigm bearing on the SSC, and (12), the paradigm bearing on the PIC.

(11) a.   Who does he want the woman to like?
     b.   Who wants the woman to like him?

(12) a.   Who does he think likes the woman?
     b.   Who thinks he likes the woman?

In the (b)-examples, the pronoun is free in reference with respect to the variable bound by *who*,[6] whereas in the (a)-examples,[7] the pronoun is construed as disjoint in reference from the variable bound by *who*. In the (a)-examples, the speaker must already know the referent of the pronoun; in the (b)-examples, he need not, but rather may be inviting the listener to provide a referent for the pronoun by answering the question. This difference is easily captured on the assumption that a Wh-trace has an anaphoric index.

Under trace theory, the derivations of (11a) and (11b) involve the following partial mappings from S-structure to LF.

(13)   (for (11a)):
   a. $[_{\bar{s}}[_C \text{ who}_3]$ $[_S \text{ does he}_1 \text{ want } [_{\bar{s}} e_3 [_S \text{ the woman}_2 \text{ to like } e_3]]]]$
   b.   (for which x_3, x_3 a person) $[_S \text{ he}_1 \text{ wants } [_S \text{ the woman}_2 \text{ to like } x_3]]$
   c.   (for which x_3, x_3 a person) $[_S \text{ he}_{(1)} \text{ wants } [_S \text{ the woman}_{(2,\{1\})} \text{ to like } x_{(3,\{1,2\})}]]$

(14)   (for (11b)):
   a. $[_{\bar{s}}[_C \text{ who}_1]$ $[_S e_1 \text{ wants } [_{\bar{s}}[_S \text{ the woman}_2 \text{ to like him}_3]]]]$
   b.   (for which x_1, x_1 a person) $[_S x_1 \text{ wants } [_S \text{ the woman}_2 \text{ to like him}_3]]$
   c.   (for which x_1, x_1 a person) $[_S x_{(1)} \text{ wants } [_S \text{ the woman}_{(2,\{1\})} \text{ to like him}_{(3,\{1,2\})}]]$

The S-structures (13a), (14a) are mapped onto (13b), (14b) by a rule which replaces a Wh-phrase with its meaning (see Chomsky (1976; 1977a) for discussion). The structures (13b), (14b) are mapped onto (13c), (14c) by a rule which assigns anaphoric indices. Further, (14c) will be mapped onto (15) by the SSC, thus accounting for the fact that *him* is free in reference with respect to the variable bound by *who*.

(15)   (for which x_1, x_1 a person) $[_S x_{(1)} \text{ wants } [_S \text{ the woman}_{(2,\{1\})} \text{ to like him}_{(3,\{2\})}]]$

In contrast, the SSC should not apply to the anaphoric index of the variable in the complement of (13c); otherwise, we lose the relevant distinction between (11a) and (11b). We conclude then that the anaphoric index of a Wh-trace is not subject to the SSC.

The analysis given above is based on a discussion of (11) in Chomsky (1976). This analysis extends naturally to the PIC cases such as (12) which were not discussed there, and in Chomsky (1980) were assumed not to exist.

Parallel to (13) and (14), the derivations of (12a) and (12b) involve the following partial mappings in (16) and (17).

(16)   (for (12a)):
   a. $[_{\bar{s}}[_C \text{ who}_2]$ $[_S \text{ does he}_1 \text{ think } [_{\bar{s}} e_2 [_S e_2 \text{ likes the woman}_3]]]]]$
   b.   (for which x_2, x_2 a person) $[_S \text{ he}_1 \text{ thinks } [_S x_2 \text{ likes the woman}_3]]$
   c.   (for which x_2, x_2 a person) $[_S \text{ he}_{(1)} \text{ thinks } [_S x_{(2,\{1\})} \text{ likes the woman}_{(3,\{1,2\})}]]$

(17)   (for (12b)):
  a. $[_{\bar{S}}[_C$ who$_1]$ $[_S$ e$_1$ thinks $[_{\bar{S}}[_S$ he$_2$ likes the woman$_3]]]]$
  b. (for which x_1, x_1 a person) $[_S$ x_1 thinks $[_S$ he$_2$ likes the woman$_3]]$
  c. (for which x_1, x_1 a person) $[_S$ $x_{(1)}$ thinks $[_S$ he$_{(2,\{1\})}$ likes the woman$_{(3,\{1,2\})}]]$

The PIC maps (17c) onto (18).

(18)   (for which x_1, x_1 a person) $[_S$ $x_{(1)}$ thinks $[_S$ he$_{(2)}$ likes the woman$_{(3,\{1,2\})}]]$

It does not apply to the variable in the complement of (16c), thereby preserving the distinction between (12a) and (12b). From this we conclude that the anaphoric index of a Wh-trace is not subject to the PIC.

Thus far, we have established (a) that a Wh-trace, which functions as a variable at LF, takes an anaphoric index, and (b) that this anaphoric index is not subject to either the SSC or the PIC. In this regard, a Wh-trace patterns like a name (cf. Chomsky (1976, 335), where the parallelism between variables and names was first discussed). Below we will consider the question of whether the referential index of a Wh-trace might be subject to the reindexing rules.

The correct representations for the "crossover cases" (11a) and (12a) follow from the rule that assigns anaphoric indices and the assumption that the trace of Wh is not subject to the SSC or the PIC. In addition, a rather natural account of violations of the COMP-to-COMP condition on Wh-Movement follows from this analysis without any further stipulations, as shown in May (1981).

COMP-to-COMP violations involve movements of a Wh-phrase from a COMP to an NP position. In term of binding, the condition prohibits the binding of a trace in COMP from an NP position in S. For the sake of exposition, we will assume that once a Wh-phrase is Wh-moved, it must end up in a COMP position. Violations of the COMP-to-COMP condition will result in structures in which a Wh-phrase binds two different NP-traces, one in a matrix S and the other in a complement S. There are two cases to consider: (i) where the complement NP-trace is in the predicate, and (ii) where the complement NP-trace is in subject position. An example of each case is given in (19).

(19) a. *Who believes George to have seen?
    b. *Who said saw George? (cf. Who did Harry say saw George?)

The strings in (19) pair with the representations in (20).

(20) a. $[_{\bar{S}}[_C$ who$_1]$ $[_S$ e_1 believes $[_{\bar{S}}[_C$ $e_1]$ $[_S$ George$_2$ to have seen $e_1]]]]$

III   II   I

b. $[_{\bar{S}}[_C$ who$_1]$ $[_S$ e_1 said $[_{\bar{S}}[_C$ $e_1]$ $[_S$ e_1 saw George$_2]]]]$

III   II   I

The Roman numerals in (20) indicate the derivational history of the Wh-phrase. In each example the second movement (II) violates the COMP-to-COMP condition.

The representations in (20) map onto those of (21) via Wh-Interpretation and the rule which assigns anaphoric indices as discussed above for (13)—(14) and (16)—(17).

(21) a. (for which x_1, x_1 a person) $[_S x_{(1)}$ believes $[_S$ George$_{(2,\{1\})}$ to have seen $x_{(1,\{1,2\})}]]$

b. (for which x_1, x_1 a person) $[_S x_{(1)}$ said $[_S x_{(1,\{1\})}$ saw George$_{(2,\{1\})}]]$

In each case the index of the variable in the complement is contradictory — in effect indicating that the intended referent of the variable must be disjoint in reference from itself. These contradictory indices are unaffected by the reindexing rules (i.e. the SSC and PIC). Therefore, we can now account for the COMP-to-COMP violations in terms of indexing — i.e. with a prohibition against contradictory indices of the form $(i,\{i\})$. (This observation is due to Robert Mary — see May (1981) for additional discussion.)

The indexing analysis of the COMP-to-COMP violations allows us to dispense with an ad hoc condition on derivations in favor of a natural condition on representations; namely, the prohibition against contradictory indices of the form $(i, \{i\})$. See Freidin (1978; 1979) for more detailed discussion of the issue concerning conditions on derivations vs. conditions on representations.

3. INDEXING AND BINDING

Under the analysis presented above, the SSC and PIC are no longer interpreted as conditions on proper binding. Rather, they function as reindexing rules and therefore become part of the algorithms for assigning indices to representations in LF. Conditions on proper binding are given in terms of the conditions on well-formed indices in (22).

(22) a. *NP$_{(0)}$
b. *NP$_{(i,\{\ldots, i, \ldots\})}$

As demonstrated in the previous section, the SSC and PIC as re-indexing rules apply to the referential index of an anaphor and the anaphoric index of a pronoun. They do not apply to the referential index of a pronoun, the anaphoric index of a Wh-trace, or either index of a name. Whether they apply to the referential index of a Wh-trace depends on the status of a Wh-trace in LF — that is, is a Wh-trace a special case of a name, or is it a fourth NP-type distinct from anaphors, pronouns, and names? In this section, we will show that the assumption that these rules do not apply to the referential index of a Wh-trace leads to a simplifica-tion in their formulation, which in turn allows for a simplication of the algorithms for assigning indices proposed in Chomsky (1980).

In previous formulations of the SSC and PIC, $\bar{S}$ rather than S was taken as the domain of proper binding for an anaphor. The ostensible reason for this choice was the assumption that a Wh-trace had the same status as an NP-trace with respect to the conditions (cf. Chomsky (1973; 1976)). We know of no other reason for choosing $\bar{S}$ over S.

In contrast, there are several reasons for choosing S over $\bar{S}$. $\bar{S}$ must be stipulated in the structural description of the reindexing rules, whereas S need not. It follows from the definition of *in the domain of* in conjunction with the phrase structure rule S → NP AUX VP that the domain of both the subject and the tensed element is S.[8] In addition to allowing for a simplification of the reindexing rules, the choice of S provides an explana-tion for why non-Wh-NPs in the domain of subject or a tensed element may not use COMP as an "escape hatch" (see Freidin (1978, 529) and the references cited there) with respect to the SSC and PIC — a possibility which was not explicitly discounted in previous formulations of these conditions.

Another reason for choosing S rather than $\bar{S}$ is that the ungrammati-cality of NPs like (23a) follows immediately from reindexing (specifically the PIC) and the filter (22a).[9]

(23) a. *the men who each other like
     b. [$_{NP}$ the men [$_{\bar{S}}$[$_C$ who$_i$] [$_S$ each other$_i$ like e$_i$]]]

If S is the relevant domain of application for the reindexing rules, then the referential index of *each other* in the representation (23b) will be deleted. If, however, $\bar{S}$ is chosen, then *each other* would not be subject to the reindexing rules since it is bound in $\bar{S}$. Thus, another means of accounting for (23a) would be required.

An alternative method of accounting for (23a) would be to specify the algorithms for assigning referential indices in such a way that representa-tions like (23b) would never be generated. One interpretation of the algorithms given in Chomsky (1980) has this effect. The algorithms and their ordering are given in (24).

(24) a. Coindex by movement (see Chomsky (1980, (4))).
     b. Index all unindexed nonanaphoric NPs in S from top to bottom
         with hitherto unused positive integers (henceforth "contraindex-
         ing").
     c. Coindex the remaining anaphoric NPs with some *c*-commanding
         NP.[10]

(24a) is part of the syntax: (24b) and (24c) belong to LF, the latter constituting part of the construal rules. (24) will not generate the representation
(23b) given the stipulation that *who$_i$* does not count as a *c*-commanding
NP.

This alternative seems needlessly complicated. Coindexing applies in
two different components, before and after contraindexing. Thus, the
indexing operation must be given as two distinct suboperations, coindexing and contraindexing.

These complications can be eliminated by taking S to be the domain of
application for the reindexing rules. Since the ill-formedness of (23b) will
fall under (22a), it does not matter if the indexing rules generate such
representations. Therefore, we might try to eliminate (24) in favor of the
optimal rule of indexing (25).[11]

(25)   Index NP

Given (25), indexing applies freely, including as a subcase coindexing, at a
single point in a derivation. There is no need to define the operation of
contraindexing or to stipulate that it applies top-to-bottom as in (24b).
Nor is there any need to stipulate that anaphoric NPs be coindexed with
some *c*-commanding NP, excluding Wh-phrase in COMP (24c). This
follows automatically from the reindexing rules in conjunction with filter
(22a).

Having established that the choice of S rather than $\bar{S}$ has several
desirable consequences, let us now return to the question of whether the
referential index of a Wh-trace is subject to the reindexing rules. If a Wh-
trace's referential index *is* subject to reindexing, then $\bar{S}$ must be taken as
the domain of application. Otherwise, the system of rules and filters would
predict incorrectly that all Wh-questions in English are ill-formed. To
maintain this position without giving up the advantages of choosing S
would require the implausible analysis in which the domain of application
for the reindexing rules is generally S, but $\bar{S}$ for the referential index of a
Wh-trace. In view of this, we conclude that neither index of a Wh-trace is
subject to the reindexing rules. Thus in LF, a Wh-trace has the same status
as a name.

We turn next to a formulation of the rule for assigning anaphoric
indices. Following Chomsky (1980), let us take the anaphoric index of an

NP_i to be the set $\{a_1, \ldots, a_n\}$, where each a_j is the referential index of an NP which c-commands NP_i. Recall that only nonanaphors are assigned anaphoric indices. Note too that it must be assumed that a Wh-phrase in COMP or its trace in COMP is ignored by the algorithm which constructs anaphoric indices. Otherwise, the algorithm would produce representations like (26) which violate (22b).

(26) $[_{\bar{S}}[_C \text{ who}_i] [_S e_{(i, \{i\})} \text{ left}]]$

Note also that anaphoric indices must be assigned after Wh-Interpretation (see section 2) in order to account for disjoint reference in another crossover case (27a), in contrast to its noncrossed counterpart (27b).

(27) a. Whose book did he read?
     b. Who read his book?

In (27b), *his* is free in reference with respect to the variable bound by *who*. By Wh-Interpretation, the trace theoretic representation of (27) is mapped onto (28) (see Chomsky (1977a)).

(28) a. (for which x_3, x_3 a person [$_S$ he$_1$ read [$_{NP_2}$ x_3's book]]
     b. (for which x_1, x_1 a person) [$_S$ x_1 read [$_{NP_2}$ his$_3$ book]]

By the algorithm for constructing anaphoric indices, (28) is mapped onto (29).

(29) a. (for which x_3, x_3 a person) [$_S$ he$_{(1)}$ read [$_{NP_{(2, \{1\})}}$ $x_{(3, \{1\})}$'s book]]
     b. (for which x_1, x_1 a person) [$_S$ $x_{(1)}$ read [$_{NP_{(2, \{1\})}}$ his$_{(3, \{1\})}$ book]]

Since *his* is interpreted as free in reference with respect to x_1 in (29b), we assume that there is some principle operative which effects the deletion of the anaphoric index 1 on the pronoun.[12]

Given that the reindexing rules follow the assignment of anaphoric indices, which in turn follows Wh-Interpretation, Wh-trace and NP-trace are distinct at the point in a derivation where the reindexing rules apply. At that point, a Wh-trace is represented as a variable, whereas an NP-trace is represented as an empty category.

4. CONSEQUENCES

We have presented a number of related arguments that Wh-trace is not subject to Opacity.[13] Chomsky (1980) is largely compatible with this position, but has one argument to the contrary, to which we now turn. Note that here we follow Chomsky's presentation in treating Opacity as conditions on logical form rather than as reindexing rules. The argument could readily be restated in the latter format, that of the appendix to Chomsky (1980).

Comparing (30) to (31). Chomsky notes that both violate Subjacency with respect to binding by the matrix COMP, yet (31) is somewhat more acceptable.

(30) $[_{\bar{S}}[_C \text{ who}_1] [_S \text{ did you wonder } [_{\bar{S}}[_C \text{ what}_2] [_S \text{ e}_1 \text{ saw e}_2]]]]$

(31) $[_{\bar{S}}[_C \text{ what}_2] [_S \text{ did you wonder } [_{\bar{S}}[_C \text{ who}_1] [_S \text{ e}_1 \text{ saw e}_2]]]]$

If Wh-trace were subject to the NIC (see note 5), then the contrast could be described as follows. While both (30) and (31) violate Subjacency, the complement subject in (30), but not in (31), would also be subject to the NIC. (Note that if the PIC is taken to be the relevant condition, (30) and (31) would not be distinguished in this way since the PIC would affect the complement object as well.) Thus, (30) violates two conditions, whereas (31) violates only one — granting that Wh-trace is not subject to the SSC.

The validity of this account requires that Opacity be split into two quite distinct constraints. The NIC must be taken "to be an 'inviolable' constraint, as compared with Subjacency (and [the SSC] ...)," the latter two being "weaker" constraints with Wh-trace as anaphor (Chomsky (1980, 37—38)). The difference in acceptability between (30) and (31) seems rather slim evidence for such a weakening and complication of the theory. It should also be noted that there are examples quite parallel to (30) in acceptability, but identical to (31) in relevant derivational properties. Consider (32):

(32) $[_{\bar{S}}[_C \text{ what}_1] [_S \text{ do you wonder } [_{\bar{S}}[_C \text{ who}_2] [_S \text{ Bill gave e}_1 \text{ to e}_2]]]]$

While (32) is just as unacceptable as (30), like (31) it does not involve the NIC, regardless of how Wh-trace is to be treated. (33) demonstrates that the unacceptability of (32) cannot be attributed to a crossed binding constraint of the type frequently discussed in the literature (cf. Fodor (1978)).

(33) $[_{\bar{S}}[_C \text{ who}_2] [_S \text{ do you wonder } [_{\bar{S}}[_C \text{ what}_1] [_S \text{ Bill gave e}_1 \text{ to e}_2]]]]$

Though (32) is of the form $x_1 x_2 y_1 y_2$, while (33) is of the form $x_1 x_2 y_2 y_1$, they are equally unacceptable — some new constraint, which presumably would generalize to (30), is required.[14]

Thus, if there is in fact a linguistically relevant contrast between (30) and (31), the NIC does not seem to be responsible. Given that Wh-trace is not subject to the NIC (PIC), it follows that the *[that—e] filter of Chomsky and Lasnik (1977) cannot be reduced to the NIC as proposed in several recent articles and unpublished papers.[15] In fact, given our conclusions above, there is no overlap at all between the filter and the condition. Thus, one argument for eliminating the filter, namely its alleged partial redundancy with the condition, is without force. Another consideration that has come up in discussions of the filter is its complexity. The "unless"-condition particularly has been criticized.[16]

(34)   *[that—e] *Filter* (2 formulations)
    a. *[$_{\bar{S}}$ that [$_{NP}$ e] . . .], unless $\bar{S}$ or its trace is in the context:
        [$_{NP}$ NP   . . .] (= C&L (68))
    b. *[$_{\bar{S}}$ ± Wh [$_{NP}$ e] . . .], unless $\bar{S}$ or its trace is in the context:
        [$_{NP}$ NP   . . .] (= C&L (85))

If this complexity actually is a problem, it is interesting to note that it can be completely eliminated. The prupose of the entire "unless"-clause is distinguishing between (on the one hand) *that* verbal complements, which always lead to ungrammaticality when in violation (35a), and (on the other hand) relative clauses and clefts (35b), which never lead to ungrammaticality when in violation.

(35) a. *Who do you believe that t left?
      b.   i.   The man that t was shouting left.
           ii. The man left that t was shouting.
           iii. It was this phenomenon that t caused difficulties.

Thus, an alternative to the "unless"-clause is the reasonable separation of complementizer *that* into two lexical items. The filter would then be stated in terms of the verbal complementizer *that* and would need no "unless"-clause at all.

The conclusion that a Wh-trace is not subject to either the SSC or the PIC bears on the analysis of strict cyclicity whereby the empirical effects of the Strict Cycle Condition are derived from independently motivated conditions on representations. In Freidin (1978), two accounts of strict cycle violations involving Wh-Movement as in (36) are proposed.

(36) a. [$_{\bar{S}}$[$_C$ who$_1$] [$_S$ did John know [$_{\bar{S}}$[$_C$ what$_2$] [$_S$ e$_1$ saw e$_2$]]]]
      b. [$_{\bar{S}}$[$_C$ who$_1$] [$_S$ did John know [$_{\bar{S}}$[$_C$ what$_2$] [$_S$ PRO to give e$_1$ e$_2$]]]]

One account assumes that Wh-trace is subject to the PIC and SSC. Thus, (36) is prohibited because e_1 in (36a) is subject to the PIC and e_1 in (36b) is subject to the SSC. Alternatively, the binding between e_1 and *who*$_1$ in both examples violates Subjacency. As argued above, the first alternative is not viable.

This situation provides an argument that Subjacency is properly construed as a condition on representations, and not a condition on movement. Note that (36a) can be derived in a way that does not violate Subjacency interpreted as a condition on movement, as in (37).

(37) a. [$_{\bar{S}}$[$_C$] [$_S$ John knows [$_{\bar{S}}$[$_C$] [$_S$ who$_1$ saw what$_2$]]]]
      b. [$_{\bar{S}}$[$_C$] [$_S$ John knows [$_{\bar{S}}$[$_C$ who$_1$] [$_S$ e$_1$ saw what$_2$]]]]
      c. [$_{\bar{S}}$[$_C$ who$_1$] [$_S$ John knows [$_{\bar{S}}$[$_C$ e$_1$] [$_S$ e$_1$ saw what$_2$]]]]
      d. [$_{\bar{S}}$[$_C$ who$_1$] [$_S$ does John know [$_{\bar{S}}$[$_C$ what$_2$] [$_S$ e$_1$ saw e$_2$]]]]

(A similar derivation can be provided for (36b).) Such derivations could be excluded given the Strict Cycle Condition (SCC) (see Chomsky (1973) and Freidin (1978) for details). However, the SCC is redundant for NP Movement, as shown in Freidin (1978), and unnecessary generally if Subjacency is taken to be a condition on representations rather than a condition on movements. It remains to be determined where in a derivation Subjacency applies.

5. SUMMARY AND CONCLUSIONS

We have shown that within the framework of Chomsky (1980) the analysis of crossover phenomena and COMP-to-COMP violations supports the conclusion that Wh-traces bear anaphoric indices which are not subject to the PIC and SSC.[17] This conclusion leads to a simpler formulation of the binding principles (now reinterpreted as reindexing rules) and the algorithms for indexing. An argument that the referential index of a Wh-trace is also not subject to the reindexing rules results. From this it follows that the *[that—e] filter of C&L (1977) cannot be reduced to some variant of the PIC and that Subjacency must be interpreted as a condition on representations if the Strict Cycle Condition is to be treated as a theorem of the theory of grammar.

ACKNOWLEDGEMENTS

A version of this material was presented at the 1979 GLOW Colloquium, Pisa, Italy. The work of the first-named author was supported by a Postdoctoral Research Fellowship from the NIMH (grant # 1F32 MH 05879—01) and also by NIH grant # HDO 5168—06AI.

NOTES

[1] For further discussion of disjoint reference, see for example Lasnik (1976), Chomsky (1980). On core grammar, see Chomsky and Lasnik (1977) (hereafter, C&L) and Lasnik and Kupin (1977).

[2] See Freidin (1978; 1979). Chomsky (1980), and Rouveret and Vergnaud (1980) for discussion of conditions on representations.

[3] S-structure is somewhat more abstract than the traditional notion of surface structure, including for example empty categories.

[4] By "name" we mean a nonanaphoric nonpronominal NP, hence not existential *there* or expletive *it*. The fact that idiom chunks like *bucket* in the idiom *kick the bucket* do not function as names indicates that only an NP with intended referent qualifies.

[5] Note that the analysis proposed here is slightly different from the one in Chomsky (1980), where the PIC is replaced by the Nominative Island Condition (NIC):

(i)   A nominative anaphor cannot be free in $\overline{S}$. (= (103))

We assume on the contrary that the relevant parameter for the finite clause condition should remain "domain of tense" rather than "nominative case". See Lasnik and Freidin (1981) for discussion of this point. Further, as discussed below, we take the domain of application to be S rather than S̄.

[6] We assume that Wh is quantifier and as such does not refer. See Chomsky (1977a).

[7] The (a)-examples are often referred to in the literature as "crossover phenomena" on the grounds that Wh-Movement over a pronoun affects coreference possibilities (see Postal (1971) and Wasow (1972)).

[8] The slight difference here from the formulation given in (3) is motivated by the need for *tense* to be introduced by Aux rather than by S. See, for example, Lasnik (1981a), for discussion.

[9] We are indebted to Dominique Sportiche for bringing this example to our attention.

[10] See Chomsky (1980, fn. 46) for discussion of how indexing might be done when a lexical anaphor receives an index in the syntax via movement.

[11] Recall that this is the rule for assigning referential indices. Whether coindexing by movement is still necessary remains to be determined. If the indices assigned via movement are referential indices, then the pied piping cases, or PP movements in general, might provide some problems for interpretation.

[12] This principle might involve deletion of the anaphoric index of a genitive pronoun. An alternative approach, suggested in Anderson (1979), would represent the pronoun in (28b) for example, as a bound anaphor, possibly a suppletive form of the nonoccurring *himself*. Under this interpretation, *his* would receive no anaphoric index at all. Thus, *his, her, their*. etc., would be systematically ambiguous between bound anaphors, on the one hand, and regular pronouns, on the other.

[13] Following the terminology of the first section of Chomsky (1980), we use this term to designate both the SSC and the finite clause condition, the PIC.

[14] The more acceptable examples in the set — such as (31) or (i) below — can possibly be thought of as derivatively generated.

(i)   What did you wonder how well he did?

In particular, the Wh-phrase introducing the embedded S might not have undergone movement at all in (31) and might have been preposed by adverb movement in (i). Thus, violation of Subjacency would be avoided. The examples would still not be fully grammatical, however, since they relax the requirement that *wonder* and *know* (in the relevant sense) require Wh-phrases in their embedded COMPs, to the less stringent requirement that the Wh-phrase simply be adjacent to *wonder* or *know*. In this way, we would not be forced to say that Subjacency is a weaker constraint in these cases. Note that no such "derivative" derivation is available for (30), (32), or (33). It should be noted, however, that the above remarks cannot be extended to the distinction between (ii) and (iii),

(ii)   Which book do you wonder how well the students read?
(iii)   Which students do you wonder how well read the book?

where (iii) seems less acceptable than (ii).

[15] See especially Kayne (1980; 1981), Taraldsen (1979), and Pesetsky (1981).

[16] Note though that complexity creates no learnability problem for a universal rule.

[17] Although the examples we presented all involve Wh-questions, the same result obtains for relative clauses. The following are parallel to (11a, b) and (12a, b):

(i) a.   The man who he wants the woman to like . . .
    b.   The man who wants the woman to like him . . .

(ii) a.   The man who he thinks likes the woman . . .
     b.   The man who thinks he likes the woman . . .

Rizzi (1980) provides independent evidence based on Wh-extraction facts that Wh-Movement in Italian relative clauses is not subject to the PIC and SSC.

HOWARD LASNIK

ON TWO RECENT TREATMENTS OF
DISJOINT REFERENCE
1981

The phenomenon of disjoint reference has received a great deal of attention. The "Unlike Person Constraint" of Postal (1966a; 1969) was one early attempt to deal with the strangeness of examples such as (1).

(1)   *We like me.

Helke (1971) extended Postal's treatment to cases of obligatory reflexiviza-tion as well. Chomsky (1973) proposed a rule of interpretation (RI) which "seeks to interpret . . . two NPs as nonintersecting in reference." (1) would thus be precluded, because *we* and *me* must intersect in reference (in a particular utterance) by virtue of their lexical meaning.

Chomsky observes that RI is subject to his Tensed Sentence Condition and Specified Subject Condition. (1) contrasts with both (2) and (3):

(2)   We think that I will win.

(3)   We proved Harry to have slandered me.

(4a—c) demonstrate the same paradigm with respect to coreference.

(4) a. *I like me.
    b. I think I will win.
    c. I proved Harry to have slandered me.

(5a—c) and (6a—c) show that third person pronouns fall under the same generalizations. In these cases, however, the (a) sentences will not be absolutely ungrammatical, but rather, ungrammatical on a particular intended reading.[1]

(5) a. They like him. [*they* ⊅ *him* in intended reference]
    b. They think he will win. [no restriction on *they, he*]
    c. they proved Harry to have slandered him. [no restriction on *they, him*]

(6) a. He likes him. [*he* ≠ *him* in intended reference]
    b. He thinks he will win. [no restriction on *he, he*]
    c. He proved Harry to have slandered him. [no restriction on *he, him*]

In Lasnik (1976), I showed that a rule very like RI exists which is not subject to the constraints of Chomsky (1973). Compare (7) with (6).

(7) a.   He likes John. [*he* ≠ *John*]
   b.   He thinks John will win. [*he* ≠ *John*]
   c.   He proved Harry to have slandered John. [*he* ≠ *John*]

This rule of non-coreference[2] seems to violate both the Tensed Sentence Condition — ex (7b) — and the Specified Subject Condition — ex (7c).

In Chomsky (1980), the two rules are combined into one, and a formalization is proposed. All NPs receive *referential indices* — integral subscripts — by rules that will not be of immediate concern here. Then, all NPs except bound anaphors (trace, reflexive, etc.) receive *anaphoric indices* as well. The anaphoric index of an NP X is the set consisting of the referential indices of all NPs that c-command X. (7a), for example, would receive an index assignment such as (8).

(8) $He_{1, \emptyset}$ likes $John_{2, \{1\}}$

The interpretation of the indices in (8) will be that *he* and *John* are disjoint in reference.[3] More generally, the NP in (9)

(9) $NP_{i, \{j, k, l \ldots\}}$

will be disjoint from the NPs with referential indices $j, k, l \ldots$[4]

Assignment of anaphoric indices, then, subsumes RI and the non-coreference rule. Note that the process is superficially too general, since it will apply in such cases as (4b, c) and (6b, c) for example. But where the c-commanded NP is a pronoun 'far enough away' from the c-commanding NP, disjoint reference does not obtain. Chomsky (1973) defined the required locality notion in terms of the conditions on rules discussed above. Chomsky (1980) replaces the earlier conditions on the application of rules with *reindexing* or *opacity* rules applying to the outputs of the initial indexing rules. When a pronoun is *free* (i) in an *opaque* domain, i is deleted from its anaphoric index, where free (i) = not c-commanded by NP_i; and the opaque domains are (a) the c-command domain of a subject and (b) nominative NP. For present purposes, (b) is indistinguishable from 'domain of tense'.[5] Crucially, reindexing does not apply to full lexical NPs. If it did, the distinction between (10) and (11) would be lost.

(10)   John thinks he is intelligent. [*John* may = *he*]

(11)   He thinks John is intelligent. [*John* ≠ *he*]

The relevant portion of the derivation of (10) is as follows.

(12) a. $John_1$ thinks he_2 is intelligent. Referential index assignment
    b. $John_{1, \emptyset}$ thinks $he_{2, \{1\}}$ is intelligent. Anaphoric index assignment
    c. $John_{1, \emptyset}$ thinks $he_{2, \emptyset}$ is intelligent. Opacity rule

Here *John* and *he* are mutually free in reference, as far as indexing is concerned. Thus *he* may (but need not) be intended as designating John. Since reindexing cannot apply to *John* in (11), *he* and *John* are disjoint.

Consider now such examples as (13) and (14):

(13)   *We like me.

(14)   We think I will win.

Their ultimate representations will be (13′) and (14′) respectively.

(13′) $We_{1,\emptyset}$ like $me_{2,\{1\}}$.

(14′) $We_{1,\emptyset}$ think $I_{2,\emptyset}$ will win.

Reindexing cannot apply to *me* in (13′) since that NP is not free (1) in an opaque domain. Ungrammaticality results, since the final indexing contradicts one aspect of the lexical meanings of *we* and *me*. On the other hand, *I* in (14′) is subject to reindexing, hence *we, I* are mutually free in reference, and in particular, free to mean what they must.

The Government Binding Theory (GB) of Chomsky (1981a; 1979) handles the above facts in a rather different way. Anaphoric indices are eliminated, obviously a technical simplification, all else equal. The effects of anaphoric indices (and reindexing of them) are captured with two Binding Principles:

(15) a.   A 'name' must be free.
    b.   A pronominal must be free in its governing category.

Referential indices are freely assigned. Then, an NP is *bound* if it is coindexed with a c-commanding NP in argument position, *free* otherwise. The *governing category* of an NP is the minimal NP or S in which that NP is governed, where α governs β if α minimally c-commands β (α a lexical category or tense).

An example such as (4a) above would potentially receive the two representations (16) and (17).[6]

(16) I_1 like me_1.

(17) I_1 like me_2.

(16), however, is ruled out by (15b), since *me* is not free in its governing category. Similarly, (6a) receives the representations (18) and (19), but (18) is excluded by (15b).

(18) He_1 likes him_1.

(19) He_1 likes him_2.

Thus far, as Chomsky (1981a) indicates, "we need have no resort to anaphoric indices." A further claimed advantage of the GB theory is less clear. Chomsky claims that, "we need introduce no mention of the property of disjoint reference." This is hardly a respect in which GB differs from the On Binding framework (OB), however. In GB, indices are randomly assigned, and the resulting string is checked against the binding principles. Thus far the property of disjoint reference is not mentioned. Similarly, in OB, anaphoric indices are assigned by rule, then reindexing takes place in accord with the opacity rules. Again, there is no mention of the property of disjoint reference.

Neither theory is yet complete, however. The index relations must now be *interpreted*. That is, to take the simplest case, in OB, (20) must be interpreted as imposing a requirement on the relationship between NP_1 and NP_2.

(20) $\ldots NP_{1, \emptyset} \ldots NP_{2, \{1\}} \ldots$

Otherwise, nothing rules out, e.g., ex. (4a) *'I like me', since there cannot be any indexing principle per se excluding structures such as (20). Thus the property of disjoint reference must ultimately be mentioned in OB, but clearly must also be mentioned in GB. Returning to the pair of representations (16), (17), while (16) is excluded by binding theory, (17) surely is not. What rules out (17)? It must be something about the interpretation of such structures as (21).

(21) $\ldots NP_1 \ldots NP_2 \ldots$

Interesting questions arise when the precise interpretation of (21) is considered. To exclude (17) it would be sufficient to stipulate that in (21), NP_1, NP_2 are non-coreferential. Since this would contradict lexical requirements in (17), ungrammaticality results. This stipulation is not strong enough to handle (22), however.

(22) We_1 like me_2.

A non-coreference requirement would contradict no lexical property in this case. In fact, the lexical properties of *we, me* entail non-coreference. What is needed is a stipulation that in (21) the two NPs are non-over-lapping, or *disjoint* in reference. Applied to (22), this gives the desired result, since disjointness does contradict lexical meaning here.

All that remains is to specify the interpretation of (23).

(23) $\ldots NP_1 \ldots NP_1 \ldots$

The obvious interpretation is overlap in reference, the complement of the interpretation of (21). Since (21) and (23) together exhaust the class of possibilities, this portion of the theory is now complete. Two problems immediately emerge. First, consider (25), the two representations the theory would provide for (24).

(24)   *We like myself.

(25) a. We₁ like myself₂.
     b. We₁ like myself₁.

(25a) will be ruled out by binding principle (26), which, together with (15) above, completes the binding theory.

(26)   An anaphor must be bound in its governing category.

(25b) meets requirement (26), though. Further, it satisfies the designated interpretation since the intended referents of the two NPs overlap. In fact, they necessarily overlap. Hence, it is not clear how (24) with representation (25b) can be ruled out. It might be suggested that the problem has nothing to do with binding, but rather with agreement. In particular, perhaps a reflexive must agree in syntactic features with its antecedent. Even this will not suffice to rule out (27), however.

(27)   They₁ like themselves. [where *they* designates John, Bob, Harry and *themselves* designates John, Tom, Sam]

Clearly this is impossible even though binding theory is apparently satisfied, binding interpretation is satisfied, and the hypothesized agreement principle is satisfied.

Note that an alternative interpretation for (23) would solve the present problem but create still worse problems. Suppose the interpretation for coindexing were coreference rather than mere overlap in reference. (25b) and (27) are then immediately excluded, since the proposed interpretation contradicts lexical requirements in the former case, and is inconsistent with the bracketed description in the latter case. But now the grammar completely excludes the possibility of grammatical partial overlap in reference. The only possibilities are *coreference* and *disjoint reference*. (28) would be excluded on both logically possible indexings (29a, b).

(28)   We think I will win.

(29) a. We₁ think I₂ will win. [disjoint reference contradicts lexical requirements]
     b. We₁ think I₁ will win. [coreference contradicts lexical requirements]

Further, (30a, b) could never have the interpretation in which *they* is intended to include *he*.

(30) a. They think he will win.
     b. He thinks they will win.

All of these predictions are totally incorrect. Further, the theory that yielded these predictions has a strange systematic gap. Hence, I conclude that the original proposal is more adequate, despite the problem raised by (25b) and (27).

The second problem with the theory as presented is both more interesting and more serious. Consider the GB indexing possibilities for (31).

(31)   John told Bill that they should leave.

(32) a.   John$_1$ told Bill$_2$ that they$_3$ should leave.
     b.   John$_1$ told Bill$_2$ that they$_1$ should leave.
     c.   John$_1$ told Bill$_2$ that they$_2$ should leave.

(32) exhausts the possibilities, since by (15a) *John* and *Bill* must have different indices. Consider now the interpretations provided by the theory for each case.

(32) a$'$.   'they' includes neither John nor Bill.
     b$'$.   'they' includes John but not Bill.
     c$'$.   'they' includes Bill but not John.

All of these are grammatical interpretations for (31). The difficulty is that one prominent reading for (31) — that in which 'they' includes both John and Bill — is simply unavailable. This is the old 'split antecedents' problem come home to roost.

To summarize, the interpretation of distinct indices must be disjoint reference if we are to handle standard cases such as (1). The interpretation of identical indices must then be overlap in reference, to exhaust the relevant domain and to allow for such sentences as (28), (30a) and (30b). The resulting system has two shortcomings. There is no clear treatment of bound anaphora, that is of necessary coreference. Further, 'split antecedents' for pronouns are incorrectly predicted to be impossible.[7]

The alternative within GB is that disjoint reference should be removed from present consideration and dealt with outside of the indexing framework entirely. Note that if examples like (1) need not be handled, indexing interpretation can be reformulated so as to avoid both major problems considered. Coindexing will be interpreted as *coreference* eliminating the problem of inappropriate antecedents for reflexives. The interpretation of distinct indexing will now be *non-coreference*. Split antecedents then disappear as a problem. Each part of the split antecedent can safely be designated as non-coreferential from the related pronoun. In (31) above, both *John* and *Bill* are in fact non-coreferential from *they*. Partial overlap in reference would be allowed. Partial overlap with plurals in general would constitute the remaining vestige of the notion 'free in reference'. This proposal of course requires a reasonable alternative treatment of disjoint reference; none currently exists. Further, it is not clear how an alternative treatment outside of the indexing framework could capture the fact that the phenomenon has essentially the same distribution as what *would* be handled by indexing. In the following section, I will argue that the extra complexity of OB indexing is well motivated in that it provides the basis for a systematic treatment of disjoint reference.

There appear to be at least three distinct cases that a theory of coreference must handle: (1) disjoint reference; (2) (obligatory) coreference; (3) partial overlap in reference.[8] The GB indexing system provides only a single index for an NP, and hence provides potential coverage for just two cases, since any two NPs have either identical or non-identical indices.

The OB theory, like its predecessor in Lasnik (1976), avoids all of the problems considered above. For example, split antecedent phenomena are handled by the notion "free in reference" made available in OB, but not in GB. More generally, there are three distinct representation types provided, exactly in accordance with the three referential possibilities discussed above.[9]

(33) a. $\ldots$ NP$_{1,\emptyset}\ldots$ NP$_1\ldots$ [Bound anaphora (including trace)]
     b. $\ldots$ NP$_{1,\emptyset}\ldots$ NP$_{2,\{1\}}\ldots$ [Disjoint reference]
     c. $\ldots$ NP$_{1,\emptyset}\ldots$ NP$_{2,\emptyset}\ldots$ [Free reference]

(33a), 'bound anaphora', is interpreted as obligatory coreference.[10] Therefore, mere overlap in reference will not satisfy the requirements of a reflexive and its antecedent. (24) is immediately ruled out. If *we* and *myself* are coindexed, they must be coreferential, but this contradicts lexical properties of the items. On the other hand, if they are not coindexed, an anaphor — *myself* — lacks an antecedent. Essentially the same comments apply in the case of (27).

(33b) is the representation of standard disjoint reference cases such as (34) or (35).

(34) a. *We like me.
     b. *We like us.

(35)   He thinks John is intelligent. [*He* ≠ *John*]

(33c) represents the case that is, in effect, unavailable in GB. A pair of NPs so indexed are mutually free in reference. Neither imposes any referential requirement on the other.

One important aspect of this possibility, as noted in Lasnik (1976), is that split antecedents cease to be problematic. Following the assignment of referential and anaphoric indices, and the operation of reindexing, (31) will have the following representation:

(36)   John$_{1,\emptyset}$ told Bill$_{2,\{1\}}$ that they$_{3,\emptyset}$ should leave.

John and *Bill* are disjoint, while *they* is entirely free. In particular, *they* can be used to designate the set consisting of John and Bill (or a larger set properly including John and Bill). This result appears to be correct.

One additional case, easily handled by an extension of (33), has been argued to exist. May (1979) and Freidin and Lasnik (1981), expanding on an argument in Chomsky (1976), show that a trace resulting from Wh-movement will, like other traces, be coindexed with the moved phrase. Unlike other traces, however, a Wh-trace will receive an anaphoric index and will not be subject to reindexing. These latter two properties follow naturally from the assumption first made explicit in Chomsky (1976) that Wh-trace, being a bound variable, will be treated as a 'name'. Taken together, these properties can result in representation (37) under certain circumstances.

(37) $\ldots wh_1 \ldots NP_{1, \{1\}} \ldots$

May argues that (37) results from 'improper movement', that is, movement of a Wh-phrase from COMP and into a sentential position. Assuming that $NP_{1, \{1\}}$ is ill-formed, a reasonable assumption since on a natural interpretation an NP so indexed will be disjoint in reference from itself, it need not be stipulated that an item in COMP can only be moved into another COMP.[11] Thus, yet another indexing possibility made available by OB turns out to be useful.

I have tried to show that the most important potential argument against OB indexing — that it is too powerful, providing descriptions for non-existent cases — is not valid. Every distinct representation made available handles a distinct referential possibility. In fact, GB as presented seems too weak in failing to adequately distinguish the existing referential types.[12] The second argument against OB, and the one actually presented by Chomsky, is that the system is needlessly complex. However, some of the apparent complexity, the notion 'disjoint reference', is shared by GB when that theory is fully articulated. The remaining complexity is needed to handle cases beyond the scope of GB.

NOTES

[1] Throughout this article, I will be concerned with *intended* reference, *intended* coreference, etc. In the analyses I will consider, grammaticality will depend not on actual reference but rather on intended reference. I will frequently refer to 'coreference', 'non-coreference', etc., but only as a shorthand manner of speaking.

[2] Ultimately, the rule is argued to be one of disjoint reference rather than non-coreference. In both (A), discussed in Chomsky (1973), and (B), discussed in Lasnik (1976), in the strongly preferred interpretation *the soldiers* and *the officers* are disjoint, not merely non-coreferential.

(A)   The soldiers shot the officers.

(B)   The soldiers think that the officers are incompetent.

[3] Higginbotham (1980) points out that the usual interpretation of disjoint reference is that the referents of two NPs in this relationship, for example *He* and *John* in (8), are purportedly distinct. He goes on to argue rather convincingly that this usual interpretation is too restrictive and should be replaced by the following:

If two NPs are contraindexed in S, then the speaker of S purports thereby not to beleive that the contraindexed items are coreferential.

The precise formulation is open to question, but this is definitely on the right track.

[4] It is now clear why anaphors do not receive anaphoric indices. If they did, structures such as (A) would always result.

(A) $John_{1,\emptyset}$ hurt $himself_{1,\{1\}}$.

This is incorrect since it requires that *himself* be both coreferential to, and disjoint from, *John*, a contradiction. (A) also seems to require that *himself* be disjoint from itself, also a contradiction, presumably. Such contradictory representations will be further considered below.

[5] See Lasnik and Freidin (1981) and Freidin and Lasnik (1981) for further discussion.

[6] The precise integers chosen are, of course, of no importance. All that matters is whether the two indices are the same or different.

[7] Note that split antecedents *are* impossible for bound anaphors:

(A)   *John told Bill about themselves.

The GB system seems to err in failing to distinguish sufficiently between pronouns and bound anaphors.

[8] Significantly, there are no obligatory cases of the third type.

[9] In (33), I abstract away from all potential interactions with additional NPs in a given sentence.

[10] If referential indices are assigned completely freely — the simplest system — an additional possibility, combining properties of (33a) and (c), arises.

(i) $\ldots NP_{1,\emptyset}\ldots NP_{1,\emptyset}\ldots$

Thus, 'John thinks he is intelligent' could have either representation (i) or (33c). (i) could then be used for stipulated coreference. In the case at hand, then, a 'free' reading could be distinguished from a 'reflexive' reading.

[11] See Chomsky (1979) for a potential argument against this account.

[12] Note that both theories are reasonably successful in capturing the generalization that bound anaphors and disjoint reference obtain in the same sorts of structures. The one major exception to the generalization — genitive determiners — is problematic for both. Thus, in (A), either a reciprocal or a coreferential pronoun is possible.

(A)   We read $\left\{ \begin{array}{l} \text{our} \\ \text{each other's} \end{array} \right\}$ books.

OB could describe this two-way possibility by characterizing NP as an opaque domain, thus allowing the pronoun, and stipulating that as a marked option *each other* will not reindex to zero in this particular opaque domain. It is not immediately clear how to characterize this possibility in GB.

ILLICIT NP MOVEMENT:
LOCALITY CONDITIONS ON CHAINS?
1985

1. CONDITIONS ON NP MOVEMENT

One of the major syntactic discoveries of the early 1970s was that in certain central respects, NP movement obeys the same constraints as the process associating an anaphor with its antecedent. Chomsky (1973) proposed that this fact is simply a special case of the generalization that *all* rules obey the Tensed-S Condition and the Specified Subject Condition. The significance of such an approach was that it allowed for a great reduction in the descriptive power of transformations, leading ultimately to the current "Move α." (1) and (2) are representative examples of illicit reflexive binding and movement, respectively.

(1)   *John believes [that [Mary likes himself]]

(2)   *John is believed [that [Mary likes ___]]

(1) and (2) each violate both constraints.

Note that this approach does not claim that NP movement and anaphor binding are a "natural class" of processes. They pattern alike only because all rules behave this way. Of course, in Chomsky (1973), it was noted that pronominal coreference did not in fact obey the constraints; and Wh-movement obeyed them only by stipulation. Moreover, the costraints were specifically stated in such a way that COMP-to-COMP movement was granted an exemption. Apparently, then, certain rules had to be designated as obeying the constraints, others as not obeying them.

Chomsky (1976) proposed an alternative. There is exactly one type of rule conforming to the constraints: namely, rules of construal (which concern themselves with antecedent relations). Other rules are not constrained.[1] Thus, NP movement itself is not constrained. Rather, the trace of such movement is an anaphor, subject to the same rule of construal as any other anaphor. This approach ultimately led to binding condition A of Chomsky (1981).

(3)   An anaphor must be bound in its governing category.

This theory asserts that the abstract distribution of trace is identical to that of lexical anaphors,[2] while movement itself is unconstrained.[3] Once we

134

abstract away from other concomitant difference between Chomsky (1973) and Chomsky (1981), it is difficult to find any empirical differences in the treatment of NP movement.

2. AN UNEXPECTED CONDITION A LOOPHOLE

There is one construction on which the two accounts diverge. Example (4) is indistinguishable from (2), as far as the Tensed-S Condition and the Specified Subject Condition are concerned.

(4)   *John is believed [(that) [he likes ___]]

The movement of *John* unequivocally violates both conditions. Now consider representation (5).

(5)   *John$_1$ is believed [(that) [he$_1$ likes e$_1$]]

(5) is the result of the movement illustrateed in (4). Yet e$_1$, the trace of that movement, conforms to binding condition A. The governing category of e$_1$ is the embedded S, and in that embedded S, e$_1$ is bound by he$_1$.

A return to the framework of Chomsky (1973) is presumably not the answer, because of the conceptual problems noted above. The modular character of the Government-Binding theory provides a number of potential accounts of the ungrammaticality of (5) — none of them completely satisfactory, as we shall see.

3. A CLASS OF NONSOLUTIONS

The ungrammaticality of (5) cannot be ascribed to Subjacency, because (5) does not violate Subjacency. Movement takes place across one S and one S'. This must be licit, or long-distance Wh-movement would never be possible.

The functional determination algorithm of Chomsky (1982) is initially more successful in excluding (5). This algorithm presupposes that empty categories (ECs) are not intrinsically specified for the features [±anaphoric] and [±pronominal]. Rather, these features are functionally determined according to the position occupied by the EC at S-structure. Consider again the relevant configuration.

(6)   *John$_1$ is believed [(that) [he$_1$ likes e$_1$]]

Here, e$_1$ is not a variable, since it is not locally Ā-bound. According to the algorithm, "an EC that is not a variable is a pronominal if it is free or locally A-bound by an antecedent with an independent θ-role" (Chomsky (1982, 35)). Since he$_1$ has an independent θ-role and locally A-binds e$_1$, e$_1$ is therefore determined to be pronominal. But now, the structure is irredeemable. By binding condition B, a pronominal must be free in its governing category; hence, e_1 (now determined to be pronominal) violates the binding theory.

This account is successful to the extent that functional determination is valid. But in fact its validity has been called into serious question. Brody (1984) points out a number of problems. First, there is an empirical problem, since there are locally Ā-bound ECs that are not variables. In (7) that first EC is apparently the pronominal anaphor PRO, rather than the non-pronominal nonanaphoric "variable."

(7)   Who$_1$ did EC$_1$ losing the race annoy EC$_1$

         PRO   variable

Next, Brody points out a number of potential conceptual problems. The one most relevant to our concerns is summarized as follows (p. 367).

In order for [the algorithm] to tell us which categories are pronominal, we must ... know which elements have an independent θ-role. But in order to know that, we must know which categories are pronominal, since if a category is not in a θ-position, then whether or not it has an independent θ-role will depend on what sorts of empty categories it binds.

That is, the procedure is, at least in part, circular.

Epstein (1984) raises still another problem. Consider (8).

(8)   *Who$_1$ did he$_1$ try [[e$_1$ to win the race]]

Since the EC in embedded subject position is locally A-bound by he_1, an antecedent with an independent θ-role, it is [+pronominal].[4] If this EC is also [+anaphoric], as allowed by the algorithm, it will be PRO. But this should be allowed. The position of the EC is ungoverned; hence, the binding theory is satisfied. The particular requirement of PRO, control, is also apparently satisfied. Further, under a "visibility" approach to the Case Filter (as in Chomsky (1981), for example), *who* need not have Case, since it is not an argument and hence need not receive a θ-role. The requirement on *who*, that it bind some variable, is met. Under the general theory including functional determination (as in Sportiche (1983)), a variable crucially need not be a [−anaphoric, −pronominal] EC. The overt pronoun *he* can serve as a variable. Epstein concludes that ECs are not functionally determined, but instead have intrinsic features.[5] Returning to (6), the intrinsic features of the EC there are [+anaphoric, −pronominal], since it is the trace of NP movement (i.e. movement to an A-position). As we have already seen, if the EC has those features, the binding conditions are satisfied.

Next, consider an approach in terms of Case. Note that the A-chain in (6), (John$_1$, e$_1$), consists of two Case-marked elements, if it is stipulated that Case assignment is obligatory. It has occasionally been proposed, most recently in Davis (1984), that such a configuration is impossible.[6] A slight alternation in (6) can provide a test for whether this "double Case" violation is all that is involved.

(9)   *Bill tried [[John$_1$ to be believed [(that) [he$_1$ likes e$_1$]]]]

Here the chain has just one Case-marked element, e$_1$, since *John* is not even in a governed position, yet grammaticality is not improved.

Even though the chian in (9) has exactly one Case, perhaps there is a more specific requirement: that the head of the chain be in a Case-marked position. *John$_1$* would violate this constraint. However, the head of a chain need not be Case-marked in general. Rather, it must be either Case-marked or PRO. Once again, a minimal alteration in the example can test the efficacy of that constraint.

(10)   *Bill$_1$ tried [[PRO$_1$ to be believed [(that) [he$_1$ likes e$_1$]]]]

The head of the chain is not in a Case-marked position; yet, being PRO, it need not be in such a position, as shown in (11).

(11)   Bill$_1$ tried [[PRO$_1$ to leave]]

One final Case approach might be to stipulate that NP-trace not be in a Case-marked position, as suggested in Bouchard (1984) and Sportiche (1983). This would correctly exclude (6), (9), and (10). However, it would not rule out (12).

(12)   *John$_1$ is believed [(that) [he$_1$ is proud e$_1$]]
        (cf. *It is believed that John is proud of himself*)

Here, the A-chain has exactly one Case-marked member, *John$_1$*, and the trace of *John* is not in a Case-marked position. If *of*-insertion were stipulated to be obligatory, (12) would be excluded. Then (13) would be ruled out by virtue of containing a Case-marked NP-trace.

(13)   *John$_1$ is believed [(that) [he$_1$ is proud of$_1$ e$_1$]]

However, obligatory *of*-insertion would also incorrectly exclude (14).

(14)   Rome's$_1$ destruction e$_1$

Further, stipulated obligatoriness would create massive redundancy in the system, since Case requirements alone force the insertion of *of* in all grammatical instances. Without obligatory *of*-insertion, the problem of illicit NP movement remains.

Neither bounding theory, functional determination, nor Case theory has provided an answer. Further, binding theory failed immediately. A revision of binding theory can handle (6), but creates even more severe difficulties. Suppose that binding principles must be satisfied at D-structure as well as S-structure. The D-structure representation of (6) is (15), assuming free indexing at D-structure.

(15)   ___ is believed [that [he₁ likes John₁]]

This clearly violates binding condition C, since *John₁* is A-bound. (16), with D-structure representation (17), would also be excluded.

(16)   He₁ is believed [that [he₁ likes e₁]]

(17)   ___ is believed [that [he₁ likes him₁]]

This time binding condition B is violated, since *him₁* is A-bound in its governing category. Finally, consider D-structure representation (18).

(18)   ___ is believed [that [he₁ likes himself₁]]

This is well-formed. However, the S-structure representation resulting from movement of *himself₁* would violate binding condition A:

(19)   Himself₁ is believed [that [he₁ likes e₁]]

But if the binding conditions must be satisfied at D-structure, a number of well-formed sentences will be ruled out. The D-structure representation of (20) is (21), where *each other* is free in its governing category.

(20)   We₁ seem to each other₁ [e₁ to be intelligent]

(21)   ___ seem to each other [we₁ to be intelligent]

There is also evidence that binding condition C need not be satisfied at D-structure. In the D-structure representation of (22), *John* is c-commanded by *he*, yet the sentence is well-formed.

(22)   Who that John₁ knows does he₁ respect

The hypothesized revision of the binding theory must be rejected.

Since a moved NP and its [+anaphoric, −pronominal] traces must constitute an A-chain, the properties of such chains are relevant to the problem at hand. For example, it has been proposed in Aoun (1982) that S′ breaks a chain. If this is so, then *John₁* and *e₁* in (6) cannot constitute a chain, since only the latter is contained within the embedded S′. A violation of the θ-Criterion results, since *John₁* is not in a θ-marked position, nor is it the head of a chain with a θ-marked member. Though this seems to work, it substantially overlaps with the standard claim that NP-trace is an anaphor. Nearly all instances of an NP-trace free in its governing category would also violate other principles. In (23), for example, binding condition A is superfluous because the chain is broken by S′.

(23)   John₁ is believed [that [Mary likes e₁]]

At any rate, even if S′ does in general break a chain, one would expect this property to follow from independent principles.

4. TOWARD A SOLUTION

Another property of chains has been postulated. Chomsky (1981, 333) includes the following as one of four defining characteristics of (A)-chains.

(24) α_i locally A-BINDS α_{i+1}

(The α_i are members of the chain.) Chomsky gives no actual argument for a condition this strong.[7] He merely notes that "In the chains discussed in chapters 2 and 3, each link was a case of local binding" (p. 332). But note that precisely this condition is violated in our problematic example. In (6), repeated here as (25), the θ-Criterion demands that there be two chains: $(John_1, e_1)$ and (he_1).

(25) $John_1$ is believed [that [he_1 likes e_1]]

Chomsky's condition does not permit $(John_1, e_1)$ to be a chain, since *John*$_1$ does not locally bind e_1. Rather, *he*$_1$ does. Thus, the θ-Criterion cannot be satisfied. Note that this result is largely independent of how chains are actually constructed. One might regard them as histories of movement. Alternatively, one might consider the simplest chain formation algorithm: optionally construct a chain out of an NP in an A-position and any of the A-position NPs that it binds. General principles, especially the θ-Criterion, will exclude almost all of the ill-formed possibilities that result.

The configuration in (25) is reminiscent of the results of another case of illicit movement.

(26)   *Who_1 does he_1 think [that [Mary likes e_1]]

As noted by Chomsky (class lecture, Fall 1983), strong crossover creates structures in which an Ā-chain must be (who_1, e_1), but in which *who*$_1$ does not locally bind e_1. Suppose we generalize (24) to (27), which may be thought of as a generalized strong crossover constraint.

(27)   If α_i and α_{i+1} are successive links in an A/Ā-chain, then α_i locally A/Ā-binds α_{i+1}.

This condition rules out all derivations with the abstract properties of (28).[8]

(28)

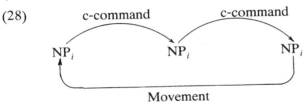

Movement

Rizzi (1986) provides another argument for the locality requirement on chains, based on certain unexpectedly ungrammatical NP movement chains in French and Italian. In these cases a clitic chain overlaps with an NP movement chain in such a way that locality is violated in the latter:

(29)   *Gianni$_1$ [$_{VP}$ si$_1$ è stato affidato e$'_1$ e$''_1$]
        Gianni   to himself was   entrusted
        'Gianni was entrusted to himself.'

Here, e', the trace of NP movement, is not locally bound by *Gianni*, the head of its chain. Rather, the nearest binder is the trace of the clitic. A related example, called to my attention by an LI reviewer, suggests that (27) should be limited to A-chains, as in Chomsky (1981). (30) seems to indicate that clitic chains, unlike A-chains, do not conform to the locality requirement.[9]

(30)   Gianni$_1$ si$_1$ vuole [PRO$_1$ vedere e$_1$]

        Gianni himself wants   to see
        'Gianni wants to see himself.'

If (27) is limited to A-chains, crossover (as in (26)) will no longer be in its purview, but that is perhaps just as well. To rule out the binding of a lexical R-expression or an anaphoric epithet, condition C of the binding theory is necessary, regardless of the outcome of the present investigation. It seems essentially cost-free to extend it to variables; hence, the locality condition would do no work in this case.

Given the limitation to A-chains, one might conjecture that the real constraint is not one precluding intervening binders, but rather something along the lines of (31).

(31)   An NP-trace must be bound in its governing category by a member of its A-chain.

This would render example (i) of footnote 8 innocuous regardless of its structure, while correctly excluding (4), etc. Further, if (32) is derived via raising, it is a problem for any locality constraint but not for (31).

(32)   They$_1$ strike each other$_1$ [as e$_1$ intelligent]

On the other hand, Rizzi discusses this example and observes that a Wh-trace in the position of the object of *strike* can at least marginally support a parasitic gap (PG) in the small clause complement.

(33)   ?Who$_1$ did the pamphlet$_2$ strike e$_1$ [as e$_2$ being insulting to PG$_1$]

This would not be expected if e_1 c-commanded PG$_1$. But if it does not, locality is not violated. Further, (31) itself is not without defects. First, it replaces binding condition A, but only for nonlexical anaphors. In effect, we would have two separate versions of condition A. Second, (31) does not handle (29), since the NP-trace in that example is bound in its governing category by *Gianni*, a member of its A-chain.

Apparently, we are left with (27), perhaps restricted to A-chains, as suggested. If only that constraint itself could be deduced from more basic properties, we would have a full-fledged explanation of the initial phenomenon — the impossibility of "illicit" NP movement.

ACKNOWLEDGEMENTS

I would like to thank Noam Chomsky, Sam Epstein, Bob Freidin, Yinxia Long, Luigi Rizzi, Dominique Sportiche, Tim Stowell, and an anonymous LI reviewer for helpful suggestions. This research was supported in part by the MIT Center for Cognitive Science under a grant from the A. P. Sloan Foundation's particular program in Cognitive Science.

NOTES

[1] This account is not entirely accurate. Following Lasnik (1976), Chomsky noted that one need not posit a rule of sentence grammar for pronominal coreference. Hence, (i) does not display any violation of the constraints.

(i) $John_1$ thinks Mary likes him_1.

However, the disjoint reference rule of Lasnik (1976) seems to be a rule of the same general character as the rule operative in (ii).

(ii)   *$John_1$ likes him_1

Yet only the latter rule obeys the constraints.

(iii)   *He_1 thinks Mary likes $John_1$

(iv) $John_1$ thinks Mary likes him_1

[2] The *actual* distribution of NP-trace and lexical anaphors is complementary, as has frequently been noted. But this complementarity can be entirely traced to independent principles, in particular those determining Case and θ-assignment. Abstracting away from these effects, the distribution is essentially identical.

[3] Except, of course, by Subjacency, which will not concern us here.

[4] The trace in the lower Comp has been omitted, based on the conclusions in Lasnik and Saito (1984). Assuming that Subjacency is a constraint on movement (rather than on representation), a Wh-phrase can move through a Comp to satisfy Subjacency but can optionally fail to leave a trace. Note that even if a trace were present in Comp, it would not count as a relevant Ā-binder, as discussed in Chomsky (1982).

[5] An anonymous reviewer suggests that (8) is ruled out because English lacks resumptive pronouns. As Epstein shows, this depends on the precise nature of the parameter yielding this effect. For example, suppose that the parametric property is that English does not allow the existence (or alternatively, the indexing) of base-generated operators in Comp. This could exclude classic resumptive structures, but would still allow (8). A second possibility is that English disallows locally Ā-bound pronouns. This would indeed exclude

(8) along with the classic cases. But it would also exclude strong crossover entirely. I a crossover configuration the nearest (relevant) binder is always the operator in Comp. Thus, functional determination would be rendered superfluous for the central phenomenon that it could handle and would therefore be called into serious question, just as Epstein implies.

[6] More precisely, for Davis, *John* itself would be doubly Case-marked.

[7] Chomsky does observe that "an element in COMP breaks a chain ..." (p. 322). However, he considers no alternative accounts of this fact.

[8] Examples like (i) are counterexamples, if *each other*$_1$ c-commands e_1.

    (i)   We$_1$ seem to each other$_1$ [e$_1$ to be intelligent$_1$]

In this connection, notice that coreference is difficult in (ii).

    (ii)   ?It seems to him$_1$ that John$_1$ is intelligent

On the other hand, (ii) seems substantially better than (iii).

    (iii)   *He$_1$ thinks that John$_1$ is intelligent

Let us tentatively assume, then, that the dative NP in (i) and (ii) does not c-command the complement sentence.

[9] This observation is somewhat mitigated by the fact that such "clitic climbing" is limited to a small set of so-called restructuring verbs.

ANDREW BARSS AND HOWARD LASNIK

A NOTE ON ANAPHORA AND DOUBLE OBJECTS
1986

This squib is concerned with English V NP_1 NP_2 (double-object) constructions, as in (1), and in particular with the implications of such
constructions for phrase structure principles governing certain anaphoric
relations:

(1) a.   I gave John a book.
    b.   I denied Fred his pay.

We will present several phenomena demonstrating an asymmetrical relation between NP_1 and NP_2 (some of which have been noted before, some
of which we believe are noted here for the first time). In each case it will
be seen that NP_2 is in some sense in the domain of NP_1, but NP_1 is not in
the domain of NP_2.

1. THE BINDING PRINCIPLES

As is well known, in the sequence [V NP_1 NP_2] NP_1 can bind NP_2, but not
conversely (see Kuno (1986)):

(2)   I showed $\left\{ \begin{array}{l} \text{John} \\ \text{him} \end{array} \right\}$ himself (in the mirror).

(3)   *I showed himself John (in the mirror).

These examples constitute two independent pieces of evidence for our
claim. Condition A of the binding theory (Chomsky (1981)) is presumably
satisfied by (2), showing that the first NP binds the second. Further,
conditions B and C are evidently *not* violated in (2). Hence, the second
NP does not bind the first. (3), on the other hand, evidently violates both
condition A and condition C. The condition A contrast in (4) and (5)
seems to replicate that in (2) and (3):

(4)   I showed the professors each other's students.

(5)   *I showed each other's students the professors.

2. QNP-PRONOUN RELATIONS

Ignoring some complex cases that we abstract away from,[1] in order for a
pronoun to be related to a quantificational NP (QNP) as a variable, it

143

must be in the structural domain of the QNP at S-Structure.[2] As (6) and (7) show, there is an asymmetry consistent with that seen in section I:

(6) a.   I denied each worker his paycheck.
    b.   I showed every friend of mine his photograph.

(7) a.   I denied its owner each paycheck.
    b.   I showed its trainer every lion.

In (6a—b), but not (7a—b), the pronoun can be a bound variable.

3. WH-MOVEMENT AND WEAK CROSSOVER

Cases that are parallel to (7), except that they involve moved Wh-phrases in place of the quantifier, exhibit weak crossover; cases like (6) do not:[3]

(8) a.   Which worker$_i$ did you deny e_i his$_i$ paycheck.
    b.   Who$_i$ did you show e_i his$_i$ reflection in the mirror.

(9) a.   *Which paycheck$_i$ did you deny it$_i$s owner e_i.
    b.   *Which lion$_i$ did you show it$_i$s trainer e_i.

4. SUPERIORITY

In a double-object verb phrase, both NPs may be (separately) extracted:

(10) a. Who did you give a book?
     b. Which book did you give John?
         ((10a) is somewhat awkward; see note 3)

However, if the two NPs are *both* Wh-phrases, the second one must not move overtly:

(11) a. Who did you give which book?
     b. *Which book did you give who?
         ((11b) is grammatical only on the echoic reading)

The Superiority Condition of Chomsky (1973) requires, roughly, that given any two Wh-phrases, the structurally higher ("superior") one must move, if either does.[4] Many Superiority effects, for example (12), have been subsumed under the Empty Category Principle (ECP in more recent work (Chomsky (1981), Lasnik and Saito (1984)):

(12)   *[$_{S'}$ What$_i$ [$_S$ did who see e_i]]?

However, as Pesetsky (1982) and Hendrick and Rochemont (1982) note, some Superiority violations in other constructions are not reducible to the ECP.[5] (13) is such a case:

(13)   *What did you [$_{VP}$ persuade whom [$_{S'}$ [$_S$ PRO to buy t]]]?

(13) is not ruled out by the ECP, since each Wh-phrase is a direct object and each trace will therefore be lexically governed. Note that the ungrammaticality of (11b), like that of (13), is apparently not attributable to the ECP, since (10) indicates that both objects are properly governed. But if Superiority is to handle (11b), then the first object must be superior to the second.

5. THE EACH . . . THE OTHER CONSTRUCTION

Consider the following:

(14)   I gave each man the other's watch.

(15)   *I gave the other's trainer each lion.

It is not clear to us what the structural requirements for this relation are, but a plausible candidate is to suppose that the minimal NP in which *each* appears must have *the other* in its domain; the failure of this relation in (15) would account for its ungrammaticality.

6. POLARITY *ANY*

Our final phenomenon involves polarity *any*, which is only licensed in the scope of negation, modals, yes/no questions, and other scope-bearing elements (Klima (1964), Lasnik (1972), Horn (1972), Kroch (1974), Linebarger (1980)):

(16)   I didn't see anyone.

(17)   *I saw anyone.

We note that there is a sharp distinction between (18) and (19):

(18)   I gave no one anything.

(19)   *I gave anyone nothing.

This distinction is reminiscent of those discussed above.

7. DISCUSSION

To sum up the data, we have noted a number of anaphoric relations that distinguish the two NPs in a V NP NP sequence, each indicating that the second NP is in the domain of the first, but not vice versa.

We now must seek a more formal characterization of this asymmetry in "domain." The standard notion of "domain" in the Extended Standard Theory is *c-command*; two definitions are commonly utilized in variants of the theory:

(20)   X c-commands Y iff every maximal projection that dominates
        X also dominates Y. (Aoun and Sportiche (1981))

(21)   X c-commands Y iff the first branching node dominanting X
        dominates Y. (Reinhart (1976))[6]

The problem now is to determine how it is that the first NP in a double-
object VP asymmetrically c-commands the second NP, and this requires
discussion of the phrase structure of these VPs. Consider the possibilities
((23) is from Kayne (1981a); (24) is from Chomsky (1980)):[7]

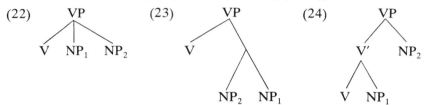

(22) and (23) must be rejected immediately, since in these structures the
hierarchical relation between the two NPs is utterly symmetrical. This
holds true regardless of which definition of c-command is chosen. The
third structure, the left-branching (24), is even worse, making backward
predictions with respect to domains if we choose definition (21): the *first*
NP will be in the domain of the *second*, and not conversely. If we choose
definition (20), then again the two NPs are symmetrical with respect to
domain, contrary to what the evidence suggests.

   These are the most obvious ways to assign structure to the V NP NP
sequence without a discontinuous constituent.[8]

   With a discontinuous constituent, asymmetric c-command of the required sort between the two NPs could be obtained with a structure
something like (25):

(25)

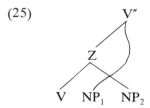

(25) is not permitted within the theory of phrase structure advanced in
Chomsky (1955) and somewhat revised in Lasnik and Kupin (1977); in
that theory it is axiomatic that for any nodes X and Y, either one precedes
the other or one dominates the other. In (25) the node Z (which dominates
V and NP$_2$) neither dominates nor is dominated by NP$_1$. Since NP$_1$
neither precedes nor is preceded by Z, structure (25) is not permitted.

The less restrictive conceptions of phrase structure advanced by McCawley (1982) and Higginbotham (1983), on the other hand, *do* permit such a structure as (25) to occur; in these theories precedence and dominance relations are separated, permitting discontinuous constituents.

There is another possibility. Suppose that one of the structures rejected earlier is correct, and that the two NPs do in fact mutually c-command. The problem then would be to distinguish the domain of NP_1 from that of NP_2 in terms of something other than c-command. Linear precedence is the obvious candidate.[9]

Consider the following definition of *domain of*:

(26)   Y is in the domain of X iff X c-commands Y and X precedes Y.

The various anaphora conditions (binding principles A, B, and C, the scope condition on polarity *any*, etc.) might be reformulated in terms of this definition: for example, "X binds Y iff Y is in the domain of X and X and Y are coindexed." This will properly distinguish all of the grammatical and ungrammatical pairs given above.

ACKNOWLEDGMENTS

We wish to acknowledge the helpful suggestions of Luigi Rizzi and two anonymous *Linguistic Inquiry* reviewers.

NOTES

[1] Specifically, donkey-sentence anaphora and inversely linked quantifiers. See Haïk (1984), Higginbotham (1983), May (1977; 1985), and the references cited there for much discussion.

[2] Relations between quantifiers and pronouns are treated in the literature in a number of ways. Our observation is independent of any particular treatment of this relation. A number of authors assimilate the failure of QNP-pronoun anaphora to weak crossover; the next section points out a weak crossover asymmetry in double-object verb phrases.

[3] Sentences (8a) and (8b), like (10a), are less than fully grammatical. They illustrate the general fact that the center NP in such verb phrases weakly resists extraction (see Jackendoff and Culicover (1971)). Though we have no explanation for this, we emphasize that it has nothing to do with the quantifier-bound pronoun relations in (8). What is relevant to our discussion is the strong contrast between (8) and (9). Furthermore, the difference can be repeated with Wh-in-situ questions, which do not exhibit this weak extraction constraint:

(8')   Which woman gave [which man]$_i$ [his$_i$ paychecks]?

(9')   *Which woman gave [it$_i$s author] [which book]$_i$?

[4] The Superiority Condition is stated as follows (p. 246):

No rule can involve X, Y in the structure
$$\ldots X \ldots [_a \ldots Z - WYV \ldots] \ldots$$

where the rule applies ambiguously to Z and Y and Z is superior to Y
... the category A is "superior" to the category B in the phrase marker if every major
category dominating A dominates B as well but not conversely.[27]
[27] We use the term "major category" in the sense of Chomsky (1965, p. 74), that is, N,
V, A and the categories that dominate them.

[5] See Pesetsky (1982), which collapses the ECP, the Superiority Condition, and several
other conditions into one general constraint on extraction.
[6] This is actually just one of several definitions of c-command that Reinhart considers.
[7] Stowell (1981) presents an analysis of double-object constructions that involves a word
formation rule adjoining NP_1 to the verb. Stowell gives two possible structures:

    (i) $[_{V'} [_V \text{ V } NP_1] NP_2]$
    (ii) $[_{V'} [_V \text{ V } NP_1] NP_2 \text{ } e_1]$

The first, geometrically similar to (24), has the same problem noted for that structure. In
the second, which Stowell analogizes to cliticization, the crucial relation is that between
NP_2 and the empty category, and once again symmetry obtains. A *Linguistic Inquiry*
reviewer observes that if e is actually outside V', as in (iii), it will asymmetrically c-command the second object under definition (21):

    (iii) $[_{V'} [_{V'} [_V \text{ V } NP_1] NP_2] e_1]$

However, note that the second object (NP_2) will asymmetrically c-command the "clitic"
NP_1 and, of course, everything within the clitic. Examples such as our (3), (5), (7), (9),
(15), (19) are thus still problematic.
[8] There are other structures that might be assigned without discontinuous constituents, for
example (i) or (ii):

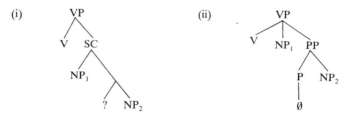

(i) would be an elaboration of Kayne's proposed structure (23), with the node ? a null
preposition or Infl, or, as Kayne suggests, a null *have* or *be*. These would allow the
representation of asymmetrical c-command of NP_2 by NP_1, as required. Further research is
needed to determine whether it is appropriate to postulate such structures. One concern
with the null verb or preposition proposal is that a range of such verbs and prepositions
would presumably be required. In (2), for example, *have* and *be* would be inappropriate.
[9] In including linear as well as hierarchical information, (26) is reminiscent both of the
early anaphora proposal of Langacker (1969) and of the modification presented in Lasnik
(1976).

HOWARD LASNIK

ON THE NECESSITY OF BINDING CONDITIONS
1986

I will be concerned in this paper with the binding conditions — the structural requirements governing certain anaphoric relations. I will give particular attention to "Condition C" effects, and will argue that, contrary to a currently popular view, something like Condition C does indeed exist. That is, I will display a wide variety of facts motivating Condition C which cannot be handled by, for example, independently motivated pragmatic constraints (see Reinhart (1983) for extensive discussion of such constraints) or by core properties of the theory of "Linking" (Higginbotham (1983)). A number of the arguments will be seen to carry over to Condition B as well. [It is on these grounds, of course, rather than on logical or biological grounds, that I will attempt to motivate the "necessity" of binding conditions, as one can surely conceive of an organism, even an evolutionarily successful one, whose linguistic system allows, say, the binding of a pronoun within its governing category.] In the course of the discussion, it will become evident that a partial reformulation of Condition C is in order, but its basic nature as a structural constraint on binding will remain intact.

It cannot be denied that there are some discourse based or pragmatic restrictions relevant to coreference relations. For example, there seems to be a mild prohibition, reasonably regarded as extragrammatical in nature, against repetition of R-expressions. The effect of this can be seen in the slight oddness of a sentence like (1) or a sequence of sentences like (2). [Throughout, I will be concerned only with readings involving coreference (or overlap in reference). I will, thus, suppress indices. Inevitably, this will result in certain issues being suppressed as well. See the Appendix below, as well as Lasnik (1981), Higginbotham (1983), Sportiche (1985), Lasnik and Uriagereka (1988) for relevant discussion.]

(1)   ?After John walked in, John sat down.

(2)   ?John walked in. Then John sat down.

This repetition constraint would also be relevant in (3) and (4), presumably, but, unaided, is too weak to account for the sharp contrast between these examples, on the one hand, and (1, 2), on the other.

(3)   *John regrets that John wasn't chosen.

(4)   *John thinks that I admire John.

149

This patterning of facts constituted a central part of the argument of Lasnik (1976) for a non-coreference rule. A coreference rule merely *permitting*, or even *requiring*, coreference does not, of itself, preclude coreference, even when such a rule fails to apply. An additional constraint disallowing coreference is needed. Note that this additional constraint seems grammatical in nature, in at least two respects. First, it is crucially dependent on hierarchical structure: the less acceptable examples such as (3, 4) invariably involve c-command. Second, its effects run directly counter to a plausible discourse principle favoring clarity. The acceptable sentences expressing the contents of the unacceptable (3, 4), namely (5, 6), are more, rather than less, vague than their counterparts.

(5)   John regrets that he wasn't chosen.

(6)   John thinks that I admire him.

Here I disagree with Reinhart (1986). Reinhart presents a pragmatic Gricean analysis of non-coreference effects. In the following quotation, the term 'bound anaphora' is intended to include not just the usual case of lexical anaphors, but also pronouns used as bound variables, that is, all bound pronouns for Reinhart.

> In a rational discourse we would expect that if a speaker has the means to express a certain idea clearly and directly he would not choose, arbitrarily, a less clear way to express it. When syntactically permitted, bound anaphora is the most explicit way available in the language to express coreference, as it involves direct dependency of the pronoun upon its antecedent for interpretation. So, if this option is avoided we may conclude that the speaker did not intend coreference. (p. 143)

The difficulty with this, paradoxically enough, is that the notion 'explicit' is unclear. As suggested earlier, there is no clear respect in which (5, 6) are more explicit than (3, 4) respectively in their presentation of coreference relations. Just the opposite is true. Thus, the above paradigm is unexplained in these terms.

It is also significant that we find Condition C effects even in unacceptable examples that lack acceptable meaning-preserving bound pronoun counterparts. Anaphoric epithets represent one such striking case.

(7)   *John thinks that I admire the idiot.

While (6) is, perhaps, a reasonable paraphrase of (4), it does not seem to be a reasonable paraphrase of (7), since it clearly lacks information represented in the latter example. Further, even the mild prohibition against repetition is without effect in such cases. Analogues to (1, 2) with epithets are not even slightly unacceptable.

(8)   After John walked in, the idiot sat down.

(9)   John walked in. Then the idiot sat down.

Finally, note that Condition C effects are even evident in cases not involving coreference, but mere overlap in reference.

(10)   They told John to leave. [They ⊉ John.]

(11)   They told John to visit Susan. [They ⊉ John. They ⊉ Susan.]

In these cases, it is particularly clear that there is no well-formed alternative to the ill-formed examples. To account for these cases, apparently we need two things: (1) a prohibition on binding (or a requirement of freedom); and (2) a principle giving semantic import to lack of binding. Here, I am particularly concerned with the former requirement. (See Lasnik (1981) for discussion of the interaction between these two mechanisms.)

Arguments similar to some of those above can be constructed for Condition B, as well. For example, (12) seems unacceptable even though it lacks a grammatical bound anaphora alternative, as indicated by (13).

(12)   *We like me.

(13)   *We like myself.

(14) is a further case.

(14)   *John and Mary like him/himself.

(15) is an example of this general type illustrating both Condition B and Condition C effects.

(15)   *John told them that Mary should leave.

Thus, even so comprehensive a pragmatic account as Reinhart's seems quite insufficient to account for the full range of effects.[1]

The mechanism of linking was advanced to deal with some of the limitations of binding theory, including those of the type pointed out in Lasnik (1981) involving plural NPs. The proposals put forward were partially successful (an alternative to the account of split antecedence in terms of the formalism of Chomsky (1980) was provided, for example[2]) but a number of issues remained unresolved, in particular, some of those outlined above. Further, despite Higginbotham's claim that with linking "no analogue of Chomsky's (C) . . . is required", the attempted elimination of Condition C was not entirely satisfactory, even for a simple case such as (3) above. To account for (3) in terms of linking, one must first prohibit either occurrence of *John* from being linked to the other. Further, one must explain why coreference is precluded in the absence of a link. Higginbotham, essentially following Evans (1980), denied the factual basis behind the second mechanism, apparently reducing (3) to (1) or (2), an incorrect reduction, I have argued. For the first mechanism, he prohibited 'downwards' linking quite generally. And finally, he prohibited R-expressions from being linked. A direct prohibition would have been tantamount to the postulation of Condition C, but Higginbotham argued that no such direct prohibition is required (or desired). Rather, the impossibility of linking an R-expression is a special case of (16).

(16)   The interpretation of an expression is given in one and only one way.

The idea behind (16) is that since R-expressions receive interpretation internally, by virtue of their lexical content, they cannot also receive interpretation via an antecedent. As it stands, (16) is arguably too strong. As observed by Paul Gorrell (personal communication), in (17), plausibly, *himself* receives some of its interpretation internally — person, gender, number — even though it not only allows, but requires, an antecedent.

(17)   Leslie likes himself.

A reasonable response in this case is that there is, in fact, no internal contribution to the interpretation of *himself.* Rather, the observed person, gender, and number reflect a pure agreement phenomenon and not true lexical conent. But now note that the semantic difference between reflexives and reciprocals makes it quite clear that anaphors do make an "internal" contribution to the meaning of a sentence. (18) and (19) are not synonymous. Since the antecedent is evidently the same in both cases, the difference resides in the choice of anaphor.

(18)   They like themselves.

(19)   They like each other.

Suppose, then, that we consider a weaker version of (16) as in (16'):

(16')   If all of the interpretation of an expression is given one way, then none may be given another way.

(16'), unlike (16), correctly allows examples (18) and (19). In these cases, some of the interpretation of the anaphor is given via the content of the antecedent and some (the difference between a reflexive and a reciprocal) is given internally. As required, (16') still rules out a linked representation for (3), and, for that matter, an upward linked representation for (3'), since all of the interpretation of a name is given internally.

(3')   He regrets that John wasn't choosen.

But now consider again example (7), or the modification of it in (7').

(7')   *John thinks that I admire the idiot.

(7')   *He thinks that I admire the idiot.

Surely, it would be desirable to analogize these to (3, 3'). And, in fact, the analogy is basically correct. It was argued on essentially these grounds in Lasnik (1976) that anaphoric epithets are like names with respect to binding. That is, in current terms, anaphoric epithets are R-expressions. However, according to Higginbotham (1983), the only relevant property of R-expressions is that they have lexical content. No condition refers directly to R-expressions, a claimed virtue of the theory, and the only indirect reference is in (16). Since we have been forced to reject (16) in favor of (16'), the question now arises whether (16') can account for (the upwards linked representations of) (7) and (7'). The answer would seem to be in the negative. Unlike names, epithets evidently are able to take antecedents. If (8) above is not an instance of antecedence (*John* being the antecedent of *the idiot*), then the notion is rather obscure. But, as noted, (8) is entirely well-formed. Thus, (16') cannot account for (7, 7') without incorrectly ruling out (8). Apparently, the correct generalization is that epithets, and R-expressions more generally, cannot be *bound*, a generalization that linking theory is, in principle, unable to state. It is in part for this reason that Higginbotham (1986) reintroduces a version of Condition C (and one of Condition B as well), formulated in terms of 'obviation'.

An examination of patterns of coreference in a variety of languages provides further evidence for a grammatical approach to disjoint reference effects, in particular, a Condition C type approach. The oddness of an English example like (3) or (4) is a fact which must be explained. But in many other languages, this fact does not obtain. Evidently, such a distribution constitutes evidence against a pragmatic approach, unless one is willing to posit that speakers of Thai, for example, are less interested in effective communication than are speakers of English. The variation that we find seems parametric in an interesting sense, in ways explicable in terms of the notions of syntactic description, and perhaps only in these terms. In Thai (20) and Vietnamese (21), for example, an R-expression need not be completely A-free:

(20)   cɔɔn khít   wâa cɔɔn chàlaàt
        John thinks that John is smart

(21)   John tin   John sẽ thǎṅg
        John thinks John will win

But within a clause, these two languages diverge:

(22)   cɔɔn chɔɔp cɔɔn
        John likes   John

(23)   *John thủóng John

       John likes   John

As a first approximation, we have the following: An R-expression is free (English); An R-expression is free in its governing category (Vietnamese); No requirement (Thai). However, if the first NP in (20—23) is replaced by a pronoun (*no* in Vietnamese or *khǎw* in Thai), all four examples become ungrammatical, just as they are in English:

(20′) *khǎw khít   wâa cɔɔn chàlaàt

       he   thinks that John is smart

(21′) *No' tin   John sẽ thǎng

       he   believes John will win

(22′) *khǎw chɔɔp cɔɔn

       he   likes John

(23′) *No' thủóng John

       he   likes   John

Apparently, Condition C is really two conditions, and the one just observed, unlike any of the standard binding conditions, involves reference to the binder as well as the bindee:

(24)   An R-expression is pronoun-free.

That is, a pronoun may not bind an R-expression. As far as I know, (24) is universal. (24) was not seen as a property of English in earlier work, since its effects all fall under [the English parametrization of] Condition C. If an R-expression must be entirely free, then, in particular, it must not be bound by a pronoun. (24) is not masked in this way in Thai or Vietnamese.

As predicted, sentences with the structure of (7) above are well-formed in both Thai and Vietnamese.

(25)   cɔɔn khít   wâa ?âybâa chàlaàt

       John thinks that the nut is smart

(26)   John tin   thǎng chỏ dẻ   sẽ thǎng

       John believes the son of a bitch will win

In Vietnamese, unsurprisingly given (23), anaphoric epithets must be free in their governing categories:[3]

(27)   *John thủóng cải thǎng chỏ dẻ

       John likes   the son of a   bitch

What is surprising is that this requirement holds in Thai also, a language in which R-expressions need not be free, as seen in (22) above.

(28)   *cɔɔn chɔ̂ɔp ʔâybâa
        John likes   the nut

Momentarily, I will return to the problem raised by (28).

In all of the languages under discussion, in fact universally as far as I know, a pronominal must be free in its governing category. For Thai, this is illustrated in (29).

(29)   *cɔɔn chɔ̂ɔp khǎw
        John likes   him

I suggest that (28) should be analogized to (29), that is, that (28) actually falls under Condition B rather than under any version of Condition C. In particular, I propose that epithets are not merely R-expressions, but rather, are pronominal R-expressions. We have already seen substantial evidence in English of name-like behavior for epithets. Obviously, no direct evidence of the type provided by (7) above is available in Thai, given the lack of pure Condition C effects. However, it is quite clear that epithets in Thai have lexical content, just as they do in English. It is reasonable to conjecture on this basis that they are R-expressions. Further, as bindees, they behave like R-expressions with respect to condition (24), as shown by (30):

(30)   *khǎw khít   wâa ʔâybâa chàlàat
        he   thinks that the nut is smart

The parallelism between (30) and (20′) above is especially revealing in this connection.

However, there is equally strong evidence indicating pronominal nature for epithets. For example, again as far as (24) is concerned, ʔâybâa as a *binder* behaves like a pronoun, *khǎw*, rather than like a name. (31) too has the status of (20′).

(31)   *ʔâybâa khít   wâa cɔɔn chàlàat
         the nut thinks that John is smart

Significantly, (31) contrasts sharply with the well-formed (20). Thus, in (31), as in (28), it is evidently the pronominal character of epithets that is playing a crucial role, in the present case, with respect to condition (24), and in the earlier case, with respect to Condition B.

This same effect obtains in Vietnamese as well. (32) is completely parallel to (31).

(32)   *cái thằng chò dẻ   tin   John sẽ thắng

          the son of a   bitch thinks John will win

Recall from (21) that R-expressions may be bound in a structural configuration such as this one. What is disallowed is the binding of an R-expression by a pronominal, as in (21', 23') above. Plausibly, it is this constraint that is responsible for (32), once again suggesting a pronominal status for epithets.

As observed earlier, epithets generally share one significant property with pronouns: they can have antecedents, as in (8), repeated here as (33).

(33)   After John walked in, the idiot sat down.

There is yet another similarity between epithets and pronouns. Both can participate in Left Dislocation constructions:

(34)   John, I think he should be fired.

(35)   John, I think the idiot should be fired.

An R-expression in place of the pronoun or epithet is far less acceptable.

(36)   ?*John, I think John should be fired.

Evidently, it is not Condition C that is implicated in (36) since first, there is no A-binding here; and second, Condition C would not be expected to distinguish between (35) and (36). Apparently, something like predication is required in this construction, and this demands an open sentence, or a nearly open sentence. The target must not be a complete description. Notice, by the way, that contrary to the proposal of Chomsky (1977), Left Dislocation and the 'as for' construction must be kept distinct, for they differ markedly in this regard. For example, (37) is much better than (36).

(37)   ?As for John, I think that John should be fired.

This is in accord with the observation that 'as for' constructions do not involve predication but merely relevance. No open sentence is required, in sharp contrast to Left Dislocation in English. The following contrast is representative.

(38)   As for sports, I like baseball best.

(39)   *Sports, I like baseball best.

Thus, a variety of properties all follow from the assumption that anaphoric epithets are pronominal R-expressions.

Thus far, we have seen substantial evidence that anaphoric epithets are pronominal R-expressions and that R-expressions may not be bound by pronouns (24). Before examining further, potentially problematic, data, I would first like to consider the question of how the present proposals might be instantiated within the theory. Note that the standard feature analysis of nominal categories of Chomsky (1981; 1982) will not do. According to that theory, there are two independent binary features, [+/−a] and [+/−p], yielding four types of nominals. The [+a] categories — lexical anaphors, NP-trace, and PRO — all satisfy Condition A. The [+p] categories — pronouns, PRO, pro — all are subject to Condition B. The one remaining feature complex, [−a, −p], is a sort of default. The categories instantiating this feature complex — fully lexical NPs, Wh-trace — satisfy Condition C. There is clearly no place in this system for a pronominal R-expression. Such an expression would, of necessity, be [+p]. It would not be pronominal otherwise, and hence, would not be constrained by Condition B. However, to be an R-expression, it would have to be [−a, −p]. Neither of the feature complexes including [+p] satisfies Condition C. Let us tentatively explore alternatives to the standard categorization in an attempt to overcome this difficulty. It is important to keep in mind that the problem is essentially technical, rather than conceptual. A priori, a pronominal R-exprssion is no more impossible than, for example, a pronominal anaphor, or an anaphoric R-expression, as in the 'Generalized Binding Theory' of Aoun (1984).

If we wish to maintain a limit of four classes of expressions, obviously we must maintain a limit of two binary features. Suppose we begin by making R-expressions a substantive category, rather than a default, by positing a feature [+/−r]. Lexical NPs, Wh-trace, and anaphoric epithets have the plus value for this feature, by hypothesis. To maintain our limit, one feature must now be abandoned. Evidently, [+/−p] must be kept, since the point of the exercise is to allow for the description of pronominal R-expressions. Thus, we have (40):

(40)   [+p, +r]   [+p, −r]   [−p, +r]   [−p, −r]

The first of these, [+p, +r], is the complex for epithets. As desired, being [+p], they must conform to Condition B, and being [+r], they must conform to Condition C. The second, [+p, −r], will be pure pronominals, while the third, [−p, +r], will be pure R-expressions. This leaves, essentially as a default, the class of anaphors — [−p, −r]. This is not obviously incorrect, but there is a substantial cost associated with it. While before, we could not accomodate the hybrid category pronominal R-expression, now we cannot accomodate the hybrid pronominal anaphor. This raises the question of how to analyze PRO. Clearly, controlled PRO cannot be [+r], since it does not conform to Condition C. This leave just two possibilities: [+p, −r] and [−p, −r]. The first of these satisfies Condition B, but not Condition A. The second satisfies Condition A, but not Condition B. There is then no description for a category satisfying both Conditions A and B, thus, no possibility of deducing the 'PRO theorem'. According to a number of recent proposals, this consequence is not undesirable. For example, Bouchard (1984) argues at some length that PRO is sometimes pronominal and sometimes anaphoric but never both simultaneously. Bouchard's account is thus entirely consistent with the feature analysis being considered. However, the only analysis of PRO that I am aware of that fully gives the distributional fact that PRO must not be governed is that of Chomsky (1981) (or its close variant in Chomsky (1986)), in which PRO is crucially a pronominal anaphor. [See Chomsky (1981), Huang (1983), and Lasnik and Uriagereka (1988) for problems with trying to deduce the distribution from other properties, including Case requirements.] For this reason, I will tentatively assume that (40) is incorrect.

If a theory with two binary binding features does not provide enough distinctions, the obvious next move is to consider a theory with three features. [I will not consider non-binary features here, but they are not to be excluded a priori, I assume.] Suppose, then, that we have the three features $[+/-a]$, $[+/-p]$, and $[+/-r]$, where the content of each feature is as before. This gives eight categories, of course, presumably too many. Nevertheless, let us explore the consequences. We require at least five categories — that was why two binary features did not suffice — and these will be as in (41).

(41) a. $[+a, +p, -r]$ PRO
     b. $[+a, -p, -r]$ anaphors
     c. $[-a, +p, -r]$ pronouns
     d. $[-a, -p, +r]$ 'pure' R-expressions
     e. $[-a, +p, +r]$ anaphoric epithets

Apparently, there are now three additional predicted but non-existent categories:

(42) a. $[-a, -p, -r]$
     b. $[+a, +p, +r]$
     c. $[+a, -p, +r]$

But are they really all non-existent? I would like to suggest, first, that (42a) does satisfy a theoretical need. A category with this feature complex would have no binding requirement — it would not have to be free in its governing category, bound in its governing category, or A-free. Now it has become increasingly evident that there is a substantial amount of redundancy in the constraints on the distribution of NP trace. Case requirements, chain requirements, bounding requirements, proper government requirements, as well as binding (Condition A) requirements have all been argued for. For discussion, see Lasnik (1985), Chomsky (1986), among many other references. The binding requirement is, perhaps, entirely redundant. It is extremely difficult to find an ungrammatical instance of NP movement which violates only Condition A. In part for this reason, Chomsky (1986) proposes that the 'NIC' case of Condition A should be eliminated in favor of the ECP. If this situation obtains more generally, it would be desirable to remove NP trace from the domain of Condition A entirely. However, it does not seem possible to effect this removal by wholesale elimination of the remainder of Condition A. Central properties of lexical anaphors evidently still must be accounted for in terms of SSC requirements. Suppose, then, that we simply assert that NP trace does not fall under Condition A. How can this be instantiated? Within the traditional categorization, there seems to be no way. In that system, if NP trace is [−a], to exempt it from Condition A, then it will be either [−a, +p] or [−a, −p]. In the former case, NP trace will have to be free in its governing category. In the latter, it will have to be entirely free.[4] Neither of these is an acceptable consequence, it would appear, since, descriptively, NP trace is always bound in its governing category, hence bound. But now note that (42a) in the three-feature system has precisely the desired properties.

Consider now the remaining two cases in (42), [+a, +p, +r] and [+a, −p, +r]. Both of these nominal types would have to bound in their governing categories by virtue of being [+a]. Further, they would both have to be free, a near contradiction reminiscent of Chomsky's analysis of PRO. The two possibilities thus collapse to one. In this case, as in the case of PRO, the expression could only occur in a position where it had no governing category. It could not then be overt, for it would lack Case, being ungoverned, of necessity. Thus, what is predicted is a null category (or two such) which must be ungoverned and A-free. In principle, such a category could exist. Possibly, it does so-called arbitrary PRO seems a not implausible candidate. Arbitrary PRO, like controlled PRO, must be ungoverned. Further, it is not clear that it can ever be bound. Note in particular that when a potentially arbitrary PRO is bound in (43), it no longer is arbitrary, but rather behaves like a controlled PRO. Its value varies with that of its binder.

(43)   John$_1$ thinks [that [[PRO$_1$ playing soccer] is easy]]

This is apparently true even when the binder is itself an arbitrary PRO, as in (44).

(44)   It is important [[PRO to think [that [[PRO playing soccer] is easy]]]]

It is, then, at least possible that the 'extra' categories shown in (42) actually occur. Thus, it is at least possible that the three feature system is correct. However, I would now like to examine some further data that suggests that an alternative description is in order. Recall constraint (24), repeated here as (45).

(45)   An R-expression is pronoun-free

This constraint handled a wide range of phenomena, including a variety of ill-formed examples in languages lacking a general Condition C effect. Recall further that epithets cannot be bound in their governing categories, even when they are not required to be entirely free, suggesting pronominal binding status for epithets. (See (27, 28) above.) Finally, recall that with respect to (45), epithets as binders pattern with pronouns, while as bindees, they pattern with names. Taken together, these properties suggest a consequence that turns out to be completely false. In particular, an epithet should not be able to bind an epithet, yet Vietnamese sentences such as (46), for example, are acceptable.

(46)   cái thằng chó dẻ   tin   cái thằng chó dẻ sẽ   thắng
        the son of a   bitch thinks the SOB   will win

Under the assumptions developed thus far, (46) is evidently in violation of (45), since a pronominal R-expression (hence, a pronominal) binds a pronominal R-expression (hence, an R-expression), an incorrect result. For the present type of case, it might be thought that 'pronoun' in (45) should be understood as 'pure pronoun', thus excluding epithets. However, this would give just the wrong result for cases such as the Vietnamese (32), repeated here as (47), or the Thai (31), repeated here as (48).

(47)   *cái thằng chó dẻ   tin   John sẽ   thắng
        the son of a   bitch thinks John will win

(48)   *?âybâa   khít   wâa cɔɔn chàlaàt
        the nut thinks that John is smart

In both of these cases, the violation stems from the binding of an R-expression by an epithet. Thus, it does not seem desirable to limit the domain of (45) in the way under consideration. Similarly, 'R-expression' in (45) cannot be understood as 'pure R-expression' in order to allow (46), as this would incorrectly allow such an example as Thai (30), repeated here as (49).

(49)   *khǎw khít   wâa ?âybâa chàlaàt
        he   thinks that the nut is smart

A pronoun binding an epithet is no better than a pronoun binding a name.
     The entire array of facts including (46) does not seem amenable to analysis simply in terms of features which cross-classify the nominal expressions in the way considered above. Before proceeding, I will summarize all of the binding relationships between two nominal expressions not in the same governing category. Most of these have been illustrated above. The rest are straightforward.

(50)   *Bindee*

	pronoun	epithet	name
Binder			
pronoun	ok	*	*
epithet	ok	ok	*
name	ok	ok	ok

I have arranged the categories in (50) in what might be regarded as increasing referentiality, from pronoun to name (and name-like definite descriptions). In a sense, this is reflected in the feature analysis proposed, as in (51). [The feature [−a] is suppressed, as it is shared by all three categories being discussed at this point.]

(51) $[+p, -r] < [+p, +r] < [-p, +r]$

This establishes a kind of referentiality hierarchy among the discrete categories given by the features. In these terms, the generalization emerging from (50) is that a less referential expression may not bind a more referential one. (45), the requirement that a pronoun not bind an R-expression, emerges as a special case, as do the other requirements we have seen — that an epithet may not bind a name and that a pronoun may not bind an epithet. However, an epithet is correctly permitted to bind an epithet. For ease of exposition, I state the generalization as (51′).

(51′)   A less referential expression may not bind a more referential one.

One might expect that [+a] categories would also fall under (51′), and there is, in fact, some evidence that this is the case. For example, quite generally, an anaphor cannot bind an R-expression. Further, in Japanese, an anaphor may not bind a pronoun, a phenomenon quite reminiscent of the one we have been examining.[5] The contrast between (52), with a pronoun *kare* binding an anaphor *zibun*, and (53), with the anaphor binding the pronoun, is representative.

(52)   John-ga [s kare-ga [s zibun-ga tensai da to] omotte iru to] itta
        (koto)

        John said that he thinks that self is a genius

(53)   *John-ga [s zibun-ga [s kare-ga tensai da to] omotte iru to] itta
        (koto)

        John said that self thinks that he is a genius

This contrast obtains in Korean as well:

(54)   ?John-nɨn [s kɨ-ga [s caki-ga chənjaelako] sengakhanta ko] mal-
        haetta

        John said that he thinks that self is a genius

(55)   *John-nɨn [s caki-ga [s kɨ-ga chɘnjaelako] sengakhanta ko] mal-
        haetta

        John said that self thinks that he is a genius

This suggests that an approach in terms of something like (51) has applicability beyond the treatment of anaphoric epithets.[6]

To summarize, we have seen a variety of phenomena in a number of languages that receive a natural account in terms of principles based on the structural relation of binding. In particular, it has been argued that Condition C does exist, and, in fact, that it is parametrized, holding in English, for example, but not holding in Thai. Beyond this parameterized requirement that an R-expression be free, there is the further requirement, possibly universal, that a pronoun not bind an R-expression. This requirement is, perhaps, best viewed as one instantiation of a general prohibition on the binding of a more 'referential' expression by one that is less so. Conditions on binding thus seem to play a central role in determining the distribution of nominal expressions of various types.

APPENDIX

As is well-known, the phenomenon of split antecedence raises difficult problems for the theory of indexing. See Lasnik (1981), Higginbotham (1983) for detailed discussion. Here, following Sportiche (1985) [and a discarded proposal of Higginbotham (1983)], I will present a version of indexing that circumvents these problems to a significant extent.

Suppose that an index is not a single integer, but rather, is a non-null set of integers. Suppose further that indices are freely assigned, in the sense that an NP receives an arbitrary set of integers as its index. Consider now the following relational notions:

(1)   A binds B if A c-commands B and the index of A is identical
       to the index of B.

(2)   A is free with respect to B if either B does not c-command A
       or the intersection of the indices of A and B is null.

The binding principles will be the standard ones, with Condition C revised as in the text. Notice that with the definitions in (1) and (2), while free entails not bound, not bound does not entail free. That is, an NP might be neither bound nor free, as in (3).

(3)   They$_{(1, 2)}$ like him$_{(1)}$.

In (3), *him* is not bound, since its index is distinct from that of *they*. However, *him* is also not free, since its index overlaps with that of *they*. (3) thus violates Condition B. The representation of split antecedence might now be as follows:

(4)   John$_{(1)}$ told Bill$_{(2)}$ that they$_{(1, 2)}$ should leave.

In a complete account, the semantic representation would also be specified. Sportiche indicates that set indexation will be provided "with the obvious interpretation". Here I will attempt, in a preliminary way, to explicate the notion "obvious interpretation".

As is customary in studies of anaphora, I will ignore the problems inherent in such terms as 'coreference', 'disjoint reference', and the like. For a clear presentation of a number of these problems, see Higginbotham (1980), and for a promising approach towards a solution, see Heim (1982). For present purposes, I will adopt the pretense that the terms need no explication.

In Lasnik (1981), it was shown in some detail that indexing must be given semantic as well as syntactic import, and further, that assignment of semantic import has non-trivial consequences. Obviously, such an argument carries over from a theory with integer indices to one with set indices. Consider, then, the following interpretive conventions.

(5)   If the index of A is identical to the index of B, then A, B are coreferential.

(6)   If the intersection of the index of A and the index of B is null, then A, B are disjoint in reference.

(5) makes explicit something that is presumably taken for granted in investigations of anaphora. It is required, for example, to guarantee that a reflexive and its 'antecedent' corefer. (6) will be part of the account of the ill-formedness of (7).

(7)   *I like me.

If *I* and *me* are coindexed, Condition B is violated. If they are contra-indexed, (6) contradicts the lexical requirements of those NPs: In a particular utterance, *I* and *me* must be coreferential, hence cannot be disjoint. Now notice that this account generalizes to (8).

(8)   *We like me.

Suppose the indices of *we* and *me* overlap. Then, once again, Condition B will be violated, given the definition of 'free' in (2). But if the indices do not overlap, then by (6), the two NPs will have to be disjoint in reference, contradicting lexical properties: In a particular utterance, the reference of *we* must include the reference of *me*.

Returning now to split antecedence, neither (5) nor (6) is relevant to example (4). Thus, *they* is not required to be coreferential with either of the other NPs, nor is it required to be disjoint from them (since, while it is not free, it *is* free in its governing category). Thus, *they* is free to include John and Bill in its reference. This is essentially the analysis of Lasnik (1976) restated in the terms of Chomsky (1981), except with set indices replacing integer indices. One might speculate about whether such a representation as (4) should have a more determinate interpretation. Some evidence that it should comes from (9).

(9)   Every violinist$_{(1)}$ told some pianist$_{(2)}$ that they$_{(1, 2)}$ should play a duet.

Here, the notion 'free in reference' does not suffice. *They* cannot be freely picking up the reference of *every violinist* and *some pianist*. Rather, we seem to have true split antecedence: the reference of *they* is *determined* by that of the variables bound by the two quantified NPs. This suggests that (10) should be added to (5) and (6).

(10)   If the index of A is included in the index of B, then the reference of A is included in the reference of B.

Given this syntactic and 'interpretive' machinery, the standard cases receive a natural account. Higginbotham (1985, fn 25), however, argues that such an account in terms of set indices must be rejected in favor of a theory based on linking. I will briefly comment on his arguments. His most detailed discussion concerns the ambiguity of (11).

(11)   They told each other that they had better leave.

For (11) to be true, each might have told the other (a) "I had better leave"; (b) "We had better leave"; or (c) "You had better leave". Under linking, Higginbotham points out, (c) can be distinguished from (a) and (b). In the former case, the second *they* would be linked to the first. In the latter case, *they* would be linked to *each other*. Indexing can make no such distinction, if we assume, as is standard, that *each other* and the first *they* must have the same index. Then, obviously, if the second *they* is coindexed with one of those NPs, it is also coindexed with the other. This gives just one representation, rather than the two provided by linking. Note that even under linking, (a) and (b) are not syntactically distinguished, as Higginbotham acknowledges. Nor does linking provide any account for the ambiguity of (12), from Higginbotham (1981).

(12)   They thought they loved each other.

Intuitively, either *they* can be the antecedent of *each other*, yet *each other* must be linked to the lower *they* and only to the lower *they*. To handle all of these cases by the same mechanism, Heim, Lasnik, and May (forthcoming) propose a syntactic analysis in which *each other* is not, in fact, coindexed with its 'antecedent'. Rather, roughly along the lines of Lebeaux (1983), *each* undergoes raising at LF, its landing site determining the interpretation. The apparent locality constraints on *each other* will now be constraints on the relation between the trace of *each* and *each* itself. To the extent that such an analysis proves successful, the force of this argument against indexing is correspondingly lessened.

Higginbotham's second argument is that without linking, "We would lose the account of the distinctions . . . in Montalbetti (1984)". I assume that what Higginbotham has in mind is Montalbetti's argument that in one variety of Spanish, an overt pronominal subject cannot be linked to a formal variable (i.e., to the trace left by operator movement). Montalbetti shows that such a pronoun may, in fact, be *bound* by a formal variable, but only if there is an intervening (null) binder. The implication is that while this is straightforwardly statable in terms of linking, such is not the case with binding. However (13) captures nearly all of the facts under consideration.

(13)   An overt pronominal subject may not be locally bound by a formal variable.

The notion 'local binding', which has wide application in syntactic theory, is that of Koopman and Sportiche (1982) and Chomsky (1982). Essentially, A locally binds B if A binds B and there is no intervening binder. There is just one class of facts not amenable to this description, illustrated in (14) [Montalbetti's Ch. 3, ex. (59)]:

(14)   Nadie pensó que las fotos que él tomó probarían que [pro] estuvo ahí.

        Nobody thought that the picture he took would prove that [pro] was there.

Montalbetti reports that this example is fine on the relevant reading, even though *el* is locally bound by the LF trace of *nadie*. This follows immediately for Montalbetti, since *el* need not be linked to that trace, but rather, may be linked to pro, which is in turn linked to the trace. Thus, linking receives some empirical support.[7] It might be noted, though, that Montalbetti's approach, for reasons that I cannot go into here, relies heavily on a transitivity condition on linking that Higginbotham, in his treatment of (11) above, explicitly rejects. Thus, it is not clear that the phenomenon in (11) and the phenomenon in (13) can simultaneously be arguments for linking.

Finally, Higginbotham raises the question of the interpretation of set indices:

The interpretation could not be that the number *n* [the cardinality of the set] gives the intended number of the referent; for it must be possible to wave at a crowd without knowing how many people one is waving at. (p. 573)

Surely this claim is correct. Hence, one cannot claim an interpretive *advantage* for indexing, even set indexing, vis-à-vis linking. That is, there is no principled correlation between the cardinality of an index on an NP and the cardinality of the set designated by that NP. Rather, the interpretation of indices is precisely as in (5), (6), and (10) above. An individual set index has no interpretation in this theory, just as an individual integer index has no interpretation in standard versions of indexing. Choice of, say, 5 rather than 17 as the index for a particular NP is of no semantic import. There is nothing necessarily 5-like about the referent of an NP with index 5. It is only the relationship between this index and another — identity or non-identity — that is of consequence. Similarly for set indices. Their contribution to interpretation is purely relational. In this respect, indexing shares a central property of linking.

NOTES

[1] There is one further problem for Reinhart's pragmatic account that might be noted. Consider an example such as (i) [(8) in Reinhart (1986)]:

i.   Charlie Brown talks to his dog and my neighbor Max does too.

In line with a tradition going back at least to Ross (1967), Reinhart observes that this example is ambiguous. Reinhart characterizes the readings as (1) Max talks to Charlie's dog ['pragmatic coreference']; (2) Max talks to Max's dog ['bound variable']. Reinhart argues, in fact, that the first conjunct of (i), even in isolation, is always ambiguous, even if the ambiguity is not always evident. The now familiar characterization of sloppy identity as involving variable binding is also to be found in Lasnik (1976, p. 20), where it is argued that the structural requirements governing sloppy identity are precisely those on pronouns used as variables bound by overt quantifiers. The following claim of Reinhart (1983, p. 63) is thus not entirely accurate: "What has gone unnoticed in the studies of sloppy identity is that, in fact, it obeys precisely the same conditions as quantified NP anaphora . . ."

Consider now the particulars of the pragmatic analysis of Reinhart (1986):

a. *Speaker's strategy*: When a syntactic structure you are using allows bound-anaphora interpretation, then use it if you intend your expressions to corefer, unless you have some reasons to avoid bound-anaphora.

b. *Hearer's strategy*: If the speaker avoids bound anaphora options provided by the structure he is using, then, unless he has reasons to avoid bound-anaphora, he didn't intend his expressions to corefer.

Note that these strategies are inconsistent with the claim that the first conjunct of (i) is ambiguous, in the relevant respect, in isolation. This is so because if the hearer intends coreference, bound anaphora must be used in this case, as there are no apparent reasons for avoiding it. Similarly, the hearer will assume that bound anaphora (rather then mere coreference) is being employed. Thus far, this conclusion is without obvious problematic consequences, even if it contradicts Reinhart's claim. Note, in particular, that the initial phenomenon, the ambiguity of (i), is not excluded. Obviously, the bound anaphora reading is made available. Further, pragmatic coreference is possible just in case the speaker has a reason for avoiding the use of a bound variable. And in this case, there is a reason: If the speaker intends to report that Max talks to Charlie's dog yet still wants to use an elliptical construction, then he will choose pragmatic coreference. Now, however, consider the following discourse.

ii.   Speaker 1: Charlie Brown talks to his dog.
            Speaker 2: My neighbor Max does too.

As far as I can tell, exactly as in (i), the ellided constituent has both a sloppy and a non-sloppy reading. However, the latter reading should not be possible in this case. By hypothesis, Speaker 1 intends coreference. Further, there is evidently no reason whatsoever for that speaker to avoid bound anaphora. Finally, there is no reason for Speaker 2 to assume that Speaker 1 had a reason for avoiding bound anaphora. The conclusion is thus that Speaker 2 cannot intend by his utterance that Max talks to Charlie's dog, since the ellided material must include a bound variable. But this is clearly contrary to the facts of the matter.

2 See the Appendix above for discussion of an indexing approach to this phenomenon in the spirit of Chomsky (1981).

3 For some speakers, (23) above is acceptable. But even for them, (27) is out. Vietnamese and Thai are, thus, identical in relevant respects for such speakers.

4 This assumes, as is standard, that all nominal expressions are specified for features. For a possible alternative, see Barss (1986).

5 I have not yet been able to examine Vietnamese or Thai in this connection, but in relevant respects, Japanese seems very similar, as seen in the following examples:

i.   *John-ga ano baka-o hometa (koto)
       John   the idiot   praised

       John praised the idiot

ii.   ?John-ga [Mary-ga ano baka-o sonkeisite iru to] omotte iru
       John   Mary   the idiot   respects   thinks

       John thinks Mary respects the idiot

iii.   *ano baka-ga [Mary-ga John-o sonkeisite iru to] omotte iru
       The idiot thinks Mary respects John

iv.   ?ano baka-ga [Mary-ga ano baka-o sonkeisite iru to] omotte iru
       The idiot thinks Mary respects the idiot

6 Contrary to what we have seen in Japanese and Korean, in English, an anaphor apparently may bind a pronoun, as in (i) or (ii).

i.   John told himself that he should leave.
ii.   John believes himself to have said that he would accept the job.

That is, with respect to constraint (51), overt pronouns and anaphors are equally 'referential' in English. Why this should be the case is not clear, but Mamoru Saito (personal communication) points out a correlation. In English, both pronouns and anaphors can function as variables bound by operators. (iii) illustrates the former case.

iii.   Who thinks that he is smart?

This possibility does not exist in Japanese or Korean. Compare the Japanese (iv) and the Korean (v) with (iii).

iv.   *Dare-ga kare-ga atama-gaii to omotte iru no
v.   *Nu-ka ki-ka toktokhata-ko malhaess-ci

See Montalbetti (1984), Hong (1985) for extensive discussion.

7 There is some question about how general the phenomenon in (14) is. There are Spanish speakers who share Montalbetti's judgments, for the most part, but for whom a non-c-commanding pro cannot 'save' an overt pronoun. These speakers reject the crucial examples, those with the structure of (14).

BIBLIOGRAPHY

Akmajian, A. (1972) "Getting Tough," *Linguistic Inquiry* 3, 373—377.

Anderson, M. (1979) *Noun Phrase Structure*, Doctoral dissertation, University of Connecticut, Storrs, Connecticut.

Aoun, J. (1982) *The Formal Nature of Anaphoric Relations*, Doctoral dissertation, MIT, Cambridge, Massachusetts.

Aoun, J. (1985) *A Grammar of Anaphora*, MIT Press, Cambridge, Massachusetts.

Aoun, J. and D. Sportiche (1981) "On the Formal Theory of Government," *Linguistic Review* 2, 211—236.

Bach, E. (1970) "Problominalization," *Linguistic Inquiry* 1, 121—122.

Barss, A. (1986) *Chains and Anaphoric Dependence: On Reconstruction and Its Implications*. Doctoral dissertation, MIT, Cambridge, Massachusetts.

Barss, A. and H. Lasnik (1986) "A Note on Anaphora and Double Objects," *Linguistic Inquiry* 17, 347—354. [Reprinted in this book.]

Belletti, A., L. Brandi, and L. Rizzi, eds. (1981) *Theory of Markedness in Generative Grammar*, Proceedings of the 1979 GLOW conference, Pisa, Scuola Normale Superiore.

Berman, A. (1974) *Adjectives and Adjective Complement Constructions in English, Mathematical Linguistics and Automatic Translation*, Report NSF-29, The Aiken Computation Laboratory, Harvard University, Cambridge, Massachusetts.

Berman, A. and M. Szamosi (1972) "Observations in Sentential Stress," *Language* 48, 304—325.

Bouchard, D. (1984) *On the Content of Empty Categories*, Foris, Dordrecht.

Bresnan, J. (1970) "On Complementizers: Towards a Syntactic Theory of Complement Types," *Foundations of Language* 6, 297—321.

Bresnan, J. (1971) "Sentence Stress and Syntactic Transformations," *Language* 47, 257—281.

Bresnan, J. (1972) *Theory of Complementation in English Syntax*, Doctoral dissertation, MIT, Cambridge, Massachusetts.

Brody, M. (1984) "On Contextual Definitions and the Role of Chains," *Linguistic Inquiry* 15, 355—381.

Chomsky, N. (1955) *The Logical Structure of Linguistic Theory*, unpublished, Harvard University, Cambridge, Massachusetts. [Published in part in 1975 by Plenum Press, New York.]

Chomsky, N. (1957) *Syntactic Structures*, Mouton, The Hague.

Chomsky, N. (1964) *Current Issues in Linguistic Theory*, Mouton, The Hague.

Chomsky, N. (1965) *Aspects of the Theory of Syntax*, MIT Press, Cambridge, Massachusetts.

Chomsky, N. (1970) "Remarks on Nominalization." in R. A. Jacobs and P. S. Rosenbaum, eds. (1970).

Chomsky, N. (1973) "Conditions on Transformations," in S. Anderson and P. Kiparsky, eds., *A Festschrift for Morris Halle*, Holt, Rinehart and Winston, New York.

Chomsky, N. (1975) *Reflections on Language*, Pantheon Books, New York.

Chomsky, N. (1976) "Conditions on Rules of Grammar," *Linguistic Analysis* 2, 303—351.

Chomsky, N. (1977) "On Wh-Movement," in P. Culicover, T. Wasow, and A. Akmajian, eds., *Formal Syntax*, Academic Press, New York.

Chomsky, N. (1979) Unpublished transcript of lectures presented at the Scuola Normale Superiore, Pisa, Italy.

Chomsky, N. (1980) "On Binding," *Linguistic Inquiry* 11, 1—46.

Chomsky, N. (1981) *Lectures on Government and Binding*, Foris, Dordrecht.

Chomsky, N. (1981a) "Markedness and Core Grammar," in A. Belletti et al., eds. (1981).

Chomsky, N. (1982) *Some Concepts and Consequences of the Theory of Government and Binding*, MIT Press, Cambridge, Massachusetts.

Chomsky, N. (1986) *Knowledge of Language*, Praeger, New York.

Chomsky, N. (1986a) *Barriers*, MIT Press, Cambridge, Massachusetts.

Chomsky, N. and H. Lasnik (1977) "Filters and Control," *Linguistic Inquiry* 11, 1—46. [Reprinted in H. Lasnik (1989).]

Davis, L. (1984) *Arguments and Expletives*, Doctoral dissertation, University of Connecticut, Storrs, Connecticut.

Donnellan, K. (1966) "Reference and Definite Descriptions", *Philosophical Review* 75, 281—304.

Dougherty, R. C. (1969) "An Interpretive Theory of Pronominal Reference," *Foundations of Language* 5, 488—508.

Dougherty, R. C. (1970) "A Grammar of Coordinate Conjointed Structure: I," *Language* 46, 850—898.

Emonds, J. (1970) *Root and Structure Preserving Transformations*, Doctoral dissertation, MIT, Cambridge, Massachusetts.

Epstein, S. D. (1984) "A Note on Functional Determination and Strong Crossover," *The Linguistic Review* 3, 299—308.

Evans, G. (1980) "Pronouns," *Linguistic Inquiry* 11, 337—362.

Fiengo, R. (1974) *Semantic Conditions on Surface Structure*, Doctoral dissertation, MIT, Cambridge, Massachusetts.

Fiengo, R. and H. Lasnik (1973) "The Logical Structure of Reciprocal Sentences in English," *Foundations of Language* 9, 447—468. [Reprinted in this book.]

Fodor, J. D. (1978) "Parsing Strategies and Constraints on Transformations," *Linguistic Inquiry* 9, 427—473.

Freidin, R. (1978) "Cyclicity and the Theory of Grammar," *Linguistic Inquiry* 9, 519—549.

Freidin, R. (1979) "Misgeneration: Conditions on Derivations vs. Conditions on Representations," unpublished.

Freidin, R. and H. Lasnik (1981) "Disjoint Reference and Wh-Trace," *Linguistic Inquiry* 12, 39—53. [Reprinted in this book.]

Geach, P. (1962) *Reference and Generality*, Cornell University Press, Ithaca, New York.

Haïk, I. (1984) "Indirect Binding," *Linguistic Inquiry* 15, 185—223.

Heim, I. (1982) *The Semantics of Definite and Indefinite Noun Phrases*, Doctoral dissertation, University of Massachusetts, Amherst, Massachusetts.

Heim, I., H. Lasnik, and R. May (forthcoming) "Reciprocity and Plurality."

Helke, M. (1971) *The Grammar of Reflexivization*, Doctroal dissertation, MIT, Cambridge, Massachusetts.

Hendrick, R. and M. Rochemont (1982) "Complementation, Multiple Wh, and Echo Questions," unpublished, University of North Carolina and University of California at Irvine.

Higginbotham, J. (1980) "Anaphora and GB: Some Preliminary Remarks," in J. Jensen, ed., *Cahiers Linguistiques d'Ottawa*, Proceedings of the Tenth Annual Meeting of NELS, Department of Linguistics, University of Ottawa, Ottawa, Ontario.

Higginbotham, J. (1980a) "Pronouns and Bound Variables," *Linguistic Inquiry* 11, 679—708.

Higginbotham, J. (1981) "Reciprocal Interpretation," *Journal of Linguistic Research* 1.3, 97—117.

Higginbotham, J. (1983) "Logical Form, Binding, and Nominals," *Linguistic Inquiry* 14, 395—420.

Higginbotham, J. (1983a) "A Note on Phrase-Markers," *Revue Quebecoise de Linguistique* 13.1.

Higginbotham, J. (1985) "On Semantics," *Linguistic Inquiry* 16, 547—593.

Hong, S. (1985) *A and A' Binding in Korean and English*, Doctoral dissertation, University of Connecticut, Storrs, Connecticut.

Horn, L. (1972) *On the Semantic Properties of Logical Operators in English*, Doctoral dissertation, UCLA, Los Angeles, California.

Huang, C.-T. J. (1983) "A Note on the Binding Theory," *Linguistic Inquiry* 14, 554—561.

Jackendoff, R. (1969) *Some Rules of Semantic Interpretation for English*, Doctoral dissertation, MIT, Cambridge, Massachusetts.

Jackendoff, R. (1972) *Semantic Interpretation in Generative Grammar*, MIT Press, Cambridge, Massachusetts.

Jackendoff, R. and P. Culicover (1971) "A Reconsideration of Dative Movements," *Foundations of Language* 7, 397—412.

Jacobs, R. A. and P. S. Rosenbaum, eds. (1970) *Readings in English Transformational Grammar*, Ginn and Co., Waltham, Massachusetts.

Karttunen, L. (1971) "Definite Descriptions with Crossing Coreference," *Foundations of Language* 7, 157—182.

Kayne, R. (1980) "Extensions of Binding and Case-Marking," *Linguistic Inquiry* 11, 75—96.

Kayne, R. (1981) "Two Notes on the NIC," in A. Belletti et al., eds. (1981).

Kayne, R. (1981a) "Unambiguous Paths," in R. May and J. Koster, eds., *Levels of Syntactic Representation*, Foris, Dordrecht.

Kayne, R. (1984) *Connectedness and Binary Branching*, Foris, Dordrecht.

Klima, E. (1964) "Negation in English," in J. Fodor and J. Katz, eds., *The Structure of Language*, Prentice-Hall, Englewood Cliffs, New Jersey.

Koopman, H. and D. Sportiche (1982) "Variables and the Bijection Principle," *The Linguistic Review* 2, 139—160.

Kroch, A. (1974) *The Semantics of Scope in English*, Doctoral dissertation, MIT, Cambridge, Massachusetts.

Kuno, S. (1986) *Functional Syntax*, University of Chicago Press, Chicago.

Lakoff, G. (1968) "Pronouns and Reference," Distributed by Indiana University of Linguistics Club. [Reprinted in J. McCawley, ed. (1976), *Syntax and Semantics, Volume 7: Notes from the Linguistic Underground*, Academic Press, New York.]

Lakoff, G. (1970) *Irregularity in Syntax*, Holt, Rinehart and Winston, New York.

Langacker, R. (1969) "On Pronominalization and the Chain of Command," in D. Reidel and S. Schane, eds., *Modern Studies in English*, Prentice-Hall, Englewood Cliffs, New Jersey.

Lasnik, H. (1972) *Analyses of Negation in English*, Doctoral dissertation, MIT, Cambridge, Massachusetts.

Lasnik, H. (1975) "On the Semantics of Negation," in D. Hockney, W. Harper, and B. Freed, eds., *Contemporary Research in Philosophical Logic and Linguistic Semantics*, Reidel, Dordrecht.

Lasnik, H. (1976) "Remarks on Coreference," *Linguistic Analysis* 2, 1—22. [Reprinted in this book.]

Lasnik, H. (1981) "On Two Recent Treatments of Disjoint Reference," *Journal of Linguistic Research* 1.4, 48—58. [Reprinted in this book.]

Lasnik, H. (1981a) "Restricting the Theory of Transformations: A Case Study," in N. Hornstein and D. Lightfoot, eds., *Explanations in Linguistics*, Longmans, London. [Reprinted in H. Lasnik (1989).]

Lasnik, H. (1985) "Illicit NP Movement: Locality Conditions on Chains?" *Linguistic Inquiry* 16.3, 481—490. [Reprinted in this book.]

Lasnik, H. (1989) *Essays on Restrictiveness and Learnability*, Reidel, Dordrecht.
Lasnik, H. (in press) "On the Necessity of Binding Conditions," in R. Freidin, ed., *Principles and Parameters in Comparative Grammar*, MIT Press, Cambridge, Masschusetts. [Reprinted in this book.]
Lasnik, H. and R. Fiengo (1974) "Complement Object Deletion," *Linguistic Inquiry* 5, 535–571. [Reprinted in this book.]
Lasnik, H. and R. Freidin (1981) "Core Grammar, Case Theory, and Markedness," in A. Belletti et al., eds. (1981). [Reprinted in H. Lasnik (1989).]
Lasnik, H. and J. Kupin (1977) "A Restrictive Theory of Transformational Grammar," *Theoretical Linguistics* 4, 173–196. [Reprinted in H. Lasnik (1989).]
Lasnik, H. and M. Saito (1984) "On the Nature of Proper Government." *Linguistic Inquiry* 15, 235–289. [Reprinted in H. Lasnik (1989).]
Lasnik, H. and J. Uriagereka (1988) *A Course in GB Syntax: Lectures on Binding and Empty Categories*, MIT Press, Cambridge, Massachusetts.
Lebeaux, D. (1983) "A Distributional Difference Between Reciprocals and Reflexives," *Linguistic Inquiry* 14, 723–730.
Lees, R. (1960) "A Multiply Ambiguous Adjectival Construction in English," *Language* 36, 207–221.
Lees, R. and E. Klima (1963) "Rules for English Pronominalization," *Language* 39, 17–28.
Linebarger, M. (1980) *The Grammar of Negative Polarity*, Doctoral dissertation, MIT, Cambridge, Massachusetts.
May, R. (1977) *The Grammar of Quantification*, Doctoral dissertation, MIT, Cambridge, Massachusetts.
May, R. (1979) "Must Comp-to-Comp Movement Be Stipulated?" *Linguistic Inquiry* 10, 719–725.
May, R. (1985) *Logical Form: Its Structure and Derivation*, MIT, Cambridge, Massachusetts.
May, R. (1981) "Movement and Binding," *Linguistic Inquiry* 12, 215–243.
McCawley, J. (1970) "Where do Noun Phrase Come From?" in R. Jacobs and P. Rosenbaum, eds. (1970).
McCawley, J. (1982) "Parentheticals and Discontinuous Constituent Structure," *Linguistic Inquiry* 13, 91–106.
Montalbetti, M. (1984) *After Binding*, Doctoral dissertation, MIT, Cambridge, Massachusetts.
Newmeyer, F. (1969) "English Aspectual Verbs," *Studies in Linguistics and Language Learning* VI, University of Washington, Seattle, Washington.
Perlmutter, D. (1968) *Deep and Surface Constraints in Syntax*, Doctoral dissertation, MIT, Cambridge, Massachusetts.
Pesetsky, D. (1981) "Complementizer-Trace Phenomena and the Nominative Island Condition," *The Linguistic Review* 1, 297–343.
Pesetsky, D. (1982) *Paths and Categories*, Doctoral dissertation, MIT, Cambridge, Massachusetts.
Postal, P. (1966) "On So-Called 'Pronouns' in English," in F. Dineen, ed., *19th Monograph on Language and Linguistics*, Georgetown University Press, Washington, D.C.
Postal, P. (1966a) "A Note on 'Understood Transitively'," *International Journal of American Linguistics* 32, 90–93.
Postal, P. (1969) "Review of A. McIntosh and M. A. K. Halliday, *Papers in General Descriptive and Applied Linguistics*," *Foundations of Language* 5, 409–439.
Postal, P. (1970) "On Coreferential Complement Subject Deletion," *Linguistic Inquiry* 1, 439–500.
Postal, P. (1971) *Cross-Over Phenomena*, Holt, Rinehart and Winston, New York.
Postal, P. (1972) "Some Further Limitations of Interpretive Theories of Anaphora," *Linguistic Inquiry* 3, 349–371.

Postal, P. and J. R. Ross (1971) "¡Tough Movement Si, Tough Deletion No!," *Linguistic Inquiry* 2, 544—546.

Reinhart, T. (1976) *The Syntactic Domain of Anaphora*, Doctoral dissertation, MIT, Cambridge, Massachusetts.

Reinhart, T. (1983) "Coreference and Bound Anaphora: A Restatement of the Anaphora Questions," *Linguistics and Philosophy* 6, 47—88.

Reinhart, T. (1986) "Center and Periphery in the Grammar of Anaphora," in B. Lust, ed., *Studies in the Acquisition of Anaphora, Volume I*, Reidel, Dordrecht.

Riemsdijk, H. van and E. Williams (1986) *Introduction to the Theory of Grammar*, MIT Press, Cambridge, Massachusetts.

Rizzi, L. (1980) "Violations of the Wh Island Constraint and the Subjacency Condition," *Journal of Italian Linguistics* 5, 157—195.

Rizzi, L. (1986) "On Chain Formation," in H. Borer, ed., *Syntax and Semantics, Volume 19: The Grammar of Pronominal Clitics*, Academic Press, New York.

Rosenbaum, P. S. (1967) *The Grammar of English Predicate Complement Constructions*, MIT Press, Cambridge, Massachusetts.

Ross, J. R. (1967) *Constraints on Variables in Syntax*, Doctoral dissertation, MIT, Cambridge, Massachusetts.

Ross, J. R. (1967a) "On the Cyclic Nature of English Pronominalization," in *To Honor Roman Jakobson*, Mouton, The Hague.

Ross, J. R. (1969) "Guess Who?" in R. Binnick et al., eds., *Papers from the Fifth Regional Meeting of the Chicago Linguistic Society*, Department of Linguistics, University of Chicago, Chicago, Illinois.

Rouveret, A. and J.-R. Vergnaud (1980) "Specifying Reference to the Subject," *Linguistic Inquiry* 11, 97—202.

Safir, K. (1984) "Multiple Variable Binding," *Linguistic Inquiry* 15, 603—638.

Sportiche, D. (1983) *Structural Invariance and Symmetry in Syntax*, Doctoral dissertation, MIT, Cambridge, Massachusetts.

Sportiche, D. (1985) "Remarks on Crossover," *Linguistic Inquiry* 16, 460—469.

Stockwell, R. P., P. Schachter, and B. H. Partee (1973) *The Major Syntactic Structures of English*, Holt, Rinehart and Winston.

Stowell, T. (1981) *Origins of Phrase Structure*, Doctoral dissertation, MIT, Cambridge, Massachusetts.

Taraldsen, K. T. (1978) "On the NIC, Vacuous Application and the *That*-Trace Filter," unpublished, MIT, Cambridge, Massachusetts.

Wasow, T. (1972) *Anaphoric Relations in English*, Doctoral dissertation, MIT, Cambridge, Massachusetts.

INDEX OF NAMES

173

INDEX OF SUBJECTS

175

STUDIES IN NATURAL LANGUAGE
AND LINGUISTIC THEORY

Managing Editors

JOAN MALING and LUIGI RIZZI

Luigi Burzio, *Italian Syntax: A Government-Binding Approach.* xiii+468 pp., 1986. ISBN 90–277–2014–2; 90–277–2015–0 (pbk).

William D. Davies, *Choctaw Verb Agreement and Universal Grammar.* xi+202 pp., 1986. ISBN 90–277–2065–7; 90–277–2142–4 (bpk).

Katalin É. Kiss, *Configurationality in Hungarian.* 268 pp., 1987. ISBN 90–277–1907–1; 90–277–2456–3 (pbk).

Douglas Pulleyblank, *Tone in Lexical Phonology.* xii+249 pp., 1986. ISBN 90–277–2123–8; 90–277–2124–6 (pbk).

Lars Hellan and Kirsti Koch Christensen, *Topics in Scandinavian Syntax.* vii+273 pp., 1986. ISBN 90–277–2166–1; 90–277–2167–x (pbk).

K. P. Mohanan, *The Theory of Lexical Phonology.* xii+219 pp., 1986. ISBN 90–277–2226–9; 90–277–2227–7 (bpk).

Judith L. Aissen, *Tzotzil Clause Structure.* xxiii+290 pp., 1987. ISBN 90–277–2365–6; 90–277–2441–5 (pbk).

Takao Gunji, *Japanese Phrase Structure Grammar: A Unification-Based Approach.* ix+239 pp., 1987. ISBN 1–55608–020–4.

Wolfgang Wurzel, *Inflectional Morphology and Naturalness.* (forthcoming)

Carol Neidle, *The Role of Case in Russian Syntax.* xvi + 208 pp., 1988. ISBN 1–55608–042–5.

Claire Lefebvre and Pieter Muysken, *Mixed Categories: Nominalizations in Quechua.* xvii + 304 pp., 1988. ISBN 1–55608–050–6; 1–55608–051–4 (pbk).

Karin Michelson, *A Comparative Study of Lake-Iroquoian Accent.* x + 197 pp., 1988. ISBN 1–55608–054–9.

Karen Zagona, *Verb Phrase Syntax: A Parametric Study of English and Spanish.* xv + 206 pp., 1988. ISBN 1–55608–064–6; 1–55608–065–4 (pbk).

Randall Hendrick, *Anaphora in Celtic and Universal Grammar.* xi + 284 pp., 1988. ISBN 1–55608–066–2.